By Harry Golden

AT THE WHITE HOUSE, AUGUST 28, 1963, a group of leaders of the
March on Washington meet with the President. Left to right: Whitney
Young, National Urban League; Dr. Martin Luther King, Christian
Leadership Conference; John Lewis, Student Non-Violent Coordinating
Committee; Rabbi Joachim Prinz, American Jewish Congress; Dr.
Eugene P. Blake, National Council of Churches; A. Philip Randolph,
AFL-CIO Vice President; President Kennedy; Walter Reuther, United
Auto Workers; Vice President Johnson, rear, and Roy Wilkins, NAACP.

Mr. Kennedy and the Negroes

HARRY GOLDEN

THE WORLD PUBLISHING COMPANY

CLEVELAND AND NEW YORK

Published by The World Publishing Company
2231 West 110th Street, Cleveland 2, Ohio
Published simultaneously in Canada by
Nelson, Foster & Scott Ltd.
Library of Congress Catalog Card Number: 64-12060
FIRST EDITION
WP364
Design is by Jack Jaget.

A DEDICATION

THIS BOOK was not conceived after the assassination of President John F. Kennedy in Dallas, Texas, on November 22, 1963. In fact, on the day before the assassination I had completed the first five chapters, roughly half the book.

The subject of the social revolution of the American Negro has concerned me for the last twenty-two years. In a way, I have been mulling over this kind of book in all my books, and in the essays, stories, and editorials I have written both for my own newspaper, *The Carolina Israelite,* and for some of the national magazines. Every writer in the South has a book like this in mind, and one day each and every Southern writer will come to it.

The South made me a writer by providing a panoramic view of America's greatest domestic news story of the twentieth century—the industrialization and urbanization of a vast agricultural society and the changing of its social order. This change has caught up forty-four million people, Southerners all, white and black, people I know and love.

For this purpose, I must concentrate in this book on the South. I must concentrate on the South, not only because

I live there, and I know it, but because the South is central to the story.

If the Montgomery Bus Strike had not succeeded, I do not believe Negro students would have boycotted the New York City public schools last February; without the Negro demonstrations in Greensboro, North Carolina, Albany, Georgia, and Birmingham, Alabama, I do not believe Negro pickets would have paraded in Philadelphia.

The evil of racial segregation, to be sure, afflicts nearly every major city of our country, but the inflammation is centered in the South, and there it will be cured.

Over these last two decades I doubt if I have missed a printed word or public address on the problem of how the Negro will gain his rights.

But, of course, the book needed a John F. Kennedy. It would be futile and silly to deny that the Boston Irishman inspired me.

I began the planning of the book in late 1962 and by the time of the March on Washington on August 28, 1963, I had begun the actual writing. It was at that point I decided to call the book *Mr. Kennedy and the Negroes* because the late Mr. Kennedy was the first President of the United States since Lincoln to declare publicly that racial segregation and discrimination are morally indefensible. He was the first President to support the Negro's drive for equality by making public announcement that the security of the nation, its sacred honor, and its future are inseparable from its guarantee of civil rights.

These declarations were some of the reasons why the people loved John Fitzgerald Kennedy. They loved him much as philosophers loved the Idea of the Good. Good things decay but the Idea lives on.

John F. Kennedy was an Idea to the people of the United States. More than the man he was and the office he held he was an Idea of what we could become, what we could be, what we could achieve.

Both John F. Kennedy and the country were still in the process of *becoming* on November 22, 1963. But many of us felt we were as near the state of pure being then as we had been when Abraham Lincoln preserved the Union and Franklin D. Roosevelt preserved the country.

In July, 1963, when I told Mr. Kennedy I intended to call my "requiem for Jim Crow" *Mr. Kennedy and the Negroes,* he made no comment, but he was most generous in directing his civil rights aide, Lee C. White, to give me what data I might require. I did not ask for, nor did I receive, from the White House or from the office of the Attorney General, any materials not otherwise available to other writers and reporters, but the warmth of cooperation I did receive was of inestimable value.

I dedicate this book to the memory of our second "Emancipator President," John F. Kennedy, thirty-fifth President of the United States of America.

HARRY GOLDEN

Charlotte, North Carolina
January 10, 1964

CONTENTS

CONTENTS

ACKNOWLEDGMENTS

MY ELDEST SON, Richard Goldhurst, edited the entire book and helped in the rewriting; United States Attorney General Robert F. Kennedy, Mr. Burke Marshall, Deputy Attorney General, Chief of the Civil Rights Division; Mr. Edwin Guthman, Special Assistant for Public Information, Department of Justice; Mr. John Doar, Assistant United States Attorney General; and Mr. Lee C. White, Assistant Special Counsel to the President, gave me valuable time in granting lengthy interviews between July, 1963, and January, 1964; Judge J. Spencer Bell, United States Court of Appeals for the Fourth Circuit, contributed knowledgeable suggestions for the handling of my materials on the civil rights cases; Martha Williamson Huntley, my research assistant, checked all references; Dr. Joseph Morrison, School of Journalism, University of North Carolina, read the galley proofs and saved me from several grievous pitfalls; and Maureen Titlow, my secretary, suffered through six and seven rewrites of each chapter.

MR. KENNEDY
AND THE NEGROES

CHAPTER ONE

SEGREGATION AND TREASON

ON SEPTEMBER 30, 1952, I was part of a crowd numbering well over 35,000 who came to hear Dwight D. Eisenhower speak from the steps of the South Carolina capitol in Columbia.

The Democratic Governor, James F. Byrnes, introduced the General and said in his peroration: "Ladies and Gentlemen, I give you the next President of the United States."

The band struck up "Dixie." General Eisenhower leaped from his chair, grabbed the microphone, and shouted: "I always stand up when they play that song."

South Carolinians cried and hugged each other for joy. But when the General said it was the first time since the Confederate war that a Republican candidate was bidding for Dixie votes, the crowd went wild. I have never seen an ovation more spontaneous, more intense, nor more prolonged.

Some years later, a more meditative Eisenhower, now nearing the end of his second term as President, sat in the White House study talking to his speech-writer. In *The Ordeal of Power*, Emmet John Hughes describes the President as saying, "You take the attitude of a fellow like Jimmy Byrnes. We

15

used to be pretty good friends, and now I've not heard from him even once for the last eighteen months—all because of the bitterness on this thing . . ." [1] "This thing" was the social revolution of the American Negro, probably one of the biggest domestic news stories of the twentieth century. Jimmy Byrnes didn't want to sing "Dixie" with Dwight D. Eisenhower any more. He didn't want to sing "Dixie" because Eisenhower had dispatched units of the 101st Airborne Division to enforce a federal court order against state interference with plans to integrate Central High School in Little Rock, Arkansas.

It is only fair to say that President Eisenhower's attitudes on the civil rights movement had been changed and modified since he made campaign statements to the cheering South Carolinians, but his confession of a friendship lost makes a highly significant revelation about James F. Byrnes.

Remember, James F. Byrnes was, and still is, a lifelong Democrat. Not only as his party's governor did he introduce the Republican candidate for President, but publicly backed him against the candidate of his own party. Governor Byrnes, a former senator, former Supreme Court justice, former secretary of state, confidant of Democratic Presidents Franklin D. Roosevelt and Harry S. Truman, deserted his political party, and then deserted the Republican he had helped make President. He did all these things, because he was a Southern politician and therefore would resist with all his prestige, power, and influence any man who dared challenge racial segregation as Adlai E. Stevenson had. He would forever call enemy any man who would send troops into the South to carry out a federal court order as Dwight D. Eisenhower had.

Byrnes came to believe that legally enforced racial segregation was an article of faith for the Southerner; that support of legally enforced racial segregation offered the only oppor-

[1] Emmet John Hughes, *The Ordeal of Power* (New York, Atheneum Publishers, 1963), p. 201.

tunity for any Southerner to prove his loyalty to the South and to his Southern heritage. Cole L. Blease, an earlier governor of South Carolina, was one of the few Southerners who repeated the secret oath in public: "Whenever the Constitution of the United States comes between me and the virtue of the white women of the South, I say to hell with the Constitution." W. J. Cash, in his classic, *The Mind of the South,* commented: ". . . the whole tradition of extravagance, of sectionalism and Negrophobia in Southern politics had come to its ordained flower, and descended at last fully to the level of the most brutal viewpoint in Dixie." [2]

In the past seventy years noble Southerners have raised their voices against immorality and injustice but have remained mute about racial segregation because to condemn it made them traitors. It is Southerners' unswerving fidelity to this principle that has precipitated the tragedies of Clinton, Tennessee; Little Rock, Arkansas; Oxford, Mississippi; and the horror and shame of that September Sunday in Birmingham, Alabama, when the Sixteenth Street Negro Baptist Church was bombed, killing four little girls.

To denounce the cause of legally enforced segregation is a form of treason to Southerners. I say a form because though most men do not worry about being traitors, Southerners do. Their own common sense and humanity may conspire to make them privately critical, but publicly they remain loyal Southerners, loyal even at their own expense.

The first attempt at token integration in Charlotte came on September 4, 1957, when attractive fifteen-year-old Dorothy Counts entered Harding High School. A crowd of jeering teen-agers spat and hissed at her. During her second week of school these teen-agers reviled her in the halls and hit her with an eraser and a piece of tin. Inflamed bands of high-school

[2] W. J. Cash, *The Mind of the South* (New York, Alfred A. Knopf, 1941), p. 248.

children followed her home every day. When her brother, Herman Counts, a twenty-year-old college student, drove to the school to pick her up, he was greeted with catcalls and a rock cracked the rear window of his car.

Dorothy finally withdrew from the school. In the Charlotte *Observer* of September 11, 1957, her father, the Reverend Herman L. Counts, professor of Christian Theology at the School of Religion, Johnson C. Smith University, made the statement: "It was with compassion for our native land and love for our daughter, Dorothy, that we withdrew her as a student from Harding High School."

With several members of the local Human Relations Council, I called on the Counts family. Our purpose was to urge the Reverend Mr. Counts to permit Dorothy to stay in the previously all-white school.

At one point Reverend Counts showed us a diary in which he had listed the names of the people who had called to express sympathy and compassion for Dorothy's ordeal. We looked over this list in wonder and chagrin. The list was a fair representation of Charlotte society, the white leaders of the religious, political, and philanthropic structure of our city. Why hadn't any of these people called the school board, or the mayor, or written a letter to the editor expressing their views? The embattled editors of the Charlotte *News* and the Charlotte *Observer* were hungry for such an expression. But none came—publicly. Such action would have meant a betrayal.

Six years later under a new administration, Attorney General Robert F. Kennedy was attempting to enforce federal court orders which enjoined the end of racial segregation. He ordered his staff: "Go the last mile with the Southern officials." When James Meredith, armed with a federal court order, sought to register as the first Negro student at the University of Mississippi, the Attorney General tried his system. When nearly everything else had failed, he called one of the most famous football heroes of the nation, a Southerner and a graduate of the University of Mississippi, Charlie Conerly, the quarterback of the New York Professional Football Giants. Mr. Kennedy asked Conerly for a statement, not praising integration, merely urging compliance with the law to save the honor of beloved Ole Miss. Conerly, who played on a team of which Negroes Rosey Brown, Roosevelt Grier, and Johnny Counts were members, thought it over for three days. Sadly he gave the Attorney General his answer, "I cannot do it."

That mile is an eternal mile, and every step along the way diminishing and weakening the resolve and determination of men of good will. I recall meeting Luther H. Hodges, Secretary of Commerce, but then the Governor of North Carolina, in 1955 in the rotunda of the State Capitol in Raleigh. I had just come from a press conference at which Governor Hodges had outlined the legislation which would attempt to circumvent the Supreme Court's ruling for public school desegregation. I asked him why he championed such laws, for I knew that privately he did not share all of the views of his segregationist colleagues.

Governor Hodges told me he had carried in his pocket for several months a petition signed by legislators from the eastern and rural parts of the state, who threatened to close the public schools if somehow North Carolina could not maintain the *status quo*.

"I will do anything, anything," said Governor Hodges, "to keep the schools open."

This fear of treason makes decent Southerners accomplices in criminal violence and terror. They refuse to point out or testify against criminals who bomb Negro churches and homes. As often as these good people deplore these crimes, they can never bring themselves to bear witness against the perpetrators. In Mississippi, for instance, in 1959, a Negro named Mack Parker, charged with the rape of a white woman, was spirited from jail and lynched. The lynchers never stood trial though their names were known to nearly everyone. There was no trial because Southerners in Mississippi would not betray their oath to white supremacy; they would not speak treason.

I have always found it interesting that I could thrive in the South, denouncing racial segregation in hundreds of essays and speeches while friends of mine, editors, clergymen, salesmen, stating views far more reserved, lost their jobs and community position. I think the basic reason is that no one considers me a Southerner. I am not a renegade. I live in the South and love the South, but no one considers me a Southerner, least of all I myself. I never swore that oath.

It is true that Jews lived in the South before there was a South. They came with Oglethorpe to Savannah in 1733, and established the indigo trade in South Carolina in the 1750s. Yet, the surrounding society never thinks of them as Southerners, not really, and when an occasional Jew joins a White Citizens Council, thinking perhaps he has been accepted as a bona fide Southerner, his enthusiastic initiation merely signals the defector. My own views on the racial problem have been inspired mainly by those few Southerners who did indeed renege, who did betray their tradition and inheritance and risked their livelihood and their place in a stable community to speak out against the evil of segregation.

One of these is the truly great Southerner of our generation, Lillian Smith, a Georgia girl who, reviewing *Gone with the Wind* in 1936, called it "the swan song of white supremacy" and earned the enmity of neighbors and friends. It was Miss Smith and her friend, Paula Snelling, who edited the first antisegregation publication below the Mason-Dixon line. If anyone can be said to have "discovered" the Negro writers of

our country, it was they in their magazine, *South Today*.
Until they put this magazine together, no Southern newspaper had ever reviewed a book by a Negro novelist, no Negro
poet had ever lectured to a local writing group, no professor
or clergyman had ever discussed the meaning of Negro writing
from his desk or pulpit. But when Lillian Smith reviewed
a century of Negro writing in America, she wrote, "Whatever
it did for readers, it was one of the most moving times of my
life as I discovered how Negroes felt, dreamed, created, suffered as human beings."

Thirty years ago this Georgia girl understood that the overpowering corruption of the oath to support legally enforced
racial segregation was that it made its adherents blind. She
understood that the only way to expose and resolve the
terrible injustice of second-class citizenship which weakens
America is somehow to persuade these Southerners to forget
their oath long enough to talk to Negroes, for few of them
really know how Negroes feel, dream, create, suffer as human
beings.

Even in 1964 there is hardly any communication between
Negro and white except at the city hall where the local sit-in
leaders or Freedom Riders sign some makeshift truce with the
mayor or the city council or the state attorney general's deputy.
During the upheaval in Birmingham, Alabama, after the death
of four little girls in the Negro church, and two other Negro
children in the riots that followed, there was a considerable
attempt made by both the national administration and the
white leaders of Birmingham to get together and discuss the
problem. Dr. L. H. Pitts, president of Miles College, a Negro
institution in Birmingham, wrote to the President: "I think
there are good men in the economic power structure of this
city who want to do something. They are good men, but they
don't know me. By that I don't mean Dr. Pitts, I mean they

do not know the Negro." At the bottom of this tragedy is the complete lack of communication between the races. They speak the same words but not the same language.

Since he cannot, since he is prohibited from, communicating, the Negro must demonstrate.

"Negroes do not want integration," said Governor Marvin Griffin of Georgia. "My maid told me so." Now even if the former governor were an educated man, that oath he swore would have kept him from realizing what the Lillian Smiths of the South knew—that the American Negro has two codes of behavior, one which he reserves for whites and the other which he saves for himself. One is a disguise and the other is real.

Any governor who asks his maid, "Do you want integration?" is not likely to get "Yes" for an answer. Far likelier is: "Governor, we never reads the papers." It is an answer which satisfies the governor and saves her job. For the maid knows —she is probably a volunteer worker for the local chapter of the National Association for the Advancement of Colored People—that her making the governor momentarily happy is not going to change the decisions of the federal courts which can be counted on to make the governor permanently unhappy. The governor has only himself to blame. He allowed himself to be trapped by a myth, a myth which he himself invented. The myth insists the Negro is happy.

So fine an intelligence as that of William Faulkner, certainly the best writer to come out of the South if not out of America, was trapped by the same myth. In his novel *The Reivers,* which he published in 1962, mind you, when the Negro revolution was in full swing, he could still put in the mouth of his Negro hero, Ned William McCaslin, the old canard, "If you could just be a nigger one Saturday night, you wouldn't never want to be white again as long as you live." It is hazardous to say that William Faulkner was politically liberal about the race question—it would seem from his writing he was not—but he had a large and generous sympathy for Negroes, and in his way admired them. Yet he could believe the colored man was satisfied with his "place" and hoped his readers could believe it too. If the myth could corrupt the shrewd imagination of a William Faulkner, think of the less astute it enslaved, and think of the malice it encouraged.

Senator James Eastland of Mississippi once told a Charlotte audience of which I was a member, "The Negroes are the happiest people in my state." It struck me immediately that Senator Eastland was not only blind in the way segregationists are blind, but deaf too. He must never have heard the songs these "happy" people sing: "Nobody Knows the Trouble I've Seen," "Father, Let me be Rid of This World," and "Let My People Go!"

But there were those who heard the songs and knew of the Negroes' inexpressible sadness and weariness. Back in 1908, young Howard Odum made the Negro the subject of his doctoral dissertation. Three years before, Ray Stannard Baker began his famous series on lynching for *McClure's* Magazine. By the end of World War I, Will Alexander, with the help of Mrs. Dorothy Tilly, Mrs. Jessie Daniel Ames, and R. B. Eleazer, had organized the first interracial committee in the United States.

They had precious little help. I remember going to Raleigh some years ago to appear as a witness before the North Carolina legislature investigating the ramifications of the Supreme Court decision outlawing segregation in the public schools. I was waiting my turn, seated beside a fellow I had known for years, who was the chairman of Patriots of America, Inc., Charlotte's white citizens organization.

The Reverend James Dees, an Episcopalian minister from Statesville, was testifying in favor of the Pearsall Plan, a

carefully managed program of token integration, which indeed the Legislature passed (though the Bishop Coadjutor of
the Episcopal Diocese of North Carolina, the Right Reverend
Richard H. Baker, testified against it and against racial segregation). I listened to the exercised Reverend Mr. Dees and
turning to the white supremacist sitting next to me, I said
matter of factly, "This is the strongest segregationist speech
I have ever heard from a Christian minister."

"Damn right," he replied, "this man is a real Christian.
All those other fellows are for brotherhood." (Author Burke
Davis overhead the conversation and reported it in the
Greensboro, N.C., *Daily News,* July 18, 1956.)

I knew another Charlottean whose ancestors had worshiped
for five generations in the same Presbyterian church. When
the North Carolina Presbyterian Synod passed a resolution by
a voice vote to support the Supreme Court's ruling against
racial segregation in the public schools, he became so incensed
he called his minister and asked him how he voted.

"I voted yes," said the minister.

"I resign from your church."

It took this man three days of telephoning finally to locate
one minister who had shouted "nay" and it was to that church
he thereafter drove his family for their Sunday devotionals.
This man not only could not communicate with the other
Southerners who shared his South, he refused to share religion
with men who only said they *wanted* to communicate. A
revolution surges around him and he goes looking for the
little old church in the vale.

At this advanced date people everywhere are still asking,
"What will the Negro want next? After we give him this, will
he want that? When, O when, will he ever be satisfied?" The
lack of communication has absolutely insulated them. They
do not realize that what the Negro wants is not theirs to
give—in fact, they have nothing to give that was not the

Negro's the day he or she was born on American soil. But despite the vagaries of the William Faulkners and the malignancies of the James Eastlands, a spectacular change has colored the South: The Negro has overtaken us, one and all.

In his earliest campaigns for simple justice, the Negro, perhaps mistakenly, relied upon the leadership of whites who were sympathetic, who tried to help by telling him to wait. But it was when he himself—the black man—began to fight that the limits of legal racial segregation narrowed, access to franchise and education widened, and he began to realize that he will get what is his because he and he alone will finally force communication and recognition.

The Negro is a unique revolutionary. Most revolutionaries vault the moat and scale the walls to storm the castle. They form the Continental Congress, or liberate the Bastille, or throw a bomb at the carriage of the czar, or behead their king. The American Negro revolutionary wants to change nothing. He is, in fact, enamored of our existing institutions. He wants *in,* he wants full participation in all public facilities and access to all public institutions.

In this revolution he uses two remarkable weapons. One is the writ, the brief, the court argument. In short, he uses the law, the oldest complex in our Anglo-American civilization. The second weapon is even more remarkable. It is Christianity, the oldest complex in our Western civilization.

Precisely because he refused to communicate, the white Southerner failed to grasp what future historians surely will, that the decisive weapon in the civil rights struggle was the very complex that the white Southerner most insistently pressed upon the Negro slave—Christianity and the Gospels.

The white Southerner wanted the Negro to believe in redemption, the better to silence any protests by promising future rewards. But the Negro is using Christianity to save himself here and now. The evangelical plantation owner saw no relationship between religion and politics. He forgot that while Christianity is a group effort to realize the joys of an afterlife, that effort is realized only through an individual ethic in the here and now, an ethic which often demands sacrifice, humility and faith, and is all the more powerful and influential for these demands. Little did the Southerner suspect that one day the descendants of slaves would wield Christianity as a finely tooled political weapon, asking jobs, schools, wages, and hospitals in its name.

If Christianity is saving the Negro, so is he saving Christianity. It is the twentieth-century Negro in America who rediscovered Christianity's ethic and upon rediscovery, made that ethic an effective ethic. He has done the white Southerner an immeasurable service, for he has proved Christianity does indeed have its uses. Christianity did not save whites from the ravages of the Depression, nor did it save the Jews of Europe, nor did Christianity bring into being the emergent states of Africa. But Christianity is bringing the Negro to the threshold of first-class citizenship in the United States.

The Negro does not use Christianity to terrorize the bully-boy sheriff nor does he hope it will pacify the police dogs. Nor does he use Christianity to intimidate or discipline others. He uses it to discipline himself, to give himself order and cohesion and a rationale. Eleven million Negroes in the South, many of them unable to read or write, untutored in the sophisticated ways of the city, certainly exploited on their rural tenant farms, still all of them understand their movement, and collectively they have not made one serious mistake in their demand for justice. The Negroes have used Christianity to contain their revolution and though the Negro is in the streets, he is in the streets with prayer and humility, not with rifle and incendiary grenades.

At the moment this insurgent felt his real power, John F.

Kennedy became President of the United States. Whether he willed it or not, the late Mr. Kennedy became the nation's second "Emancipator President."

The first, of course, was Abraham Lincoln. Kennedy may have been even more strict an *emancipator* than Lincoln. Lincoln's cruel test was to save the Union, a threat not now menacing America. The revolution of the Negro is bloodless because the sovereignty of the Federal Government, though condemned throughout the South, is everywhere recognized. John F. Kennedy's crucial task in his two years and ten months as President was not, on that account, less easy.

"Abraham Lincoln was not fighting a cold war with a frighteningly large and strong nuclear power; the balance of world power did not daily shift with the emergence of new nations; the invasion of Mexico by Napoleon III was successfully resisted by the Mexicans themselves, whereas internal revolution against Castro in Cuba is most improbable.

President Kennedy knew that every move the American Negro made had its effect throughout the world. He knew that every move he himself made affected his chance for re-election, a campaign he was already preparing when struck down by an assassin. To say that he was playing politics is naive. Any President of the United States perforce plays politics with each and every issue. He dooms his administration and the hopes of the majority which elected him when he refuses to meet issues politically, as Herbert Hoover refused to meet the issues of the Depression in 1930 politically, and William Howard Taft refused to meet the issues of the growing labor movement in the early 1900s politically. I think that Theodore Sorensen, special counsel to President Kennedy, states clearly in his book, *Decision-Making in the White House:*

. . . the major forces or sources of influence which shape the presidential decision itself [are] grouped under three frames of reference: presidential politics, presidential advisers, and the presidential perspective. . . .

Some purists—if not realists—may blush at the fact that politics heads the list. But we are discussing our prime political office and the nation's prime politician, a man who has been chosen by his party as well as the people. Some Presidents may assert that they are "above politics," yet politics, in its truest and broadest sense, still colors their every decision (including the decision to appear non-political) . . .[3]

There is sufficient evidence to demonstrate that Lincoln's Emancipation Proclamation was a political move, prompted in part by Lincoln's desire to pacify the antislavery critics who kept insisting the Civil War be fought to free the slaves when Lincoln knew he had a Union to preserve.

General John C. Frémont had issued his own emancipation proclamation for Missouri as had General David Hunter for Georgia, Florida, and South Carolina. Both of whom were overruled by Lincoln. In point of fact, Lincoln by the Emancipation Proclamation freed the slaves where they could not be freed—in the Confederate states—and kept them bound where they could be freed—in the Border states. Lincoln probably hoped that, having stalled his critics at home, he had also eliminated any possibility of recognition for the Confederacy from abroad and he could use the ensuing months to bring Congress and the country to accept a plan of gradual emanicipation, perhaps even resettling the freedmen outside the country.

Having issued his Proclamation, Lincoln faced up to such charges as that he was opportunistic, purely political, and merely trying to placate a pressure group. His torments are

[3] Theodore C. Sorensen, *Decision-Making in the White House* (New York, Columbia University Press, 1963), p. 43.

too well known to need recounting here. His vacillations on the subject of slavery are known and recorded acts. He is still known as the Great Emancipator, however, because he prepared his Emancipation Proclamation on a moral foundation and that moral foundation endured.

Lincoln played politics successfully, first because he played politics for moral issues and, second, because the Union armies checked the Confederates at the Battle of Antietam. Lincoln, it should be remembered, awaited the outcome of the battle before issuing the Emancipation Proclamation.

This book is an attempt to assess how successfully Mr. Kennedy had played politics as an *emancipator* or civil rights President. Whether he was a civil rights President because of political expediency, or because he could not avoid being a civil rights President, or because he believed in this cause with all his intellectual fervor and being—all this is irrelevant. He remains the civil rights President.

What impressed itself quite clearly in the third year of Mr. Kennedy's presidency was that his politics had to include a total commitment to the social revolution of the American Negro.

In 1941, President Franklin D. Roosevelt asked A. Philip Randolph, the Negro labor leader, to cancel a proposed march on Washington, D.C. In 1956, President Eisenhower refused to see A. Philip Randolph and his committee. E. Frederic Morrow, a presidential aide, writes in his diary, *Black Man in the White House,* "I went to New York to talk to Randolph about his request to see the President, and was authorized to tell him that a conference would be granted him as soon as the President was well enough." Mr. Morrow adds that the President's Committee on Appointments decided "It would not be wise at this time to see A. Philip Randolph . . . because it would incense Southern Governors and other persons who have wanted to talk to the President about the race situation and have been denied." [4] In 1963, President Kennedy gave the August 28 "March on Washington" his blessing and simply asked Randolph in what "unofficial" way the Government could help keep the March peaceful and under responsible control, and where shall we deliver the box lunches and portable rest rooms?

To some extent President Kennedy had signaled his commitment to the cause of Negro civil rights even before he was elected. During the campaign of 1960, he telephoned Mrs. Martin Luther King when her husband, the religious leader of the protest movement of the Southern Negro, was given a four-month prison sentence technically for not having a Georgia driver's license. Perhaps Mr. Kennedy's call was dictated by a humane concern for the welfare of Dr. King, but the opposition nevertheless interpreted his telephone call politically, and it is also true that Mr. Kennedy made political capital on it. Thus the careers of Martin Luther King and John F. Kennedy coincided in decisive fashion during the 1960 presidential campaign. Writes Theodore H. White in *The Making of the President, 1960:*

> The father of Martin Luther King, a Baptist minister himself, who had come out for Nixon a few weeks earlier on religious ground, now switched. "Because this man," said the Reverend Mr. King Senior, "was willing to wipe the tears from my daughter (in-law)'s eyes, I've got a suitcase of votes, and I'm going to take them to Mr. Kennedy and dump them in his lap." Across the country scores of Negro leaders, deeply Protestant but even more deeply impressed by Kennedy's action, followed suit . . . when one reflects that Illinois was carried by only 9,000 votes and that 250,-000 Negroes are estimated to have voted for Kennedy; that

[4] E. Frederic Morrow, *Black Man in the White House* (New York, Coward-McCann, 1963), pp. 87-88.

Michigan was carried by 67,000 votes and that an estimated 250,000 Negroes voted for Kennedy; that South Carolina was carried by 10,000 votes and that an estimated 40,000 Negroes there voted for Kennedy, the candidate's instinctive decision must be ranked among the most crucial of the last few weeks.[5]

It is fair to say as well that Nixon's *failure* to act was politically motivated. Says Mr. White:

On the afternoon of the sentencing of Martin Luther King to four months of hard labor in Georgia, the Department of Justice—at the suggestion of a wise yet shrewd Republican Deputy Attorney General (Judge Lawrence E. Walsh) —composed a draft statement to support the application for release of the imprisoned minister. Two copies of the draft were sent out immediately for approval—one to the White House, one to Mr. Nixon's traveling headquarters (on that day in Ohio). No one has yet revealed who killed this draft statement that was so critically important in the tense politics of civil rights. Either President Eisenhower or Vice-President Nixon could have acted—yet neither did. However obscure Eisenhower's motivations were, Nixon's are more perplexing, for he was the candidate. He had made the political decision at Chicago to court the Negro vote in the North; only now, apparently, he felt it quite possible that Texas, South Carolina, and Louisiana might all be won to him by the white vote and he did not wish to offend that vote. So he did not act—there was no whole philosophy of politics to instruct him.[6]

Senator John F. Kennedy and Vice-President Richard M. Nixon, as had Presidential candidates before them, thought

[5] Theodore H. White, *The Making of the President, 1960* (New York, Atheneum Publishers, 1961), p. 94.
[6] *Ibid.*, p. 97.

of the Negro in terms of a momentary political advantage. Each planned a gambit for white and Negro votes. It was a political gamble for both Kennedy and Nixon. Robert Kennedy's first reaction to the news of Dr. Martin Luther King's sentence was: "Four months for a traffic violation?"

The Kennedy commitment on behalf of the victimized Dr. King may have been shrewd politics, but the Kennedys had no way of knowing that this momentary intervention by its very nature had to become an absolute policy. Nor did Mr. Nixon realize that his decision not to intervene on that particular day would end all hopes of his participation in the social revolution of the American Negro.

There is no doubt that Robert Kennedy envisioned his role in his brother's Administration mainly as the Attorney General who would finally prosecute James R. Hoffa, boss of the Teamsters Union. Swearing his oath of office, Robert Kennedy had no idea that the pursuit of James Hoffa would become insignificant compared to his work preparing fifty-eight civil rights cases in addition to the inspection of the voting records in over one hundred counties of the Southern states in his first thirty months as the Attorney General. Did Robert Kennedy imagine he and his staff would spend midnight hours in communication with the public officials of Alabama and Mississippi, persuading these men to let Negro college students attend classes and at the same time preserve order?

I doubt very much that when John F. Kennedy decided to intervene on Martin Luther King's behalf he realized that his presidency would eventually be identified, above all other accomplishments, with the social revolution of the American Negro.

And in the struggle of the Negro for his rights, Robert F. Kennedy, the man with his finger forever on the political button, was to become, not the Attorney General who happened to be a Roman Catholic, but a New England Puritan who happened to be the Attorney General. Within eighteen months Robert F. Kennedy had caught up on three hundred years of history of the American Negro. From the naive exclamation, "Four months for a traffic violation?" he was soon repeating over and over again, "But it is wrong!" in each of his conversations with Southern governors, senators, and law enforcement officers. He had come face to face with a wrong, to his mind a wrong so monstrous, that he could not even understand it fully, and for the moment at least, he had taken his finger off that political button. It is not so strange that the one considered the *most* political, should have become the *most* personally involved.

As President, John F. Kennedy, like other Presidents, had indicated he would lend the power of the Executive office to change conditions in the national interest on a broad and far-reaching scale. Why was this political prerogative on behalf of the Negro so bitterly contested? Who said "playing Negro politics" is wrong? In itself bad?

This criticism came mainly from Southern segregationist politicians who owe all their political success to that most important principle of twentieth-century Southern politics—"holler nigger first." In 1938, when Olin D. Johnston of South Carolina tried to unseat Senator "Cotton Ed" Smith, he charged that the incumbent Senator was a "nigger-lover." "Cotton Ed," said Johnston, "voted for a bill that would permit a big buck nigger to sit by your wife on a railroad train."

Cotton Ed retaliated by boasting to his constituents he had walked out of the Democratic National Convention in 1936 when a Negro minister was asked to recite a prayer. "The purpose of that prayer," said Senator Smith, "was not to invoke divine assistance but to invoke colored votes." "Cotton Ed" Smith won the election. Editor Josephus Daniels recorded it in his Raleigh *News and Observer*, July 19, 1944: "One day when Jim Farley had called on a Negro preacher to lead the convention in prayer, Senator Smith walked out of the convention, condemning having 'a nigger to pray in a Democratic convention.' "

Again, in the bitter Senatorial race in North Carolina in which Dr. Frank P. Graham lost his seat in 1950, the forces of the late Senator Willis Smith distributed a reprint of a news photograph showing a Negro GI kissing a British girl, with the caption: "Do you want this in North Carolina?" Frank Graham had appointed a Negro on the basis of a competitive examination as an alternate to West Point. The photograph of that young Negro was distributed throughout the state with the caption, "Senator Graham appointed this Negro to West Point." The two photographs were enough to defeat him.

At a social function in Chicago I remarked that I was surprised that the "liberal" United States Senator, Lister Hill of Alabama, had signed the Southern Manifesto, a round-robin "agreement" among Southern senators and congressmen pledging every legal means to prevent integration. Newton Minow, a friend of the Senator, said, "Harry, would you rather have Lister Hill in the Senate signing the Southern Manifesto or the Alabama Power and Light Company in the Senate signing the Southern Manifesto?" Even so, some years later, Senator Hill came within a few thousand votes of losing his seat to James D. Martin, who ran on the Republican ticket. The charge against Senator Hill was that he was secretly "liberal" on the race issue.

And even Southern hospitality yields to political expediency. Governor Stanley of Virginia refused to greet the Lord Chief Justice of Great Britain at the College of William and Mary because Chief Justice Earl Warren was also an honored guest at the same function.

The late President Kennedy had one hope which he expressed to every visitor, white or Negro, who came to see him on civil rights matters. The hope was to leave the White House with the racial question substantially alleviated, with a wider use of the ballot by the Negro as well as wider educational possibilities, better prospects for employment, and integrated housing, and thus to have cut the ground forever from under the conservative Southern bloc. This would have meant that Southern politicians would have to look for another horse to ride, a dismaying search for any politician, but particularly dismaying for those who have used the issue of white supremacy throughout their political lives.

The segregationists argue that the harsh politics of exclusion and separation are of ancient origin, impossible to be dispelled, hardened by centuries of usage. C. Vann Woodward in *The Strange Career of Jim Crow* decisively proves the opposite, and pinpoints the pretext: ". . . the defenders of racial segregation have consistently maintained that such practices were the inevitable consequences of the association of two races of different characteristics and cultural attainments," [7] an argument Robert Penn Warren has termed "the Great Alibi."

Governor Ross Barnett of Mississippi taunted the President with failing to dispatch troops to Philadelphia when Negroes staged a demonstration protesting discriminatory hiring practices in building public housing projects. The taunt missed the whole point. Injustice exists in Philadelphia, Chicago, New York, and throughout the North, but that injustice is neither sanctioned by law nor sanctified by public opinion, as it is in the South. The North does not fight a federal court order and compound injustice with fire hoses and shock sticks. And in the North the Negro has the most important of all weapons, the weapon still denied him wholeheartedly in the South—the ballot. In Negro homes in the city and in Negro cabins on

[7] C. Vann Woodward, *The Strange Career of Jim Crow* (New York, Oxford University Press, 1955), pp. 64-67.

the farms of the South, a common joke runs: "In the North, the white man says, 'Nigger, go as high as you can but don't come close,' and in the South, the white man says, 'Nigger come as close as you can but don't go up.' "

It was President Kennedy's great strength that the racial politics he played were moral politics; for this reason the racial politics he initiated will eventually succeed, beyond any shadow of doubt. In the struggle for emancipation, Mr. Kennedy had more resources than Lincoln had. Lincoln had only the Union armies under Ulysses S. Grant. President Kennedy had not only the courts and the Constitution, but even more significantly he had the Negro.

There remains one more question I must touch upon in this opening chapter. It is this: What forces propelled John F. Kennedy into the role of an emancipator or civil rights President at all? Why did the United States of America need two Presidents in mid-twentieth century to cope with racial injustice? (Even the Southern segregationists confess to this injustice because they say, "Let us do it—gradually.")

Both Presidents Eisenhower and Kennedy had to deal with the problem because in 1877, when the North called off Reconstruction, as C. Vann Woodward puts it in *Reunion and Reaction:* ". . . the Southerners abandoned the cause of Tilden in exchange for the control over two states and the Republicans abandoned the cause of the Negro in exchange for the peaceful possession of the Presidency." [8]

[8] C. Vann Woodward, *Reunion and Reaction* (New York, Doubleday Anchor Books, 1957), p. 79.

CHAPTER TWO

"I WANT TO BE WHERE THE PEOPLE ARE"

ULYSSES S. GRANT led so venal and so stupid an administration that he succeeded in doing what no President before or since has ever managed: he became a terrible bore. He bored even his own professional supporters.

Nor were the Democrats of 1876 much better. Seventeen years before, they had split into two parties and for their pains saw Lincoln win. They were still two parties: a Northern and a Southern party. Liberal and conservative Democrats made contentious wagon mates in 1876 on the role of the federal government in state affairs as they disagree in 1964 on whether America is an urban country to be governed by urban legislators or an urban country to be governed by rural legislators.

Republicans chose as their candidate Rutherford B. Hayes, a graduate of Kenyon College in Gambier, Ohio. By no means a brilliant man, Hayes had a reputation for stability. He had practiced law, served as a general in the Civil War, been elected to Congress, and won three different terms as Ohio's governor. He was conservative yet flexible, honest and only occasionally astute.

The Democrats picked Samuel J. Tilden, governor of New

York. Tilden had an impressive record of incorruptibility, having helped convict members of the Tammany Hall Tweed Ring. He had also amassed a large private fortune as a railroad corporation lawyer, and he must have earned every penny for he had ulcers so severe his health was a campaign issue.

In *The Angry Scar,* Hodding Carter writes:

The United States has never witnessed a clean presidential campaign. The campaign of 1876 was dirtier than most. More importantly, it was the first since 1860 in which the outcome was seriously in doubt. The Republicans pulled out the old reliable bloody shirt, labeled the Democrats as rebels at heart and Tilden a tool of the railroads, and a tax-evading millionaire whose poor health added to his unfitness. The Democrats whaled away at hard times, the domination of the Republican Party by urban, financial, and industrial interests, at the evil-doing among the remaining Carpetbag governments, and the waste and venality of Grantism.[1]

A dirty campaign is the invariable tip-off that both sides think they will lose; it is simply a question of who is going to lose worse. In this case, it was Hayes. Tilden had a plurality of 286,000 votes and, so the Democrats thought, a plurality of 18 votes in the Electoral College, 184 to 166. Or let's say the Democrats thought he had a plurality of eighteen votes.

Not having succeeded by campaign and ballot, the Republicans tried fraud. There were three Southern states with indecisive returns: Florida, South Carolina, and Louisana. In each of these three states a Returning Board composed of four or five appointed officials whose duty was to canvass the returns and certify they were accurate. Moving a state from

[1] Hodding Carter, *The Angry Scar* (New York, Doubleday & Company, Inc., 1959), p. 327.

the Democratic electoral column to the Republican was an easy matter of invalidating more Democratic than Republican ballots—which the Returning Boards of Florida, South Carolina, and Louisiana hastened to do since they were all Grant appointees. The electoral votes of the three Southern states plus the one wavering elector in Oregon gave the Presidency to Hayes, 185 to 184.

The Democrats threatened filibusters, Senate investigations, and wholesale anarchy, all of which the Republicans avoided by a compromise, commonly called the "Compromise of 1877."

Both C. Vann Woodward, in *Reunion and Reaction,* and Hodding Carter are at pains to point out that this compromise was not effected in two afternoons of haggling, but over a two-month period of prolonged negotiations. When and how it was effected, however, is not to our point.

The Southern Democrats gave Hayes the Presidency on the condition that Federal troops leave the South and that Louisiana, Florida, and South Carolina be given home rule. Hayes also promised to spend federal money in the South and appoint Southerners to his cabinet. He entered Washington secretly in a private railroad car and took his oath of office on March 3, 1877, in the White House, virtually alone.

The South got railroads, home rule, and cabinet members. The Republicans kept their patronage. But the North finally lost the Civil War because by this compromise the South won a free hand with its Negroes, which once again made us two countries.

With the Compromise of 1877, the Federal Government abandoned the Negro to the legislatures of the several states and "gradualism" had come to the South, never to leave it (for in late 1963 Republican Senator Barry Goldwater of Arizona recommended as a solution of the racial problem that the several Southern states handle it without federal interference).

"Gradualism" to the white Southerner means one thing; to

the Negro something else. To the white Southerner the promise of gradualism is a promise he doesn't have to keep, and never has kept. To the Negro, gradualism is a continuing process of dehumanization wherein he loses franchise, civil rights, economic power, and hope. Gradualism was never an ameliorating condition, steadily improving, but a desperate condition, year by year deteriorating.

In the ante-bellum South, in the days of the plantations, segregration was not only impossible, it was undreamt of. Negro and white frequently lived in the same house, shared the same plates, and attended the same church. There was no "natural antipathy" of the races. No owner of a plantation would ever have installed one elevator for whites and another for Negroes, as indeed Atlanta ordinances so instructed building contractors in the 1920s.

Federal troops had no sooner left, however, than the South discovered an institution more peculiar than slavery. It was the convict-lease system, a legal perpetuation of slavery in which the state leased its convicts to sawmills, mines, and plantations. Not only did this system save states the expense of prison maintenance, but it turned a tidy profit for the treasury. In addition, the convict-lease system made several enterprising operators millionaires. The state could ensure a never-ending supply of labor for it was easy to arrest helpless, illiterate Negroes and give them long sentences. One of the more obvious reasons why Negroes never demonstrated in the years before the turn of the century was the prospect of long servitude under barbaric conditions.

What doomed the convict-lease system was indeed its lucrative nature. By 1880, barely six years after the system had been inaugurated, prison authorities were supplying white men and women convicts to private corporations. In 1886, Rebecca Fulton, one of the pioneers of the Woman's Christian Temperance Union, was begging the Georgia State Legislature to protect convict women forced to satisfy the lusts of cruel guards.

Even here, though the Negro was the principal victim of the convict-lease system, he was not separated. Indeed, one of the reasons the system was closed out in the 1900s was that as the segregation laws came on the books, Southern citizens were more appalled by the realization that white and colored prisoners were manacled together than they were at the horrors they had perpetrated on a helpless humanity, often unjustly and arbitrarily convicted.

Segregation as we know it today, by which we mean the *legal* exclusion of the Negro, did not come to the South until the 1890s. For fifteen years after the Civil War, though the Negro was left unprotected and therefore exploited, the state had not tried removing him from the byways of life. Southerners started removing the Negro from the byways because he had started to accumulate political power. The separate drinking fountains, the back of the bus, the segregated trolley car, the Grandfather voting clause, the poll tax—all came from the attempt by Southern cities to disfranchise the rural poor, chief of whom was the Negro.

Everything the South owned—natural resources, land, labor—had been systematically exploited by the Northern capitalists in league with Southern financiers and politicians. Farmers baled their cotton, shipped it north, and then paid one hundred times its worth for shoddy dresses made of that same cotton; they watched helplessly while the railroads seized their lands for rights of way, and promptly charged exorbitant freight charges; the money farmers had to repay banks was worth much more than the money they had borrowed; they burned their crops to keep warm because the price of fuel was so high. The climate ordered them to grow one crop, cotton, and cotton kept them hungry. In Georgia, the slogan of one political campaign less than sixty years before our present era of fabulous affluence was: "Hoke for Hunger: Brown for Bread," and neither "hunger" nor "bread" was metaphorical.

Out of this poverty came the suspicion that the currency of the country was constantly manipulated against the farmers. From this suspicion came the People's party, Populism.

One significant reason for the initial success of Populism was that it banded together the white and Negro farmers and white and Negro laborers. The one-mule farmers of the South were slowly realizing that if the Civil War freed the Negroes, it also enfranchised them. But once they did realize it, once their leaders began stumping the back country, their power grew quickly. Populism became a political force. It was responsible eventually for the nomination of William Jennings Bryan. It failed nationally, but it did not fail in the South. Populism was the poor people's politics and it gave the poor power.

In 1890 there were Southern politicians calling for brotherhood. Negroes sat on the political dais and worked in the committees. Together the back-country white and the black man began to terrify the cities. All that kept the Populists from ultimate power was the ability of the city politicians to fix elections—an American trait more habitual than the usual history book makes out. Again and again, the city politician rigged the vote in the black ghettos of cities like Atlanta, Memphis, and Charleston. Time after time, Populists swept the rural areas only to find victory denied them when counting boards added the returns from the Negro city precincts. Negroes in the city were bribed and threatened, cajoled and driven to the election booths.

City politicians whose support came from the banks and railroads knew that they couldn't fix the black districts forever, so they began to urge the disfranchisement of the Negro as the remedy for the Populist surge. Suddenly these politicians and editors and financiers discovered the races had a "natural antipathy." In 1901 Carter Glass told the Virginia constitutional convention: "Negro enfranchisement was a crime to begin with." They were to make the "natural antipathy" between the races retroactive.

City councils began introducing segregation ordinances, and legislatures began passing poll tax statutes. Editorials proclaimed the Negro a beast and a brute. Newspapers, worrying about the sanctity of Southern womanhood, encouraged and spurred on lynch mobs. (Lynching became a national problem not when the Negro was freed but when he was disfranchised.)

Seeing the struggle take this turn, the Populist leaders promptly sold out. The Populists hoped that (white) Republican and Democratic desertions to their cause would more than make up for the Negro disfranchisement and thus they would still hold the balance of power.

In the late 1890s, the Populist leader of Georgia, Tom Watson, promised not to oppose the disfranchisement laws if the gubernatorial candidate, Democrat Hoke Smith, would urge the Populist reforms. Watson argued that white men had to unite before they could divide. The compromise made Watson the undisputed political boss of Georgia until he died as senator in 1922.

Not long after the passage of laws for poll taxes and literacy tests, rising farm prices dissipated the Populist appeal. But the mania of segregation, once induced, was harder to dissipate. It had proved an effective rallying cry, an easy way to get a farmer's vote while working against his interest.

But the lynch fury that swept the nation from 1882 into the 1930s, the accelerated industrialization of the South, and World War I awakened reform. The conscience of the country began to question the South's crusade against the colored man.

The South always answered, "Let us do it gradually." The South said, "This is *our* problem." And it added, "He isn't ready."

Perhaps "gradualism" might well have eased the burdens of the South in the 1960s, increased its wealth and raised its per capita earnings, except that there was no such process as "gradualism." During World War I, countless Southern towns prohibited colored doughboys walking their streets. As late as 1942 I saw Negroes tip their hats to strange white men they passed on the sidewalk. Gradualism was more than a denial of proprieties; gradualism was four Negro women dying in childbirth for every one white woman dying in childbirth in 1958, sixty years after gradualism came. Childbirth is responsible for the second largest number of deaths in the South—Negro infant and maternal deaths. Gradualism meant an infant mortality rate among Negroes five and a half times that of whites. When I was a boy, the high infant mortality was considered inescapable—that is, it was attributed to God's will—but since then we have found that it was our fault. But Negro infant mortality is still God's will. Where tuberculosis was twelfth as a cause of death among white Southerners, it was third among Negroes—in 1962. Because there was no gradualism in public health facilities for the Negro, he died from diseases hospitals can speedily cure.

"Don't quote me," said an elected official at Good Samaritan, the Negro hospital in Charlotte, North Carolina, "but I saw a doctor operate on three people without washing his hands and he used the same needle to sew them up." That was in 1957, and I use Good Samaritan Hospital in my city because Charlotte has been, in fact, next to Atlanta, the most progressive Southern city. This "progress" will give the reader an idea of what gradualism has accomplished in the less "liberal" areas of the South.

In 1963 there was still no intern program in Good Samaritan. Negroes who enter medical practice in the South have two choices: they can attend the inferior segregated schools and start practice in a weak, segregated hospital, or they can take advantage of the policy of subsidized out-of-state study, go to a good medical school in the North, and never return to the inferior hospitals of the South. In the past few years, it is true, the University of North Carolina Medical School has accepted a few Negroes; but so far, no hospital staff membership has been open to them. And it is not likely that integrated hospitals will be a reality in the near future.

In *The South and the Southerner*, Ralph McGill writes, "There was something shameful in the hurry of the Southern states to equalize their schools." [2] I can add that there was something even more shameful and more obscene in the hurry of municipal officials throughout the South to provide call buttons, for the first time, on the beds of the Negro hospitals in the South. The Negroes who fight for the right to enter public school are fighting for more than an education. They are fighting for life or death. Public schools are the first step, adequate hospital care the second.

Gradualism, so called, meant that a surprisingly large number of Negro clergymen and educators, over fifty years of age now, have never spent a day in a tax-supported school. The poorest of the poor had no public schools and had to send their children to private, church-supported schools. Usually the teachers consisted of a husband and a wife, receiving a combined salary of one thousand dollars a year and room and board, hard money scraped together every year from poor colored sharecroppers and hard-pressed domestics. In Atlanta, for instance, the first "separate but equal" high school for Negroes was not built until 1924. In 1954, most of the Negro schools in the counties outside the two most progressive cities

2 Ralph McGill, *The South and the Southerner* (Boston, Atlantic *Monthly Press*, 1959), p. 187.

of the South, Atlanta and Charlotte, had outside toilets and were heated by potbellied stoves.

Professor Howard H. Quint [3] reveals that not until 1920 did the South Carolina Legislature appropriate as much money for Negro education as had been appropriated during any one year of the Reconstruction. In 1950, Governor James Byrnes had to warn that same legislature that if the state was to preserve its legally supported "separate but equal" facilities, it would cost South Carolina upwards of 250 million dollars to make colored schools equal to white. This was the situation in the "separate but equal" schools of the South in 1954, after seventy years of "gradualism." In six separate high schools, one each in the cities of Atlanta, Birmingham, Charlotte, Charleston, Memphis, and Jackson, the teacher-pupil ratio in Negro schools was 37.2 as against 31.9 in the white schools. The library holdings were distinctly inferior, an average of 12,157 volumes in the white school as against the average of 2,467 in the Negro school. The total value of the Negro schools was only 18.2 per cent of the total value of the schools in the six cities, although Negro pupils constituted about 30 per cent of the school population.

So much for statistics. The Negro has suffered a tragic delay, his hands securely tied behind his back during a half-century of industrial and urban expansion without parallel in the history of the world. Let not his awesome loss, however, overshadow the frightful cost to the white Southerner. Nor has the cost of paying double for everything from plumbing fixtures to schools, insane asylums, prisons, swimming pools, water fountains, and even outside privies been the biggest part of that burden.

The great tragedy for the white Southerner is that he lives in the most enchanting region on this continent and comes

[3] Howard H. Quint, *Profile in Black and White* (Washington, D.C., Public Affairs Press, 1958), p. 9.

from the most politically creative society in the western
world, but has forsaken all these natural gifts and noble traditions in order to utilize his intellect, energies, and reasoning
to prevent a few Negro children from going to previously
all-white public schools. He has far removed himself from
the traditions established by John Marshall, Thomas Jefferson, the Reverend William Tennent, Charles Pinckney, and
hundreds of others. The modern Southern authority on Constitutional law is Senator Sam Ervin of North Carolina, and
Senator Strom Thurmond is its champion of the rights of
man.

Worse, this defiance has affected the segregationist's reason.
In Birmingham, when the federal court ordered public golf
links integrated, the segregationists closed down the course.
A few hardy golfers sneaked in and played anyway. So
grown-up white Southerners plugged up the holes with cement.
(The golfers still play; they just pretend they get a hole-in-
one.) In another city, so many Negroes appeared in court
every day, arrested for demonstrating, that "white" water
fountains were endangered. There were not enough police to
protect the water fountains so city officials, some of them
descended from the men who wrote the Constitution of the
United States, cut off the water altogether.

Sacrificing his common sense, the segregationist perforce
has often sacrificed his humanity. Segregation makes him callous. Mary Louise Baker, an eight-year-old Negro child, lay
bleeding on a Montgomery, Alabama, street because a good
samaritan called a "white" ambulance instead of a "colored"
ambulance. The good samaritan acknowledged his mistake,
confessing he thought the little girl was white. A police officer and a white ambulance driver stood by idly, waiting for a
"colored" ambulance to come while the little girl's blood
spilled into the street.

Because they have become calloused, it is impossible for the vast majority of white Southerners to recognize the humanity of the Negro. Ingratiating Southerners tell me, "You don't understand the Negro; he's a child," and "He isn't ready," and, "Negroes can't think for themselves."

In fact, there are Southerners who insist the Negro is blameless in this revolution for civil rights. The entire Negro movement is charged off to Northern agitators. Professor Quint reprints in his book a resolution of the South Carolina Legislature in 1930 which demanded unequivocally that "henceforth the damned agitators of the North leave the South alone." Since he has insisted on two classes of citizens at home, the Southerner still insists the country be divided into two parts.

The segregationist not only refuses to listen to but refuses to acknowledge that Lillian Smith, Paul Green, Ralph Mc-Gill, Mark Ethridge, Frank P. Graham, Guy B. Johnson, Hodding Carter, Harold Fleming, Jonathan Daniels, James McBride Dabbs, Wilma Dykeman, her husband, James Stokely, Sarah Patton Boyle, P. D. East, Marion Wright, and Harry Ashmore, bone-of-the-bone and blood-of-the-blood Southerners, have done as much to encourage the social revolution of the American Negro as all the "Northern agitators" combined.

It is not fair, therefore, to say of the South that its resistance to integration is monolithic. The whites of the South by no means constitute a solid unit. In addition to the contemporaries I have mentioned, let no one forget, particularly Southerners, that the South itself produced some of the most fearless champions of racial justice in our nation's history. One thinks immediately of Supreme Court Justice John Marshall Harlan, a former slave owner from Kentucky who dissented and protested during all the years that the Supreme Court, dominated by Northern Republicans and contemptuously called the "bulwark of privilege," cemented the segregation laws.

Southern solidarity is a result of the politicians' solidarity. Segregation has served the interests of politicians so well during this century that it is often the only subject on which an elected Southern officeholder can philosophize at all. James K. Vardaman, the Negrophobic Governor of Mississippi in the early years of this century, told Harris Dickson, who prepared an article in 1907 for the *Saturday Evening Post*, ". . . the Negro is singularly tractable and amenable to control by his well-recognized superiors. For this reason the Egyptians, Romans and Turks paid higher prices for them than for other slaves. They never fretted in captivity; it was their natural state." On no other occasion did Governor Vardaman display such a flair for history, and I wonder what he would think of the fretful Negro today.

During an exchange of views with Governor Ross Barnett of Mississippi, Attorney General Robert F. Kennedy said, "Governor, there is not a single Negro voter registered in one of your counties which has a Negro population of eighteen thousand."

Replied Governor Barnett: "They don't want to vote. They are satisfied if left alone."

Yet every Negro grandmother tells a story about the time a grandfather or granduncle walked twenty-two miles down the dirt road to the county seat to vote, in the days before disfranchisement.

Southerners drew a line and prohibited Negroes crossing it. They doomed themselves to a lifetime of guarding that line, fearing it would be breached. Because the white Southerner must forever watch that line, the Negro intrudes upon the white at every level of life.

There are white men throughout the South who are fifty

and sixty years old and who have literally never worked. Of course, they may have helped out in a political primary now and then and perhaps been paid for driving a new car from Detroit to Atlanta, but they have never practiced a profession or followed a trade. The reason for this is that their talents or skills were not immediately sufficient to train them for a job at an upper economic or social level. Their society forbade them to use their lesser talents or skills at a lower level because that was inhabited by the Negro. So these white men did nothing.

Less than fifteen per cent of the South's two-and-three-quarter million industrial workers are unionized, mostly because of the fear of the Negro. Managers and superintendents have usually offered a subtle suggestion that if the union is voted in, the "International Office" will force Negroes into the plant.

The new immigrants from Europe had one advantage over the fifth-generation white Southerner. The immigrant was not tied to an artificial standard of superiority. He went into the mines and pits and behind a peddler's cart, he swept the city's streets and built railroads and worked in the sweat shops, and while he was indeed exploited, he had a certain reward. He—and if not he, his children—could find their level.

Fear that the Negro will cross that line leads also to the threat and use of force and violence. The threat was ever present in the personal, economic, and political relationship between the races. Fear of slave insurrections was replaced by vague and unknown menaces—social equality, the paralyzing terror of "mongrelization," and the fear somehow the Negro would replace employed whites.

Many Southern writers have examined the phenomenon of the white man's transference of sexual guilt from himself to the Negro. The "mongrelization" of which the segregationist talks has always taken place between the white male and the Negro female and because it was so endemic a sexual exploitation, the white man feared, as all men fear, reprisal, and he also felt the pangs of guilt for his own infidelity.

Nowadays the white man fears the Negro will displace him on his job. Steelworkers, truck drivers, bakers, even politicians fear this new insurgent. But with automation the fears are false. There have even been instances where the unemployed, unskilled white man, automated out of the steel mill, works on the garbage truck, a job usually reserved for the Negro. Again and again the white man transfers his own heavy loads onto the already burdened shoulders of the Negro.

Since segregation necessarily involves the renunciation of logic, no logic can prevail against it. Martin Agronsky, on an NBC program, asked Alabama's Governor George C. Wallace, "Governor, did you ever sit down and negotiate with Negro leaders on this matter?" The Governor replied, "Racial segregation is not negotiable."

Governor Ross Barnett in nearly every conversation with either the late President Kennedy or the Attorney General kept repeating, "You know how our people feel about that here?" during the Meredith crisis at the University of Mississippi. The Mississippi Governor further pleaded with Burke Marshall, Deputy Attorney General in charge of the Civil Rights Division, that his state could pay Meredith's expenses elsewhere, in another school. Barnett wanted the federal authorities to ask Meredith whether he would agree to go. Barnett said that Mississippi law permitted it and such a transfer would make everybody happier. The whole problem would be solved. "Even the Negro man would be happier." Thus the Governor of Mississippi.

What Governor Barnett proposed to Burke Marshall is one of the devices which has helped keep the South poor. Toward the end of the 1930s, many Negroes began graduating from the Negro colleges of the South. They wanted graduate degrees. Under the "separate but equal" laws, several Southern states

provided out-of-state educational funds which paid for the
Negro's education in a Northern university. The Southern
states spent hundreds of thousands of dollars of these "out-
of-state" funds. And the colored graduate student rarely came
home. The South spent fortunes to educate the Negro only
to prepare him for a job in Camden, Pittsburgh, or Detroit.
Year after year the Negro population of the South lost one
half of its high school graduates and two thirds of its college
graduates to the rest of the country, which resulted, of course,
in a disproportionate number of semiliterate, unskilled, uneducated, and elderly Negroes.

Mr. Edward R. Dudley, Borough President of Manhattan,
who holds the highest elective office ever won by a Negro in
New York City, was graduated from Johnson C. Smith University, the Negro college in Charlotte. He and thousands like
him have followed the pattern of emigration which every
survey always reveals, that of the graduates of ten Negro
colleges of North Carolina, South Carolina, and Georgia only
20 per cent still live in their home state. In all of the local
industries where Negroes are employed they perform only
menial tasks. As a result the best-trained Negro youths either
go into the professions within the Negro ghetto or emigrate.
With few exceptions, the Negro girl who completes a business
course invariably goes to Washington, D.C., for the Civil
Service examination. Negroes in the South employed as policemen, post-office clerks, and letter carriers are college graduates,
though many whites in the same positions have not completed
high school.

The renunciation of logic resulted in a mad scramble to
build magnificent Negro high schools and junior colleges
right after the Supreme Court decision of May 17, 1954.
Though Negroes boycott these schools, march in protest
against their openings, and file suit to transfer from them,
Southerners still do not get the point. As late as 1961 Char-

lotte put nearly one million dollars into a new Negro junior college, the trustees saying that it is not an attempt to perpetuate segregation since whites could go to the school if they chose to do so. When the local Human Relations Council and the NAACP tried unsuccessfully to block construction of the new school (why not put all the money into one first-rate college?), they suggested that Negro students would not go to a segregated school no matter how modern and excellent its facilities. After two years of operation, it is clear that something will have to be done with this new Negro junior college, probably sell it to the high school system or to some commercial enterprise. After five years of protest, sit-ins, pray-ins, kneel-ins, and march-ins, the authorities still do not realize that the facilities have nothing to do with it. If the separate-but-equal school (which was never equal) provided a private teacher and a private rest room for each student, it would still be evil because it denies our common humanity and because it also denies a constitutional right of an American citizen.

The Jews lived in the ghettos of Europe for nearly one thousand years, but it was not until they entered the open society of western civilization and were able to exchange ideas with others, that they produced Mendelssohn, Heine, Disraeli, Einstein, Brandeis, Waxman, and Jonas Salk. This is the point:

A Negro who bought a Pullman berth in the old days was usually given a drawing room, a broad hint to stay put. One particular conductor somehow felt that he was a guilty party to this Jim Crow process. Every time he passed the drawing room, he knocked on the door and asked, "Is everything all right?" One night the conductor knocked on the door at least three times during the long evening.

"Is everything all right?" he kept asking.

The Negro inside finally opened the door and wearily answered, "No, everything is not all right. *I want to be where the people are.*"

CHAPTER THREE

WHY THE WAIT?

For THIRTY YEARS Southern legislators and legislatures waged legal war against the Negro. They disfranchised him, denied him schools, hospitals, and access to tax-supported facilities and public accommodations. They refused to prosecute the men who lynched Negroes and refused to condemn the men who regularly defiled Negro women. The politicians of the South constantly boasted of their paternal love, knowing all the time that their strategy would help maintain the *status quo*. Nor were conditions much better in the North. Northerners penned the Negro into ghettos and kept him uneducated, unskilled, and consequently unemployed. It was a war of subjugation and I doubt seriously that the Negro was biding his time. He was humiliated and degraded, ruthlessly proscribed, pushed to the absolute conditions of survival. Yet he did not mutiny. Why?

The social revolution of the American Negro, as a matter of fact, comes at a time when those conditions of survival are appreciably better than they have ever been, considerably better than the conditions most of the rest of the world knows.

Why did the Negro wait? Why did he only begin to make

his move in the late 1930s? Why did these moves be
powerful only in the late 1950s and early 1960s? Roy Wil
head of the four hundred thousand members of the Natio
Association for the Advancement of Colored People, has gi__
his version: ". . . this new push? It's cumulative. It's the
emergence of Africa. It's being hungry. It's the G.I. Bill. It's
major-league baseball with Negroes. It's the eight thousand
to ten thousand Negroes graduating from college each year.
It's kids being impatient. . . ." [1]

The reasons are indeed manifold. They are intertwined in
political, economic, social, and psychological forces. Let us
separate them one by one and try to understand them. But let
us also understand that dissecting the past does not always give
us the whole answer to the present nor will it let us fully
anticipate the future.

In *The Origins of Totalitarianism* Hannah Arendt writes:
"If a Negro in a white community is considered a Negro and
nothing else, he loses along with his right to equality that
freedom of action which is specifically human; all his deeds
are now explained as 'necessary' consequences of some 'Negro'
qualities; he has become some specimen of an animal species,
called man." [2]

If the entire community, or even the influential part of it,
lends its assent to the proposition that a Negro is not civilized
and human in the way the white community is civilized and
human, then indeed the Negro community, or a large segment
of it, will not consider itself civilized and human in the way
whites are. This is the supreme power of the collective community, or what we sometimes call the ideological force of the
state.

Adolf Hitler tore up the Weimar Constitution and wrote

[1] *Time,* August 30, 1963, p. 14.
[2] Hannah Arendt, *The Origins of Totalitarianism* (New York, Meridian
Books, 1951), p. 301.

new laws which proclaimed the Jew as the enemy of the
Reich, and most of the law-abiding Gentiles in Germany as-
sented. Joseph Stalin and his judges insisted that some of the
old Bolsheviks were guilty and the old Bolsheviks, innocent
though they were, confessed. We insisted the Negro was undeserving and he believed us and did not mutiny.

The American community lent its assent to the proposition
that the Negro was undeserving because it believed in the terrible myth that insisted slavery is a natural state. There are
today influential men who still believe that somehow slavery,
once endured, makes the slave less than a man. The history of
the major religious movements in the world, which have
always opposed this idea, should convince us this is wrong.
Slaves are unhappier than masters, and the sons of slaves unhappier still, but never, biologically or spiritually, are they less
than men.

I do not mean to equate the prejudices of the South and
of America generally with the genocide of Nazi Germany or
the politics of murder of Stalin's Soviet Union. I mean only to
point out that the Negro is not the first man in the modern
world to be convinced of his own unworthiness. Men do not
rebel or mutiny, any more than the Jews or the old Bolsheviks
rebelled and mutinied, when convinced their plight is the
result of natural forces. The Negro contended against this
belief and eventually overcame it, at least in his own mind.
But his efforts were slow and agonized. Though a native-born
American, he lacked almost all the advantages of the newly
arrived immigrant.

The Irish immigrants who inundated the Eastern seaboard
also suffered savagery and contempt from the indigenous
Yankees. But the Irish spoke the English language and,
though condemned as Papists and persecuted for their religious beliefs, they had the Roman Catholic Church. Watch
any St. Patrick's Day parade in New York or Boston or Chi-

WHY THE WAIT? 57

cago or Albany or, for that matter, New Orleans or Los Angeles, and simply by counting the banners of the different parochial schools marching you will easily understand how an Irish Catholic finally won the Presidency in 1960. The Irish Catholics set up an educational system as vast as it was proficient. They established this school system, which included not only elementary and secondary schools but colleges, universities, and seminaries, because they had a church under which these schools could flourish.

The Jews, who succeeded the Irish, did not set up a similar school system mostly because their language, if any language was common to them, was Yiddish which would only have insulated them more. Moreover, by the time of the main Jewish immigration (1885-1914), a free public school system was already turning out citizens within a generation. The Jew had another advantage. He transplanted himself to another land with a complete social system, his own complete middle-class society. Where it was the Irish peasant who immigrated, the Jew came with peasants and philosophers, tailors and doctors, peddlers and playwrights.

As Nathan Glazer and Patrick Moynihan write in *Beyond the Melting Pot:* ". . . the Negro is only an American, and nothing else. He has no values and culture to guard and protect. He insists the white world deal with his problem because, since he is so much the product of America, they are not his problems but everyone's. Once they become everyone's, perhaps he will see they are his own, too." [3]

Few Negroes have participated in the open society of America. In 1960 there was not a single Negro-owned shoe store in our country. And though the Negro had the language, he had no proprietary rights in his church. The colored man's church, which was mainly Baptist, Methodist, and Presby-

[3] Nathan Glazer and Patrick Moynihan, *Beyond the Melting Pot* (Cambridge, M.I.T. and Harvard University Press, 1963), p. 53.

terian, was controlled and dictated to by white men who deprived Negroes of religious autonomy. (In 1950, Sewanee, an Episcopal college, refused to play Kenyon, another Episcopal college, because the Kenyon football team had a Negro right tackle.)

The Negro churches, however, often became stratified within the ghetto. The more affluent Negroes proved their collective worth when the assistant pastor of the big "white" church of their denomination came to preach the sermon twice a year, and the two churches annually exchanged choirs on Race Relations Sunday. Occasionally the white visitor was a judge, a member of the city council, or the chairman of the local Democratic county committee.

The masses, however, were attracted to the more primitive sects, notably to the organization of the late Daddy Grace and his successor prophets. Bishop Grace established churches throughout the South known as "The House of Prayer for All People," and called himself Messiah. In one two-week session, which I observed in Charlotte, he baptized two thousand candidates, charging five and ten dollars for women and men respectively. The government claim against his estate indicates that Grace had accumulated a vast fortune from what many people called a "religious racket."

Significantly, the white power structure showed considerable respect for Daddy Grace. The school authorities were tolerant of the absenteeism after a Daddy Grace revival, a police escort drove him around town, and he had easy access to the political leaders of the city. He amused and satisfied the white population. The members of a Daddy Grace church conformed to the image of the happy Negro stomping and shouting "Amen" to Grace's thunderous sermon, "The Lord has struck down dead all those who have persecuted me." The Negroes also bought "Daddy Grace Coffee," packaged in

Philadelphia and imported from the Bishop's coffee plantation in Brazil.

On the other hand, the Daddy Grace churches did provide
some degree of self-esteem to the poor and segregated Negro.
During the week the Negro was a helper on a garbage truck,
perhaps a day laborer, his wife a domestic in the kitchen of a
white home or a cleaning woman in an office building, but
on Sundays they wore blue capes with red velvet lining; he
was a Seneschal and she a Princess.

The same drive for self-esteem accounted for the success a
few decades earlier of the "Back-to-Africa" movement. Marcus
Garvey organized a nationalistic scheme for the establishment of a black "African Empire" and a Negro merchant
marine. By 1920 his organization, the Universal Improvement
Association, reported a membership of more than four million Negroes. Garvey named himself "Provisional President
of Africa," and generously conferred titles of "Duke," "Duch-
ess," "Lady-in-Waiting," and "Knight Commander of the
Sublime Order of the Nile." His disciples wore elaborate
uniforms, black and green trimmed with gold braid, and carried handbooks on court etiquette.[4] Garvey failed because the
Negroes had not the slightest inclination to leave the United
States.

In 1934 the Communist party made a determined effort to
enroll the unemployed, segregated Negroes of the South. Their
organizers were well-trained intelligent young men and
women with ample financial resources. They all went home
after a year of utterly wasted effort. John P. Roche in his
excellent analysis writes,

The solution to the Negro problem which Stalin imposed
on the American Communists was the creation of a 'Black

[4] Roi Ottley, *Black Odyssey* (New York, Charles Scribner's Sons, 1948), pp.
324-28.

Republic' where the Negroes would enjoy their own culture and exercise political sovereignty. This was madness, but by 1928 Stalin was the boss. The American Communists obediently set to work, and shortly pamphlets appeared with a map of the South showing exactly where the 'Black Republic' would lie. . . . The contemporary Black Muslims seem to espouse the same notion, but have not yet provided a map.[5]

The self-esteem provided by the Daddy Grace cult attracted large numbers of Southern Negroes. Despite the ridiculous idea of an "African Empire," Marcus Garvey also succeeded in attracting a substantial following primarily because he stimulated pride in the Negro's past. But what is highly significant is that neither Daddy Grace nor Marcus Garvey tried diluting the Southern Negro's Protestant fundamentalism. The failure of the Communists in the 1930s and the failure of the Black Muslims in the 1950s (at least in the South) is no mystery to one who has attended dozens of religious services in the Negro churches of the section. The Communists and Muslims failed because they do not depend on nor incorporate Jesus and the Gospels. The religious fundamentalism of the Southern Negro is so strong that neither the Quakers nor the Unitarians have been able to make any headway among them. This is worth noting because both the Quakers and the Unitarians have been pioneers in the struggle for racial equality since before the Emancipation.

The Communists and Muslims failed for yet another reason. The great mass of the American Negroes do not reject the existing social order, they seek only to share fully in its bourgeois blessings.

The only church in the South which at least theologically

[5] John P. Roche, *The Quest for the Dream* (New York, The Macmillan Co., 1963), p. 148.

maintained the Negro's equality was the Roman Catholic Church. For that reason, perhaps, there are today many wealthy Negroes who are Catholics, and Catholic missionary efforts among Southern Negroes have been notably successful.

Despite almost insurmountable disadvantages, the Negro did establish a small nucleus of schools. His elementary and secondary schools were rudimentary, but they were all he had until the Southern states began building some in the 1920s. These schools were church affiliated. No Choates or Xaviers, nevertheless these little schools prepared the Negro students who became graduates of Fiske, Tuskegee, Howard, Miles, Johnson C. Smith, the Atlanta University Center; Clark, Morehouse, Morris Brown, and Spelman colleges, Atlanta University, the Interdenominational Theological Center, and a great many others.

The Negro colleges are not only reputable, but often superior institutions. In the last decade, Howard University has begun a reverse integration, admitting whites, and whites now compose 25 per cent of the student body in the Negro college at Institute, West Virginia.

The courtroom career of the civil rights controversy got its first impetus in the 1930s when Negro law schools began graduating students who had thoroughly studied the constitutional guarantees. These Negro lawyers were the vanguard who pioneered the legal study and interpretation of civil rights. In those years the National Association for the Advancement of Colored People kept track of every Negro law student in the country, laying the groundwork for what would result in the most remarkable legal process in the history of a free people. Thus the Negro did not make his move earlier because he had to wait to train a body of professionals dedicated to alleviating the plight of all Negroes.

Even had these law schools and colleges begun earlier, it is still a question whether the social revolution of the American

Negro could have reached the proportions it now enjoys. It must be remembered that it was not only the Negroes who were totally segregated in the years before World War I, but also vast numbers of whites, particularly Southern whites. It would have been hard for a Negro to stage an insurrection for integration when all about him for decades he saw separate but equal poverty and separate but equal segregation.

The white millhands, who were called "lint-heads," and the white tenant farmers, who were called "croppers," by no means moved easily through the open society. If the Negro did not own his church, neither did these whites. In *Millhands and Preachers*, Dr. Liston Pope describes how the mill owners not only subsidized the Protestant churches of the mill villages but filled all the churches' important offices with mill officials. Some of the segregated churches for white millworkers were supported by the "uptown" white churches. At a 1947 meeting of the leaders of a congregation at Chester, South Carolina, one of the elders proposed that it was a waste of money to continue to support the Gayles Mill Church, because ". . . the millworkers are beginning to get automobiles and they'll soon be coming here for services." [6]

At some levels, the white millworker was even more segregated than the Negro. The Negro, using the back door, had some access to the "uptown" white society. The white millworker had none at all. When the "uptown" white boy reached the age of seven, he was old enough to be told he must no longer play with the white mill children "on the hill."

There were mills which refused to hire men who were not churchgoers. By and large, employers knew churchgoers were the men who stayed out of trouble, and to most mill owners trouble meant union activities, strikes, and demands for higher wages. The mill owners subsidized the church and the

[6] Liston Pope, *Millhands and Preachers* (New Haven, Yale University Press, 1941), p. 64.

minister and wielded an inhibiting influence on the parishioners. In many mills of the South, the men and women stood
with bowed heads at their looms as the superintendent in-
toned the invocation before the work bell rang. This influence made the lint-head consent to his poverty for it
promised him the same boss-man's Christianity promised the
Negro—salvation in the hereafter as reward for toil and exploitation in the here and now.

Until the notorious Loray Mill Strike in 1929 in Gastonia,
North Carolina, most of the cotton mill towns were virtual
prison camps. For their labors the millhands received scrip
which they exchanged for food and necessities at the company
store; they did not pass freely through the gates, save to ex-
pend themselves on the weekly Saturday night drunk.

The white sharecropper didn't send his children to a free
public school. He sent them to the fields as soon as they could
walk. This man, too, ate greens and fat back and this man,
too, watched his children die with pellagra and rickets.

If the Negro attended a segregated church, so did the "lint-
head" and the tenant farmer; if he went to segregated schools,
so did they. If the white man played free and easy with the
Negro girls, so did the son of the "uptown" white play free
and easy with the lint-head's daughter. If the Negro lived in
a ghetto, so did the white live separated and as poorly as
he. Segregation did not end with the Negro and the white
Protestant Anglo-Saxon millworker. Segregation included the
native American Indian and, throughout the South, the small
segregated enclaves of people of "questionable" origin, neither
white, Negro, or Indian. In Northampton County, in the
eastern part of North Carolina, there is a group known as
"the Portuguese," supposedly the descendants of Portuguese
women brought over to work the plantations in the 1830s
who married freed Negroes or slaves. The "conjure man"
among the slaves was usually named "Manuel." When one

"Manuel" died another "Manuel" took his place. The legend is that "Manuel" originated with the arrival of these Portuguese. Their children go to a segregated school taught by a lady of the Methodist Mission Field. They are a tragic group, considered Negro by the whites but cut off from the Negro community.

In South Carolina are "the Turks" who recently won their fight for freedom in the courts. The Turks of Sumter County live between the towns of Stateburg and Dalzell, some three hundred of them within a ten-mile radius. There has never been a recorded case of a Turk committing a crime. The story is that they were brought over by General Thomas Sumter to fight in the American Revolution. After the war General Sumter settled the Turks upon his lands but neither he nor his descendants ever gave them a deed. When they married, they married outside their community, usually with Indians. There is a story of a Turk woman who married a Negro and was at once ostracized by her people. In the early days the Turks became Baptists, members of the High Hills Baptist Church; in this church the Turks were seated on the left, the whites on the right, and the Negroes in the balcony. All of this is told in the *History of Sumter County* by Anne King Gregory.[7]

In 1950 the Turks asked the trustees of the local white high school to admit their children but the trustees refused. The Turks then brought suit in the federal district court, but the school authorities did not contest the suit and so the Turks of South Carolina won their integration fight three years before the Supreme Court decision of May 17, 1954.

In sections of North Carolina and South Carolina there were at one time five sets of segregated schools and churches:

[7] Anne King Gregory, *History of Sumter County* (South Carolina, Library Board of Sumter County, 1954), pp. 467-70.

white, millworker white, Negro, Indian, and either "Turks" or "Portuguese."

The Negro had to wait until the millworkers went out on strike, until the mill village and company store began to disappear, until the white industrial workers were covered by a minimum wage law, until their children as well as the cropper's children were guaranteed a free education. For if the South is fighting against civil rights legislation for the Negro, so did the South (and much of the country) often fight against the establishment of unions, abolition of child labor, and the setting of minimum wage and hour laws. When the poor white started to get his, the Negro said, "I want mine, too."

World War I gave many Negroes the opportunity to see that there was not equal poverty and equal segregation everywhere. Negroes who served in France quickly realized that the taboos their Southern neighbors insisted upon were not at all natural. The French and the English cheered the Negro soldier just as they cheered the white doughboy. In addition, the Negro soldier was part of the morale and camaraderie of the whole army. It could not help but make a difference. And there were thousands of other Negro soldiers who left the South for the first time and were stationed in the ports of embarkation, in the training centers, and in the hospitals of America.

While studying the history of lynching, I was amazed at the incidence of lynchers burning and hanging Negroes after World War I, the sole reason being that the Negro was wearing an army uniform. This uniform had not only made the Negro the white man's equal at least for the duration and, more than that, it had put the Negro under the protection of the Federal Government. It was a symbolic protection just as it was a symbolic equality, but the symbolism was a portent which enraged the lynchers.

The real change World War I made in the Negro's condition was to create a demand by Northern war industries for hundreds of thousands of Southern Negroes for factory work. However cruel it was, the North offered better prospects and better opportunities than the South. The North kept him bottled up in ghettos, but it did not bar the way of his son from becoming a dental technician or lathe operator, if he could make it on his own. Negroes received wages comparable with the white man's. He got jobs heretofore solely the monopoly of whites. He sent his children to school.

More and more Negroes came. And right after the war, they showed no disposition to return to what they had had before. In fact, they fought for their new life. To see how times had changed, one has only to compare the race riot which exploded in Atlanta in 1906 with the one that broke out in Chicago in 1919.

In 1906 Georgia was in the process of making absolute and final its disfranchisement and segregation of the Negro. Part of this campaign was helped by an inflammatory press which kept reporting fictitious attacks on white women by illusory black rapists. On Saturday, September 22, the newspapers reported that the assaults had reached epidemic stage. Four white women had been raped. On Peachtree and Decatur streets a mob gathered, a Negrophobe harangued them, and the mob turned and lynched a colored bystander. The animal was loose.

A thousand men marched to a Negro skating rink, there to be turned back by police. They broke into a Negro barbershop and lynched the two barbers. As the mob swelled, it took to stopping trolleys and killing the Negro passengers. Firemen tried drowning the mob with hoses, but the men laughed and moved back out of range. Already downtown Atlanta was a shambles. On the outskirts of the city, police and other citizens were warning Negroes to go home. Negro saloons, pawnshops, and homes were burned and their occupants beaten. By Sunday morning the mayor had to summon the state militia.

By this time, however, the mob was armed, having stormed the sports shops and hardware stores for guns. An armed battle broke out in Brownsville, a Negro settlement two miles outside of Atlanta. One company of cavalry stormed the settlement, killing two Negroes and capturing two hundred and fifty-seven others, all of whom were sentenced to the chain gang for carrying weapons. The infantry finally quelled the disorder and for several weeks Atlanta lived under martial law. How many Negroes were killed has never been determined. The official estimate was fifty, but that figure was obviously forwarded by the Chamber of Commerce. That many innocent Negroes were dragged from trolleys and run down in the alleys in the first hour alone.

The riot had its inception in a long political war in which both sides seized upon the "Negro issue." The two contending newspapers had long since forgotten why they had joined the war, and were building immense circulation gains with sensational stories about the violation of Southern womanhood. Atlanta Negroes were helpless and the white power structure of the city indifferent until the mob began smashing up white stores and shooting down white policemen, ambushes later conveniently attributed to Negro "rapists."

The Chicago race riot was another story. On the last Sunday of July, 1919, a Negro boy at a Chicago beach swam over an imaginary segregation line. He was immediately stoned by white boys who knocked him from a raft into the water where he drowned. Colored people rushed to the policeman and asked him to arrest the stone-throwers. The policeman refused. As the body of the drowned boy was brought to shore more rocks were thrown on both sides. The policeman held to his refusal to make an arrest. Fighting broke out on the beach, then spread to all borders of the "black belt."

Three weeks before this riot began, the Chicago *Daily News* had assigned its poet and special reporter, Carl Sandburg, to do a series of articles on the booming Negro population. His articles had been running for two weeks and were on the verge of inspiring some sort of concerted community action when the stone-throwers, followed by the delinquents and then the hoodlums, took over. "Then," writes Sandburg, "as usual nearly everybody was more interested in the war than how it got loose." At the end of three days, twenty Negroes and fourteen white men were dead and a large number of Negro houses had been burned.

Grim as it was, the Chicago race riot was a break with the past. The riot was not inspired by claims of race supremacy nor by fears of Negro sexuality, nor was the nation indifferent. It is no oversimplification to say the Chicago race riot stated the problem we still labor to resolve. The virtue of Sandburg's story is that he understood these differences: that this riot came about not because menace and terror stalked the streets but because the Negro demanded equity, the freedom to use public accommodations as he sees fit.

Three new conditions attended this 1919 riot. During the war, the Black Belt population of Chicago had doubled from fifty thousand to one hundred thousand. No new houses had been built to accommodate these people. Large numbers of returning Negro soldiers had also settled in Chicago as had thousands of Negroes imported to the city to service its wartime industries. In addition, into Chicago yearly poured streams of Negroes fleeing the lynchings in Texas, Virginia, Alabama, Tennessee, and Mississippi.

None of these Negroes, however, was helpless. The Negroes

of Chicago had political strength. A city administration had recently appointed some twenty Negro precinct officials. The mayor's opponents had failed to defeat him by calling him "nigger-lover."

The last and most significant development was that thousands of white men and Negroes stuck together during the riot. White and Negro officials of the Stockyards Labor Council asked the public to witness that they were shaking hands as "brothers" and could not be counted on for any share of the mob shouts and ravages.

A large body of mixed Americans—Poles, Negroes, Lithuanians, Italians, Irishmen, Germans, Slovaks, Russians, Mexicans, Yankees, Englishmen, Scotsmen—proclaimed their opposition to any violence to either white union men or Negro union men.

Sandburg prophesied in his little monograph, *The Chicago Race Riots,* that as the Negro drove for equality there would be fewer lynchings and more riots. For these riots would be provoked not because a large mass of illiterate, semiliterate, and unskilled workers moved in, but because the Negro would become more literate, more skilled, and more desirous of his fair share.[8] Ten years later, this same Chicago sent to the House of Representatives Oscar De Priest, the first Negro elected to national office since the Reconstruction. (Atlanta did not send a Negro to the state legislature until 1962.)

What the race riot of 1919 portended came to fruition with De Priest's election. After World War I, the Negro population of northern cities increased on an average of 500 per cent. This increase made sure that the racial problem was no longer a sectional one. In leaving the South, the Negro left a rural area where he was disfranchised for an urban area where he

[8] Carl Sandburg, *The Chicago Race Riots* (New York, Harcourt, Brace & Howe, 1920), p. 16.

had the right to vote. In the cities he was concentrated, but it was by virtue of that concentration that he could force political action.

One would think that the election of De Priest would alert politicians. But it didn't. Certainly it did not alert the Republicans whose candidate De Priest was. Instead, De Priest's arrival in Washington, D.C., posed a severe social dilemma for Mrs. Herbert Hoover whose custom it was to entertain Congressmen's wives at tea. Arthur M. Schlesinger, Jr., reports in *The Politics of Upheaval* that after three tortured weeks Mrs. Hoover finally invited Mrs. De Priest to tea, after warning all her other guests of the ordeal awaiting them.[9]

But the Democrats read the signs aright. In 1932 they nominated and elected Arthur Mitchell, a Negro, who succeeded De Priest. I do not mean the Democrats are more humane than Republicans. On the issue of Negro civil rights, however, they have assuredly made capital by their ability to recognize Negro voting power. Let us say the Democrats, since 1930, have proved to be political realists on this question and have benefited by their realism.

For in 1932 the Negroes of America were still traditionally Republicans, as they had been since Lincoln. In 1936, they overwhelmingly supported Franklin D. Roosevelt and have supported the Democratic candidate ever since. In 1948 President Truman received 70 per cent of the Negro vote; in 1952 Adlai E. Stevenson won 60 per cent; in 1956 Mr. Stevenson received 50 per cent; and in 1960 John F. Kennedy received 85 per cent. (The estimates of the NAACP and the Democratic National Committee vary only fractionally.)

Of course the Democrats had the advantage of being the political party of the big-city dwellers, and probably they are more adept at integrating minorities of all types into their

---

[9] Arthur M. Schlesinger, *The Politics of Upheaval* (Boston, Houghton Mifflin Co., 1960), p. 427.

political programs. It is also true that since 1928 the Republicans have entertained the delusion that they will capture the Solid South.

Franklin D. Roosevelt captured the Negro vote. Whether another President would have been as successful as he I cannot say. Perhaps a Republican other than Herbert Hoover might have kept Negro support. But the Hoover Administration was all but helpless in face of the white man's plight; it would have been pretty hard for it to have won Negro sympathy.

Roosevelt himself was never an open champion of the Negroes. He never, as John F. Kennedy did, made a plea to the entire electorate for justice for the Negro. When Homer Cummings, the Attorney General, refused to intercede in what became a lynching in Baltimore, Roosevelt did not countermand that decision.

Most historians agree that Roosevelt was a consummate politician ever mindful that he headed a party composed of conservative Southerners and liberal Northerners, and he kept these two wings equally in balance. But without doubt he was the champion of the minorities, ethnic, economic, and social, and among these minorities was the Negro. In his first year in office he made more appointments of qualified Negroes to the federal bench and federal office than Harding, Coolidge, and Hoover had made in the twelve years they held Presidential office.

Roosevelt convinced the workingman he cared. In convincing the workingman, he convinced the Negro. He never completely alleviated the oppression the workingman suffered nor the oppression the Negro endured, but he was aware of that oppression. It was less oppressive for both by the time he died.

And the Negro did not misunderstand Roosevelt as businessmen maliciously and stupidly misunderstood him. When the Charlotte newspaper carried the news in April, 1945, that the Roosevelt funeral train would pass through town a little after midnight on its way to Washington, D.C., I went down to the Southern Railroad station about eleven o'clock. I found it impossible to get within a block of the terminal. I have never seen so many mothers with infants in their arms. They, too, had come to wait for the passage of the train through Charlotte. It was a long wait. Then, as the train which carried Roosevelt passed slowly through, I could hear whispered prayers. I edged through the crowd and saw dozens of Negroes on their knees, hands clasped.

It was a slow exodus afterward. I waited another hour. What fascinated me were the lights on both sides of the track stretching northward as far as the eye could see. These were the lanterns and flashlights of the rural folk who had walked down to the tracks to see the passing train.

I shall always remember those Negroes praying at the Charlotte railroad station and the rural folk coming out to wait for the funeral train. They came and they prayed because the President who died had attempted for the first time in the history of man to abolish hunger. And he had succeeded. Whatever happens again in this country, depression or disaster, flood or dust storm, people will never starve. This is the important and central fact of the Roosevelt career.

The depression hit Negroes harder than any other segment of the American population. Negro writers and men of sensitivity have argued that living through it, if one was a Negro, was as arduous and as calamitous as living through slavery. Negro farmers were always the first sharecroppers dispossessed because of the crop reduction policies, Negro laborers the first fired. Like most of the rural and urban poor, the Negroes were devastated.

The significant fact about Roosevelt's relief programs was not that he salvaged the Negroes, but that these programs *included* the Negroes. *This was the first time the Negro had been made part of the whole.* Two hundred thousand Negroes went into the Civilian Conservation Corps; the Public Works Administration built schools, hospitals, and homes specifically for Negroes; Negro colleges received federal education grants; the National Labor Relations Board let Negroes vote in labor disputes. The Works Progress Administration for the unemployed white was a stop-gap: for the Negro the WPA was a momentous development in his struggle for equality. It was the first time in his history that the Negro received the same wages for the same amount of work done as the white man. It had never happened before.

A principle had been established. Though that principle could not rescue the millions who went under physically and spiritually, it did establish a federal parity for whites and Negroes. Mr. Schlesinger quotes Lorena Hickok, a Georgia newspaperwoman, who reported, "For these people to be getting $12 a week—at least twice as much as common labor has ever been paid down here before—is an awfully bitter pill for Savannah people to swallow. . . . The Federal Reemployment Director observed yesterday: 'Any nigger who gets over $8 a week is a spoiled nigger, that's all.' " [10]

Not long after I came to Charlotte in 1941, I shared a taxicab with a Negro passenger. His destination was first and he gave the taxi driver a five-dollar bill. He got his change and as we drove off the cab driver said, "God damn that Roosevelt."

"Why?" I asked.

"When the hell did a nigger ever have a five-dollar bill?" he answered.

More than the social measures introduced during Roosevelt's Administration, Negroes were encouraged by the example of the First Lady, Eleanor Roosevelt. She was the

[10] *Ibid.*, p. 433.

pioneer champion of Negro civil rights. I remember her touring a North Carolina factory in the fall of 1941 and remarking when she was through that the "white" and "colored" drinking fountains and rest-rooms were a disgrace to America and would have to go. When she attended a Conference on Human Welfare in Birmingham, she sat in the Negro section until the police asked her to move. Rather than surrender, she put her chair in the aisle between the white and Negro sections. She had her photograph taken with Negroes, a practice all her predecessors had barred. She was news and everything she did was promptly reported. When she pleaded for funds for the Colored Home for the Aged in Washington, D.C., newsmen not only repeated her sentiments but reported the need of the Home itself, which did indeed receive an appropriation from the Congress.

Her most effective blow against discrimination came in 1939 when the Washington chapter of the Daughters of the American Revolution cancelled the rental of their auditorium by a civic group sponsoring a concert by the Negro contralto Marian Anderson. Oscar Chapman, Assistant Secretary of the Interior, arranged for Miss Anderson to sing at the foot of the Lincoln Memorial. Mrs. Roosevelt not only attended the concert but publicly announced her resignation from the DAR. She had effectively shamed one element of the elite. What inspiration she must have offered to others!

These public gestures of Mrs. Roosevelt, uncompromising and deliberate, gave rise to the myth about the "Eleanor Clubs" that were supposed to proliferate throughout the South. I myself have never met an ex-member of an Eleanor Club. I can testify to their effect by the worried brows of hundreds of thousands of whites. These whites believed the Eleanor Clubs were agitating for civil rights, higher wages, and free access to all facilities. The Eleanor Clubs were as good as existing institutions even in the absence of a single charter.

The Roosevelts thus made it easier for President Harry Truman to begin to end racial segregation in the armed forces in 1948. And in turn, President Truman made it easier for the late John F. Kennedy to become the first President in this century to make public declaration (in a speech televised nationally on June 11, 1963), that the Negro's struggle for first-class citizenship was a moral issue that involved every American.

The Negro made his move when he did because he had impetus coming from the very bottom of the society and the very top. But it took more than this encouragement to give his movement momentum. The two important developments which not only insured continuing momentum in the thrust for civil rights but more or less guaranteed the ultimate victory of that thrust began coming to the fore immediately after World War II.

An ever-growing and ever-improving system of communication became a salient fact in the lives of all Americans. All communication media are not equally responsible on all occasions, but they are reasonably responsible on specific occasions. The press, for example, spent the years before World War I reporting "Black Rapist Hanged" or "Fiend Executed" to headline the lynchings that occurred on the average of three a month. Then a few responsible publications began to call a lynching a lynching with the result that lynching was no longer condoned by public officials.

It was with the Scottsboro trial in 1932 that the American press acted in concert to decry the violation of liberties the Alabama authorities perpetrated on nine Negro boys accused of raping two white girls on a night freight train. Quite possibly, the motives of the workaday press were not wholly altruistic. The trial of the Scottsboro boys was world-wide news and had world-wide implications, but the reporting was objective and often sympathetic.

I cite the Scottsboro case not intending to mean this was a turning point in either the history of American journalism or in the Negro's fight for sympathy and justice, but rather as a contemporary example of the changing mood. In alerting the country, American journalists found they had alerted the world (there were strikes in Paris, protests in Rome, petitions circulated in England). For in its stories the press considered the Scottsboro defendants as American citizens and not as obvious criminals. The press has been less than accurate and less than responsible in some instances, but it does not make unfounded assumptions on Negro criminality. It no longer passes *a priori* judgment on the Negro character. Even Southern newspapers include accurate and front-page reports on Negro demonstrations these days. Though many an editorial page seems written on another planet, whites and Negroes are reasonably accurately informed in the 1960s about Negro accomplishments, aspirations, and purposes.

In the 1930s more Americans listened to radios than read newspapers, and in the 1960s their homes have television plus radios. These two mass media made it impossible for anyone to be unaware of the Negro movement or of the proportions it has assumed. Southern demagogues may say the Negro is happier segregated, they may insist he does not deserve civil rights, they may promise never to grant those rights, but they cannot maintain that the Negro isn't demonstrating, nor can they insist that these demonstrations are isolated disorders.

Nor should we forget another highly interesting relationship which television enforces between Negroes and whites. If it informs whites about Negroes, it does more than reciprocally inform Negroes about whites. To the marginal man television and the movies are a window on the affluent society. Any man exposed often enough to the luxuries and comforts presented on "Father Knows Best" or "I Love Lucy" will want them. Any movie presents these same comforts on a colossal scale. On television and in the movies, the average American family is a two-car family with a house half black-top driveway and half washer-dryer, all of which the average white family takes for granted.

Watching television, the unemployed, segregated Negro sees that what really concerns Americans, judging by the time devoted to it, is how they smell. Every blonde on television worries about deodorants and here he is—the Negro—living in a dirt-filled yard in a house on stilts without an inside toilet.

As profoundly as the communications system has influenced life in America, there is still another development which has had an even more profound effect on the Negro. American business and industry has invited the Negro into this vast open society by making him a customer. Ford and General Motors made him a customer first. So did Westinghouse and Frigidaire—and so did the "midtown" Southern merchant, the jeweler, the furniture store, the easy credit company, the haberdasher. Every chamber of commerce in midtown Birmingham and midtown Atlanta and midtown Memphis coaxed the Negro to come in.

If the segregationist wants to establish the final responsibility for the incitement of the Negro, he will find only himself to blame. He knows that neither he nor his competitor will want to surrender one fourth of his yearly dollar volume in sales or one third of all the credit purchasing. Those statistics show to what extent the Negro participates in the Southern economy, and for Southern economy please also read Southern-Way-of-Life.

Back of it all is a paradox. The Southern segregationist first blamed Earl Warren and now blames Robert Kennedy for all his troubles. But the Southerner James Buchanan Duke probably had as much to do with it as Justice Earl Warren, or the Kennedys, or the NAACP, or Dr. Martin Luther King. When in the early 1900s the tobacco tycoon "Buck" Duke built the first power station on the Catawba River to industrialize the South, he struck the first blow against racial segregation which cannot succeed or even long continue in an industrial society. The Southern segregationist still dreams of that mythical house that stood on the hill with smoke coming out of the chimney at twilight and each man knowing his own "place." But today there is a diesel motor truck going up that hill at twilight and the truck does not care who drives it.

James Street, the novelist from Laurel, Mississippi, called the Old South "a myth and a poem" and said it was "a malady for which fortunately there is a vaccine—the industrial payroll." Street was one of those Southerners ahead of his time. I remember his telling a conference of North Carolina writers at Cape Hatteras in 1949, "Don't send the *Saturday Evening Post* your usual 'nigra' stories. That's out forever. You can't write about Uncle Remus with Ralph Bunche around."

The chambers of commerce and state legislatures have spent half their time upholding the mythical traditions of the Old South in the meetings of the White Citizens Councils, and the other half scurrying through the North looking for industry. In the past thirty years they have found it. Parts of Massachusetts, New York, New Jersey, and Pennsylvania are depressed because factories have pulled stakes and headed for the New South with its milder climate, its abundant land, its superior natural resources, and its unorganized labor.

Years ago no Southern merchant sought the Negro for a customer because the Negro was impoverished. Yet there were whites who even then found in him a source of profit. I have described in *Forgotten Pioneer* how the Jewish itinerant peddler found a role in the South by filling a great need of the Negro. The Jewish peddler supplied the rural Negroes with goods and necessities at a time when the midtown white wanted no Negro business. The peddler extended credit which no other white man ever extended. It was from this peddler that the Negro bought mattresses, shoes, clocks, and clothes for his family. The Jewish peddler let the Negro try on the garment he might wish to purchase. In a midtown store, once a Negro touched a garment he had to buy it, whether it fit or not.

Much the same might be said of the Jewish storekeeper who set up in the Negro ghetto. In their way, the Jewish peddler and slum storekeeper conspired unwittingly to keep the Negro in check. They furnished those immediate needs which, while not making the Negro contented, made him less mutinous.

But sometime around the late 1930s and early 1940s the midtown storekeeper beckoned to the Negro. The midtown white was now openly competing for the Negro purchasing power. Twelve dollars a week to an unemployed white man might be a dole, but to an unemployed Negro it was a fortune. These stores offered easy credit (and still do) and they let Negroes take goods home with no down payment. Here, too, the Negro found better quality at cheaper prices. Soon enough, the midtown white storekeeper found the Negro business a bonanza.

Hundreds of Negroes who had had no occasion to leave their slum district began making the trip to midtown. They discovered how dismaying it was to sit in the back of the bus, how unfair to contribute to an entrepreneur's profit and not be allowed to use a rest-room while doing so, how uncomfortable not to be able to eat at the snack bar while spending money in the store.

In its way it is ironic that the Negro pressed his right to

use such facilities, not in the courts but in the stores themselves. For the Negro knew the argument is not whether he shall be allowed into the store; he knows there is general agreement on that. It is how he shall be treated within. It is not whether he shall be allowed to spend his money but whether one of the clerks who takes it will be a Negro or not. So he won his point in the store by organizing sit-ins and boycotts, knowing that anything that interrupts trade panics the business community of the town. He gauged his opponent well. Throughout the South, the first segregationist to sell out is always the merchant. If the White Citizens Councils ask him to lose money while they win their fight, he simply deserts them and seeks refuge and repair in an anonymous citizens' report that urges that the store be integrated and the restrooms and water fountains made available to all.

The Negro revolt is *now*, in the 1960s, not only because the attitude of the whole country has changed, not only because the Negro's lot is appreciably better, as is the country's; not only because he, the Negro, is better educated and better informed; not only because he has had examples to sustain him; not only because the courts sustain his revolts; but also because the major overpowering institution of the country—business—is waving welcome whether it knows that it is waving or not.

CHAPTER FOUR

OPENING THE DOOR

Schools, voting rights, housing, employment, and *public accommodations.* This was the memorandum Robert F. Kennedy wrote on a legal pad in January, 1963, during a conference with Negro leaders.

In their speeches some of the Negro leaders may substitute "public accommodations" for "voting rights," while others may emphasize "employment" instead of "voting rights" or "public accommodations." But "schools" always heads the list.

I once asked Judge Thurgood Marshall, then the NAACP Legal Defense Fund chief counsel (now a judge of the United States Court of Appeals for the Second Circuit), "Why did you make your important move for the integration of the public schools—why not health, for instance?" We had been on a radio panel together and we were going back to my hotel by taxi. I went on to say there would have been much less passion about integrating health facilities. If the American people realized in the boom prosperity of 1957 that one-fifth of the deliveries of Negro babies in the South were unattended, they might well have unanimously agitated for such integration.

Judge Marshall, who successfully represented the Negro plaintiffs in one of the most important Supreme Court actions in history, *Brown v. Board of Education,* agreed that forceful action in the courts and in public protest would have resulted in wide gains in health facilities for Negroes throughout the country, perhaps even in the integration of large government-financed hospitals in the South, but he said the idea of a second-class citizenship would have remained. "We are a school-oriented society. If we desegregate the public schools of America, the whole pattern of racial segregation will inevitably collapse."

In 1964 it is easy to see the wisdom of Judge Marshall's answer. Eleven months after he took office, President John F. Kennedy issued an executive order on "Equal Employment Opportunity" providing for "sanctions and penalties" for discriminatory employment practices in all plants filling government contracts.[1] The then Vice-President Lyndon B. Johnson, who administered the Kennedy directive, called several meetings of government contractors, industrialists, and chamber of commerce executives. Mr. Johnson, who succeeded to the Presidency after the assassination of President Kennedy on November 22, 1963, had wisely included in his invitation some large employers who did not have government contracts. This enabled him to make his plea on a moral basis instead of merely emphasizing the penalties involved in not opening the employment rolls to Negroes. To each group Mr. Johnson said, "Some say Now; some say Never; let's all say Together."

Because of the efforts of the Johnson committee, seventeen hundred complaints of discrimination by government contractors were received in the first two years of Mr. Kennedy's Administration with favorable action on 72 per cent.

In the previous seven and a half years, under Richard Nixon,

[1] Executive Order 10925, March 7, 1961.

the Vice-President's Commission on Contracts had instituted six suits, only one outside the District of Columbia. A few years later in discussing the voting cases, John Doar, First Assistant Attorney General in the Civil Rights Division, told me, "Apparently the boys did not like to go South to see for themselves." Mr. Doar is a holdover, a Wisconsin Republican who had been appointed during the Eisenhower Administration. He has spent the last three summers in Mississippi, Alabama, and Louisiana courtrooms, and when he is not thus engaged he spends twelve hours a day studying dozens of charts in his office, some of them huge photographic blowups of dirt roads in the deep South, pinpointing hundreds of shacks where live Negro sharecroppers denied the right to vote. A government official showed me a letter from a professor of law at the University of Mississippi who had listened in on some of the voting cases. Wrote the professor: *"The utter unreality of proving what everybody who knows anything has known since childhood intrigues me. . . ."*

The late President Kennedy had also secured the signatures of over one hundred major industrial employers and one hundred seventeen labor unions to voluntary agreements calling for an all-out attack on discrimination in employment. He had ordered the Department of Labor to eliminate discrimination in apprenticeship and all other training programs, in referrals for employment, and in operation by labor organizations.

Helen Fuller in *Year of Trial* writes:

In October, I asked a Southern Negro leader who is not usually thankful for small favors to pass private judgment on the Johnson committee's performance to date. It has been a "clear, strong and consistent program," he said. "There has been swift and thorough follow-through from

the big contractors, such as Lockheed. . . . Policy directives
have gotten down to the least significant Government agency
and the smallest Government contractor. . . ." [2]

By September, 1963, Negroes for the first time were working in the carding rooms of Southern textile mills. Significantly, these Negroes were working beside the very white men,
the Southern cotton millworkers, who were most rigidly in-
sistent on maintaining racial segregation.

Mill superintendents explained: "We work together for the
simple reason we must if we want the government contracts.
Without these contracts, we close down." Plants in the upper
South which do not have government contracts nevertheless
have begun hiring Negroes for white men's jobs because they
anticipate bidding on these contracts. Faced with the prospect
of unemployment or integrated factories, white workers in
North Carolina and Tennessee chose work. Token school integration is widespread in these states and there are cities
where a little more than mere token integration has been
implemented by school boards. One millworker in Greensboro, North Carolina, told me why he went to work with
Negroes: "Hell, they're going to school with my kids."

The entire complex of the fight for civil rights hinges upon
the court struggle to change the law which segregates Negro
children from white children in the public school system.
Integrated schools will first of all change the composition of
society and, more importantly, changed laws will change the
hearts of men (the simple truth which eluded President
Dwight D. Eisenhower). The former President repeatedly
declared that law was not enough, that the hearts of men
must change of themselves.

It is interesting that during the 1960 Presidential campaign,

[2] Helen Fuller, *Year of Trial* (New York, Harcourt, Brace & World, 1962),
p. 131.

Vice-President Richard Nixon expressed himself on this very idea: "The issue will have to be solved in the minds and hearts of people . . . if the law goes further than public opinion can be brought along to support at a particular time, it may prove to do more harm than good."

"Acceptance of the law is the beginning of change, and knowledge that the law is going to be enforced is vital" was the philosophy Burke Marshall brought to his job as Kennedy's Assistant Attorney General in charge of civil rights. Mr. Marshall said that the suggestion that the law will not be enforced until there has been some social change has an adverse effect on the situation. Said Mr. Marshall: "The law has to lead the people sometimes."

Laws do indeed change the hearts of men. We have so consistently listened to the canard that laws do not, that we have come to doubt the whole purpose of the law itself, to make us better, more responsible men.

Thurgood Marshall's successor as Director General of the NAACP Legal Defense Fund, Jack Greenberg, writes that the "*Sweatt* and *McLaurin* decisions were crucial to the admission of thousands of Negroes to institutions of higher learning. Suits for non-discriminatory interstate rail and bus accommodations reversed segregation on carriers. The school segregation litigation was indispensable in desegregating hundreds of school districts."[3]

The law may not make white men love Negroes, but throughout the Old South white men are riding with Negroes on buses, white teachers are teaching Negro children, and white law students are studying with Negro law students.

Even the most rigid Southerner, the man who does not have to retreat, has changed. The mill owner, faced with the prospect of a union election, no longer circulates the old

[3] Jack Greenberg, *Race Relations and American Law* (New York, Columbia University Press, 1959), pp. 31-72.

photograph of labor leader Walter Reuther handing over a check from the Philip Murray Welfare Fund to NAACP head Roy Wilkins, with the slogan below: "Here is what happens to your union dues." The employer may still dislike the Textile Union as much as ever, but he has ceased this propaganda because the Kennedy "Equal Employment" directive demands he not discriminate if he wants government contracts. A few Negroes perforce are now in his factory, and for the first time these Negroes are not just cleaners and janitors; if he wants to keep the union out, he must enlist them too. This is nothing less than a "change of heart."

In Charleston, South Carolina, the very heartland of the Confederacy, on September 3, 1963, eleven Negro high school children began classes with whites in four high schools without fanfare. Charleston was only one of over five hundred Southern school districts which, though individually unaffected by a court decision, changed segregated practices because of legal decisions affecting other school boards.

The laws which first changed men's hearts and made them hard are the laws that came in the 1890s, laws which cut the Negro off from the corporate whole of society in an attempt to justify disfranchisement. Taking the ballot from a man meant not tolerating him in your restaurants, consigning his children to substandard schools, and limiting the places in which he could work. These were the laws which created the illusion that the Negroes' disfranchisement was the *result* of their undesirability, instead of fear of their political power.

This whole body of laws, growing out of disfranchisement, made ardent segregationists out of the white farmer and factory worker. The poor white of the South never could find the disfranchisement itself convincing. But the segregation laws gave life to the myth that the Negro wanted to marry the white man's sister and this was very real to him. This threat made him side with the political aristocracy whose interests ran counter to his.

The disfranchisement of the Negro made it possible for politicians such as Theodore "The Man" Bilbo to be elected Governor of Mississippi with a "majority" vote of less than 25 per cent of the total electorate. The process has made it possible for Congressman Howard Smith of Virginia and Senators Harry Byrd of Virginia and James Eastland of Mississippi to perpetuate themselves in office, and through the seniority rules of the House and Senate to wield tremendous power over a whole generation of Americans.

These old conservative Southern politicians sit in the advanced realms of power not because they are diabolic and have cynically manipulated their position. They sit there because for years the South enjoyed its traditions and its customs undisturbed by either the industrial revolution or by immigration which would have created other interests. The millions of immigrants who settled in America between 1880 and 1914 went where the industrial revolution created jobs, in the Northern and Midwestern cities. Every time one of these racial or ethnic groups advanced toward power, it pulled the group below a little higher.

But the South remained a single homogeneous society of white Protestant Anglo-Saxons except for the Negro, who was by now totally segregated. Thus each white Southerner saw in his neighbor a reflection of himself, the same tradition, essentially the same religion, and the same ideas. And he did what most people have done throughout history under similar conditions; he let his public institutions overlap his private life.

We did precisely the same thing on the Lower East Side of New York. We were a single homogeneous society, not only of Jews but of immigrant Jews, and the principal of the school, were he Jewish, spoke Yiddish to mothers and fathers.

The schools of the South, like ours, became the focal points of community life. Religious meetings, political rallies, and neighborhood protests took place in the school auditorium as well as dances, plays, and many other social functions. The Southern public schools became in effect a private club, and the teachers were called "Miss Ruth," "Miss Libby," and "Miss Jessie." The papers of the South are full of such items as "Classroom Honors 'Miss Jessie' on 60th Birthday." At this level, at least, our schools were different. We never knew the teacher's first name. Like us, however, the Southerner came to identify his school with his most exciting and sometimes his most intimate experiences. Literally, his sister married out of the local high school because that is where she met her future husband.

To the white Southerner it seems that if the Negro comes into the public school he must come into the social life of the white community. The Southerner cannot imagine that the school will become a public rather than a private institution.

I remember speaking for integration in the fall of 1955 at Davidson College, the famous Presbyterian school of the South. The first question from the audience was, "What about the senior class dances in the high school?" I told my questioner what had happened to our own homogeneous society on the Lower East Side of New York. The Italians began to move eastward across the Bowery. Pretty soon three or four Italian boys sat in each of our classrooms. Now that there were strangers in the room, the principal no longer spoke Yiddish. School was not as homey a place as it had been. But the social life outside the school remained untouched both for us and, I am sure, for the Italians, who had a Garibaldi Club as we had a Young Judea Club. Later on, in DeWitt Clinton High School, there were dances sponsored by Young Judea, the Hibernians, and the Booker T. Washingtons. You helped each other out by buying each other's tickets, but socially you stuck with your own. With so many racially different students in the room, the only common denominator was instruction which perhaps explains the superiority of the Northern school systems to those of the South, yea, even unto the university level.

With this strong family identification with the Southern classroom, the poor whites have fought desperately against the integration of the schools, a fight in which they were joined by the politicians although for a different reason. The politician has history to tell him that the integration of the public schools will eventually lead to the voting booth not only for the disfranchised Negro but for the white, seeking now a new path to self-esteem.

The integration of the schools, argues the segregationist, is due to "Northern agitation." This is a most curious, inaccurate, and illogical argument since the decisions which first sanctioned segregation were handed down by a Supreme Court composed of seven Northern and two Southern Republicans.

When Congress, in 1875, passed the Civil Rights Act which provided that public accommodations accord equal treatment to all people regardless of race, this same "Northern" Supreme Court ruled it unconstitutional, handing down its decision in 1883. The argument of the Court was that the Federal Government was powerless to prohibit discrimination on the part of the individual.

Carl N. Degler takes this crucial decision to task in an argument rare in the literature on the subject:

> Only a Southern Justice of the Court and a former slave-owner—Justice John Marshall Harlan—saw the betrayal inherent in the decisions. In a ringing affirmation of the

constitutional meaning of American freedom and citizenship, he appealed to the spirit as well as the letter of the
Fourteenth Amendment. "The white race deems itself to
be the dominant race in this country," he observed, "and so
it is, in prestige, in achievements, in education, in wealth
and in power. But in the view of the Constitution, in the
eye of the law, there is in this country no superior, ruling
class of citizens. There is no caste here. Our Constitution
is color blind, and neither knows nor tolerates classes among
citizens. . . . The law regards man as man, and takes no
account of his surroundings or of his color when his civil
rights as guaranteed by the supreme law of the land are
involved." He then went on to warn his brethen: "In my
opinion, the judgment this day rendered will, in time, prove
to be quite as pernicious as the decision made by this
tribunal in the Dred Scott case." [4]

It was this decree which paved the way thirteen years later
in 1896 for the decision the Supreme Court rendered in
Plessy v. Ferguson which finally gave the South the power
to deny rights to the Negroes solely on the basis of color.

When Southerners argue that the "Warren Court" which
outlawed racial segregation in 1954 acted on "sociology" instead of law, they make an important and critical omission.
Most of the Southern senators charged that the reference in
the 1954 decision quoting Gunnar Myrdal (author of the
classic *An American Dilemma*) on the effect of prejudice and
discrimination on personality development, proved that the
Court had neglected the legal tradition and history of Constitutional interpretation. Senator Sam Ervin of North Carolina, known as a Constitutional authority, made this charge
too, although it could be said that he is no student of Supreme

[4] Carl N. Degler, *Out of Our Past: The Forces that Shaped Modern
America* (New York, Harper & Bros., 1959), pp. 234-35.

Court decisions. For the *Plessy v. Ferguson* decision which sanctioned racial segregation was based almost entirely on sociological interpretations. In fact, it was "sociology" pure and simple and bad sociology at that. The "sociologists" in *Plessy* did not cite even a single source. It is unfortunate for the law and for logic that Southern politicians can see one "sociology" and not the other.

In the Senate civil rights hearings (September 12, 1963), Attorney General Robert Kennedy asked Senator Ervin whether he believed there was any discrimination against Negroes in Mississippi, and the Senator said he did not know. Mr. Kennedy said, "Let's go down there for a day or two and look around." And the Senator said, "No, I'm too busy up here defending the Constitution. . . ." I mention this exchange between the Senator and the Attorney General because we are witnessing in our time an amazing paradox. While both Mr. Kennedy and Mr. Ervin love the Constitution of the United States of America, the man who is putting it to the acid test, trying to find if there are ultimate limits to our love and respect, is the American Negro. It is he who will teach us if the Constitution really works. Since Chief Justice John Marshall handed down his *Marbury v. Madison* decision in 1803 it has been the established fact of American law that the decisions of the United States Supreme Court are the final word in constitutional authority. "One court of supreme and final jurisdiction," Alexander Hamilton observed, "is a proposition . . . not likely to be contested." [5]

In "Judges as Guardians of the Constitution," Alexander Hamilton in the 78th Federalist established the principle which was accepted by the Founding Fathers:

"Whoever attentively considers the different departments of power must perceive, that, in a government in which they are

[5] Alpheus Thomas Mason, *The Supreme Court* (Ann Arbor, Michigan, University of Michigan Press, 1962), p. 44.

separated from each other, the judiciary, from the nature of its functions, will always be the least dangerous to the political rights of the Constitution; because it will be least in a capacity to annoy or injure them. The Executive not only dispenses the honors, but holds the sword of the community. The legislature not only commands the purse, but prescribes the rules by which the duties and rights of every citizen are to be regulated. The judiciary, on the contrary, has no influence over either the sword or the purse; no direction either of the strength or of the wealth of the society; and can take no active resolution whatever. It may truly be said to have neither FORCE nor WILL, but merely judgment; and must ultimately depend upon the aid of the executive arm even for the efficacy of its judgments." [6]

Plessy v. Ferguson did not involve education, but it removed all doubt that the Supreme Court had bestowed its blessings on state-maintained segregated school systems.

Homer Plessy, one-eighth Negro and seven-eighths white, was arrested in Louisiana when he refused to ride in the colored coach of a railroad train as required by the Louisiana statutes. He claimed that the Jim Crow statutes violated the Thirteenth and Fourteenth Amendments and named as defendant Judge Ferguson of Louisiana, assigned to conduct Plessy's criminal trial. Plessy lost in the Louisiana courts, and the Supreme Court affirmed their rulings. Plessy had argued that state-enforced segregation stamped Negroes with a badge of inferiority. The high court disagreed. The majority opinion was delivered by Justice Henry Billings Brown:

> We consider the underlying fallacy of the plaintiff's argument in the assumption that the enforced separation of the two races stamps the colored race with a badge of inferiority.

[6] Alexander M. Bickel, *The Least Dangerous Branch* (New York, Bobbs-Merrill, 1962), p. ix.

. . . The argument also assumes that social prejudices may be overcome by legislation and that equal rights cannot be secured except by an enforced commingling of the two races. We cannot accept this proposition. If the two races are to meet upon terms of social equality, it must be the result of natural affinities, a mutual appreciation of each other's merits and a voluntary consent of individuals. . . . Legislation is powerless to eradicate racial instincts or to abolish distinctions based upon physical differences, and the attempt to do so can only result in accentuating the difficulties of the present situation. . . . If one race be inferior to the other socially, the Constitution of the United States cannot put them upon the same plane.

In short, the Court argued that segregation did not deprive the Negro of any basic rights as a citizen except through his own choice.

Dr. Charles L. Black, Jr., Henry R. Luce Professor of Jurisprudence at Yale, goes directly to the point in *The Occasions of Justice* when he writes:

The fault of *Plessy* is in the psychology and sociology of its premise. . . . History tells us that segregation was imposed on one race by the other race; consent was not invited or required. Segregation in the South grew up and it kept growing because and only because the white race has wanted it that way. . . . This fact perhaps more than any other confirms the picture which a casual or deep observer is likely to form of the life of a Southern community—a picture not of mutual separation of whites and Negroes, but of one ingroup enjoying full normal communal life and one outgroup that is barred from this life and forced into an inferior life of its own. When a white Southern writer refers to the woes of "the South," do you not know, does not context commonly make it clear, that he means "white"

Southerners? When you are in Leesville, and hear someone say, "Leesville High" you know he has reference to the white high school; the Negro school will be called something else—Carver High, perhaps, or Lincoln High to our shame. That is what you would expect when one race forces a segregated position on another, and that is what you get.[7]

What you get are "separate but equal" facilities and it is becoming harder and harder to see how a man can be a citizen under "separate but equal" justice. For the Supreme Court in its *Plessy v. Ferguson* decision was commanding Negroes to be inferior citizens of their states and to that extent rejecting them as full citizens of the United States. It is manifestly impossible to imagine how, in any operative sense, a man can be a citizen without fellow citizens once in a while associating with him.

If, for example, his citizenship results in his election as a delegate to a national convention of the Building Trades Union, the whites may (as I saw done in Charlotte some years ago) put him up in the balcony, all alone, while the chairman gives instructions to the delegates on what they are to do when they get to Philadelphia. The complete freedom *from* association exists in the home and perhaps even in privately organized clubs, religious and fraternal organizations. But the man who wants complete freedom *from* association with his fellow citizens must perforce abjure public places.

What made the "separate but equal" doctrine begin to founder and what will ultimately make shipwreck of it is not the South's inability to administer equally to men who are separate. Quite the contrary. The beginning of the end of racial segregation came when the South, in a desperate at-

[7] Charles L. Black, Jr., *The Occasions of Justice* (New York, The Macmillan Co., 1963), pp. 129-34.

tempt to maintain it, went overboard in trying to show the Negro he was "equal."

A Sikh once told me how he despised the English for making his caste into soldiers when many would rather have been professors and poets. I asked, if the English had been more generous with the Sikhs and the Hindus and the Moslems would they have controlled India longer? The Sikh replied that, under those conditions India would have had its independence in 1910, for it wasn't until Indians were treated equitably that they began demanding independence.

For the same reason, the South, before the 1954 decision, never did treat Negroes equally. The Negro schools were substandard schools and the colored man's chances substandard chances. The legal assault on segregation which reached its massive proportions in the late 1950s began in the 1930s not with the charge that "separate" was unconstitutional but rather with the charge that "equal" was not a fact.

In 1934 the NAACP (which has always centered its energies on winning the precedent-making decision) determined to begin suits against graduate and professional schools since it was patently easy to prove inequality in graduate education.

One of the first of these precedent-making decisions was the Gaines case, known technically as *Missouri ex. rel. Gaines v. Canada.*

Gaines was a colored law-school student whose education Missouri financed out of state. He argued that this practice denied him equal protection. The Supreme Court agreed, requiring Missouri thereafter ". . . to furnish him within its borders facilities for legal education substantially equal to those which the State there afforded for persons of the white race." Chief Justice Charles Evans Hughes wrote: "Petitioner insists that for one intending to practice in Missouri there are special advantages in attending a law school there, both in relation to the opportunities for the particular study of Missouri law and for the observation of the local courts, and also in view of the prestige of the Missouri law school among the citizens of the State, his prospective clients."

However, Missouri did not admit Gaines to its law school. It interpreted the ruling to allow it to build a separate law school for Negroes. But the Gaines case was the beginning of the end of the "separate but equal" doctrine. "Separate" remained, but "equal" was examined ever more closely.

More cases followed. In 1950, in *Sweatt v. Painter,* the Supreme Court ruled that a separate, makeshift law school would not do and ordered the University of Texas to admit a Negro student. In the same year, in *McLaurin v. Oklahoma,* the Court held that a specially devised system of segregation interfered with the education of a colored graduate student at the all-white University of Oklahoma.

The reason these cases were important is that the Supreme Court, as yet minus Earl Warren, still Governor of California, had put the handwriting on the wall.

Mr. Sweatt had refused to attend a separate law school in Houston. The Supreme Court upheld his refusal, ruling he had to be admitted to the school at Austin. Chief Justice Fred M. Vinson read the majority opinion, noting the factors that make for the greatness of a law school: "Reputation of the faculty, experience in the administration, position and influence of the alumni, standing in the community, tradition and prestige." The Chief Justice went to the heart of the entire matter when he said that the Negro law school "excludes" 85 per cent of the population of Texas, "and most of the lawyers, witnesses, jurors, judges, and others, with whom Mr. Sweatt would deal when he became a member of the Texas bar."

Chief Justice Vinson had more to say in the case of *Mc-Laurin v. Oklahoma.* Mr. McLaurin fought segregation rules forcing him and twenty-three Negroes to sit in different rows while attending classes with whites at the University of Oklahoma Graduate School. Holding a master's degree, he sought one as a doctor of education. Originally, he had been denied admission on racial grounds, but the Oklahoma legislature amended the state laws to allow admission on a segregated basis. Mr. McLaurin was required, the Chief Justice said, first to sit in an adjoining room away from the class, at a special desk on the mezzanine floor of the library, and eat at a different time than other students in the cafeteria. Later the situation was changed, and the graduate student was seated in a place railed off, a sign above reading "Reserved for Colored."

Such restrictions, Justice Vinson said, "set McLaurin apart" from other students and handicapped his graduate instruction, "impairing and inhibiting his ability to study, to engage in discussions and exchange views with other students, and in general, to learn his profession."

The Chief Justice observed that removing these restrictions would not "necessarily abate individual and group predilections, prejudices and choices." But, he added, the state would not be depriving Mr. McLaurin of the chance to "secure acceptance by his fellow students on his own merits."

Though my résumé is brief, it is still easy to see the tack the Supreme Court was taking. While the ruling the Supreme Court handed down in 1954 outlawing public school segregation was momentous, it was not surprising. The argument had found its secondary proposition: "equal" was incompatible with "separate."

The Court that heard the argument of *Brown v. Board of Education* was made up of Chief Justice Earl Warren, Felix Frankfurter, Hugo L. Black, Stanley F. Reed, William O. Douglas, Tom C. Clark, Robert H. Jackson, Harold H. Burton, and Sherman Minton.

The principal spokesman for the South was John W. Davis, Democratic nominee for President in 1924 and veteran of more Supreme Court battles than any other lawyer in American history. Thurgood Marshall, chief counsel of the NAACP, key figure in a quarter century of legal combat on behalf of the Negro, pleaded the cause of desegregation. Another able lawyer, Assistant Attorney General J. Lee Rankin, spoke for the United States. Associate Justice Robert H. Jackson, convalescing from a heart attack, had left his hospital bed only that morning, so that all nine justices could be together when the decision was read. His being there was the clue to the great event, but no one could be sure because the Court had not even given newsmen their usual advance printed copies of the opinion. So at 12:52 P.M., May 17, 1954, some three hundred thirty-five years after the first Negro slaves arrived in America and ninety-one years after the Emancipation Proclamation, Earl Warren, Chief Justice of the United States, began reading the Supreme Court opinion in *Brown v. Board of Education:*

Segregation of white and colored children in public schools has a detrimental effect upon the colored children. The impact is greater when it has the sanction of the law; for the policy of separating the races is usually interpreted as denoting the inferiority of the Negro group. A sense of inferiority affects the motivation of a child to learn. Segregation with the sanction of law, therefore, has a tendency to [retard] the educational and mental development of Negro children and to deprive them of some of the benefits they would receive in a racially integrated school system. Whatever may have been the extent of psychological knowledge at the time of *Plessy v. Ferguson,* this finding is amply supported by modern authority. Any language in *Plessy v. Ferguson* contrary to this finding is rejected. . . .

We conclude that in the field of public education the doctrine of 'separate but equal' has no place. Separate educational facilities are inherently unequal. . . .

The vote was unanimous. All the justices said the same thing—Republican or Democrat, Jew or Gentile, Catholic or Protestant, Northerner or Southerner, liberal or conservative. There was no minority opinion. Only two of the justices were Republicans, Warren and Burton, while three of the seven Democrats were from the South, Black of Alabama, Clark of Texas, and Reed of Kentucky.

The decision was followed on May 31, 1955, by *Brown v. Board of Education*, 349 U.S. 294, the process of the implementation of the Supreme Court's opinion holding segregated schools invalid yet speaking of taking "local conditions into account." The Associated Press reported that the ruling was widely interpreted as meaning indefinite extension of racial segregation in public schools. The absence of a desegregation deadline was noted with a sigh of relief by Southern moderates and with a note of triumph by ardent segregationists. The high court's passing the problem back to local areas was thought to mean that considerable delay, perhaps in terms of years, would be sanctioned as part of "taking into account local conditions" created by generations of segregation.

The NAACP did not criticize the court for not setting a specific date for compliance. Thurgood Marshall, chief counsel, and Roy Wilkins, executive secretary, made it plain that they thought the decision brooked no delay in ending segregation. The court's decision apparently took into account difficulties faced by several states which were ready and willing to desegregate, but which faced various problems. These states included Kentucky, Oklahoma, Kansas, Maryland, and Delaware. Apparently neither ready nor willing at that time were Texas, Louisiana, Mississippi, Alabama,

Georgia, Florida, South Carolina, North Carolina, and Virginia.

But except for the politicians in Washington and in respective state capitols the South was amazingly quiet. This remarkable quiet lasted for nearly a year after the Supreme Court's "implementation" decision of May, 1955, and has puzzled most of the Southern writers and newspapermen.

Once I asked Luther Hodges, then governor of North Carolina, about this "silence" and he said it was deceptive, that underneath the people were seething. But that was only his opinion. The people may not have been seething, they may have been waiting for direction and leadership, the leadership and direction which never came. When it did not come, the irresponsibles took over. The business community, which always represents the power structure in the South, backed off. Its members were silent, scared to death. The Protestant clergy, at least at the level of the local church, abdicated its authority in the field of ethics, retreating from a moral issue, leaving its defense to a few embattled editors, small groups of Unitarians, Quakers, social workers and assorted do-gooders who banded together into the many local chapters of the Southern Regional Council, financed by a grant from the Ford Foundation's Fund for the Republic.

This silence might have been broken by the one voice with the prestige and the influence to have set the new direction (President Eisenhower was one of the most popular Presidents in our history). But that voice never spoke. In a story datelined, Newport, Rhode Island, on February 15, 1957, the New York *Herald Tribune* reported that President Eisenhower, emerging from church services, commended a Navy chaplain on his racial sermon with the comment, "You can't legislate morality."

The entire segregationist press hailed the statement, and David Lawrence in the same newspaper on September 17,

1957, likened the Eisenhower verdict to "the wisdom of the nation's lesson with national prohibition." All of which had nothing to do with the decisions of Chief Justice Fred M. Vinson and Chief Justice Earl Warren, which merely restated the duty of the civilized citizen to insist that the other man's rights be respected as fully as his own.

CHAPTER FIVE

IN AND OUT OF THE VACUUM

Millions of Southerners were ready to comply with the inevitable in 1954. The reason they did not was that the sense of inevitability was never communicated to them (that the deep South resists the inevitable in 1964 makes the inevitable no less inevitable). The one man who might have convinced the South of the inevitable was Dwight D. Eisenhower, President of the United States. He never tried.

Is it fair to place this responsibility upon the shoulders of a man to whom our nation and indeed the free world owes so great a debt? Yes it is, for the events which transpired during the four years from the time of the Supreme Court decision on May 17, 1954, to the beginning of the school term of September, 1958, clearly show the tragic consequences which stemmed from the President's inaction. Professor Oscar Handlin, reviewing Eisenhower's book *Mandate for Change,* succinctly explains the President's indecision: "A President who doggedly believed that a strong federal government was a threat to liberty could hardly excite voters or congressmen in favor of extending federal influence in education or transportation. . . ." [1]

[1] Oscar Handlin, "The Eisenhower Administration," *The Atlantic Monthly,* November, 1963, p. 168.

Even today it is difficult to understand President Eisenhower's personal attitude. Although he appointed a Negro to the White House staff, the commission was withheld for five years, and when E. Frederic Morrow was sworn in Eisenhower absented himself from the ceremonies. This was unprecedented in the swearing in of Presidential aides. The former President's most important statement about the social revolution of the American Negro fell on unbelieving ears six months after the Supreme Court had handed down its ruling. Eisenhower was reported in the New York *Times* of November 24, 1954, as having said, ". . . he was sure America wanted to obey the Constitution but there was a very great problem involved, and there were certainly deep-seated emotions." He was saying in effect that while the Court had revealed the law it was a hard law to obey. In answer to a question at the November 23 press conference, the President replied he understood the Supreme Court had undertaken as its task to write its orders or procedure in such fashion as to take into consideration these great emotional strains and practical problems. Eisenhower was prophesying how the Supreme Court would order integration implemented. Observers noted that Presidential comments in advance on Supreme Court actions are rare in American history. The White House press secretary, James Hagerty, told reporters Mr. Eisenhower got his views from the decision of May 17, 1954, particularly that part which read: "Because these are class actions, because of the wide applicability of this decision and because of the great variety of local conditions, the formulation of decrees in these cases presents problems of considerable complexity."

Though the President was hoping the Supreme Court would not rend the emotional placidity of the American personality, his Attorney General, Herbert Brownell, and his Solicitor General, Simon Sobeloff, were not so considerate. They were for all out anxiety. Despite their chief's sentiments, they soon argued an advisory brief with the Supreme Court regarding desegregation procedures which employed such terms as "promptly" and "immediately." The Brownell brief and the Soboloff argument clearly indicated that the "moderate" President had an "extremist" Attorney General and an "extremist" Solicitor General.

The Department of Justice had asked that compliance with the desegregation decree be completed within two school terms. The NAACP's Thurgood Marshall said that two school terms was too long and suggested a period of six months. The court wisely set no timetable. It merely urged "all deliberate speed." The Negro leaders were confident that something would be done by the President to support Attorney General Brownell and Solicitor General Soboloff who had argued for swifter compliance. Nothing of the kind happened.

The disappointment over Eisenhower's failure to use the moral authority of the White House occasioned deep chagrin. The Norfolk *Journal and Guide* of November 28, 1954, a Negro newspaper, said that President Eisenhower's attitude was reminiscent of the policies set forth by President William Howard Taft who proclaimed that he would appoint no Negroes to federal offices in the South where white people objected.

Eisenhower had no hard attitude because on several occasions he called for "moderation" and on numerous other occasions he called for "determination" to make progress. Perhaps he was aloof because he thought his withdrawal would aid his chances for re-election in 1956. Certainly this aloofness did not hurt him in the South, a political fact upon which many editorials commented. On June 1, 1956, Thomas L. Stokes wrote in the Miami *Herald:* "President Eisenhower's course in keeping himself out of the raging controversy over public school integration apparently is among the factors that account for his continued popularity in the South."

This is more than suspicion. The President could not have been unaware that an American Legion audience in Los Angeles had booed Adlai Stevenson when the Democratic candidate said that we could not convince other nations that we believe in justice "when mobs prevent Negro children from lawfully attending school." [2]

Emmet John Hughes penetrates Eisenhower's characteristic caution:

> Quite like his constraint in policy toward the Congress, this determination *not* to act reflected positive *belief*. . . . In civil rights as in Congressional relations, his political faith rested on the slow, gradual power of persuasion. Our differences on this issue punctuated our reviews of almost every campaign address he made. . . . Through all the preparatory process on almost all speeches, the text on civil rights signaled the playing of a kind of rhythmic game between us, accepted but unacknowledged—I toughening every reference, he softening it, I rephrasing upward, he rewording downward. The drift of political events, however, fortified his caution, for the campaign [of 1956] had not run half its course before all reports indicated a clear chance for Eisenhower to carry such states as Florida and Texas. So on Election Eve it was quite characteristic for the President—as we sat watching elaborate telecasts of rallies across the nation—to greet a Negro speaker's salute from a Detroit rally with the wry comment: "*That* will sure win us a lot of votes in Houston!"

His feelings on civil rights, however, struck roots deeper

[2] I. F. Stone, *The Haunted Fifties* (New York, Random House, 1963), p. 112.

than such campaign superficialities. Before he had delivered even his first speech of the campaign, he voiced these feelings to me vehemently. "I am convinced," he insisted, "that the Supreme Court decision set back progress in the South at least fifteen years. . . ." [3]

Not until the end of his second term in office did Dwight D. Eisenhower make a flat statement about racial segregation. On July 16, 1959, at a press conference a questioner asked, "Do you think racial segregation is morally wrong?" The President then replied that segregation that interfered with the equality of opportunity in the economic and political fields was, in his personal opinion, morally wrong. In this brief exchange he did not mention schools, the center of the integration battle. He might morally condemn segregation but a host of Southern newspapers airily reminded their readers that General Eisenhower thought segregation was best for the Army, quoting his remarks from the *Congressional Record* of June 8, 1948, page 7358.

After retiring from the White House, private citizen Eisenhower, according to Roscoe Drummond (Washington *Post*, May 30, 1961),

> . . . no longer places any restriction on discussing his views on racial discrimination. During his eight years in the White House he refrained from expressing his personal opinions on any court decisions because as President, he felt he could better administer all the laws equally if he did not select some for special approval. Now his views can be put clearly on the record. . . . General Eisenhower believes that the unanimous decision of the Supreme Court of 1954 requiring desegregation of the public schools is constitutionally correct, but he does not agree with all the reasoning that went along with it. . . . He does not see the

[3] Hughes, *op. cit.*, pp. 200-1.

Constitution as providing for social integration. . . . Mr. Eisenhower feels that America is making progress, but that we mustn't expect laws to do it all.

Two years later the former President finally referred to the social revolution of the American Negro as a "moral issue." The New York *Post* of October 10, 1963, commented, "Mr. Eisenhower's verdict was recited exactly nine years, four months, and twenty-three days after the court had spoken. Rarely has any man so firmly resisted an impetuous judgment and looked so long before leaping."

Just why Dwight D. Eisenhower's determination not to act during his eight years in the White House reflected a positive belief is one of those verbal mysteries only he alone can eventually unravel.

It may come as a surprise to many that reactions in the South immediately following the Supreme Court decision of May 17, 1954, were favorable. Or, let us say, they were not unfavorable. Governor Francis Cherry of Arkansas said: "Arkansas will obey the law"; Theodore McKeldin of Maryland: "Our citizens and our officials will accept readily the United States Supreme Court's interpretation of our fundamental law"; James Murray of Oklahoma: "Oklahoma has always followed the law, whatever it is"; Lawrence Wetherby of Kentucky said his state would "comply with the law"; and Frank Clement of Tennessee said the Court was supreme "in interpreting the law of the land." Even Governor Thomas Stanley of Virginia, though he changed his mind six weeks later, promised he would call a meeting of local and state officials to "work toward a plan which shall be acceptable to our citizens and in keeping with the edict of the court." [4]

To be fair, President Eisenhower's hesitancy in setting a direction at a time when millions of people below the Mason-

[4] *Southern School News,* Nashville, Tenn., September 1955, p. 2.

Dixon line swore "I like Ike" was not the sole factor in hardening the South's defiance of the Supreme Court decision, the defiance that eventually led to bloodshed, riots, the use of federal troops, and the massed protest demonstrations of the Negroes. It is not only too late to assign blame, it is pointless. The target is not a solitary uncomprehending Eisenhower whom history suddenly called upon; it is hundreds of other politicians equally uncomprehending whom history asked for greatness. Elected leadership throughout the country faltered.

The entire struggle has revolved around leadership, political leadership which always determines the course of developments in a political society such as ours. The majority of the American public outside the South was indifferent and remained indifferent, really, until school integration exploded into riot and bloodshed. Even today a large segment of the American public simply wants the disturbance quelled, not the injustice set aright. How important political leadership was and could have been can be gauged by what happened in Arkansas.

After Governor Francis Cherry said: "Arkansas will obey the law . . . it always has," two school systems, Charleston and Fayetteville, voluntarily desegregated. Desegregation spread to several other communities without incident. But when the time came for Little Rock to desegregate, Orval Faubus had become the governor. Six years later, I was delivering a speech at Ewha Woman's University in Seoul, Korea, under auspices of the United States Eighth Army. I was talking about Abraham Lincoln and Carl Sandburg. Yet every question from the Korean girls was about "Little Rock, Arkansas," and why did a governor prevent Negro children from going to a public school and why did the President have to send troops to protect Negro school children. When I discussed the Hitler era at the Free University in West Berlin, one student spoke for them all when she asked about "Little

Rock" and the "oppression of the American Negro." I made the point quite clear, I hope, as I had done in other foreign places, that what they were reading about did not represent the policy of the American government as racism had indeed been the official policy of the Third Reich. I told them that the American government stands for equity, and the stories about "Little Rock" and "water hoses" are, in fact, stories about *violations* of American law.

Even among Negroes, irresponsible and uninformed and purely ambitious leadership disturbs the protest. My thought goes to the Harlem Congressman Adam Clayton Powell. I am always saddened and amused by his sneers at "white liberals." During the thirty years before the 1954 decision, it was the white liberals, and the *Southern* white liberals at that, who created the atmosphere which eventually helped the Negroes assume the leadership of their revolution. When I listen to Congressman Powell I remember United States Federal District Judge J. Waites Waring, a native South Carolinian from Charleston who told the South Carolina Democratic party in 1948 it could no longer conduct its affairs as a private club but must open its primaries, the only meaningful elections in South Carolina, to the Negroes.

The reaction against Judge Waring was sudden and bitter. A South Carolina Congressman predicted bloodshed. Judge and Mrs. Waring were socially ostracized. When lightning struck at a neighbor's summer home a sign was posted which said, "Dear God, he lives next door."

Congressman Powell's criticism is explained by the truth that all revolutions breed counterrevolutionaries. The White Citizens Council may be explained by noting the vacuum responsible Southern leadership did not try to fill. The failure of the political leadership to set a direction for the implementation of the Supreme Court's decision gave the White Citizens Councils and the Ku Klux Klan a good head start.

The first White Citizens Council was formed in the delta town of Indianola, Mississippi, in 1954. Even in Mississippi, the White Citizens Council did not win the approval of the State government until August, 1959, when Ross Barnett won a landslide victory for the Democratic gubernatorial nomina-tion. He was opposed by the State's two living ex-governors who had cautioned restraint in the race issue.

The first White Citizens Council outside of Mississippi was formed in Selma, Alabama, in October 1954, an organization which continued as one of the strongest centers of resistance in the South.

The Tar Heels, "seething underneath," as Governor Hodges would have it, did not charter a white supremacy group until October, 1957. (And one of these groups had to come to the office of my paper, the *Carolina Israelite,* to ask for copies of an exposé in the *American Jewish Congress Weekly,* written by Julian Scheer and me, which would tell them where they could get their constitution and bylaws.)

Not until 1958 did the White Citizens Councils achieve any degree of influence in South Carolina, Georgia, Virginia, or Tennessee. Inward seething, apparently, was slow erupting. Once erupted, however, it plagued all America and was par-ticularly virulent in the South. Its intensity can be gauged by what happened to the Koinonia Community near Americus, Georgia.

Koinonia, which took its name from the Greek word for fellowship, was an interracial Christian community unmo-lested since 1942. The community was founded by Dr. Clarence Jordan, a Baptist minister and native white Georgian who had college degrees in agriculture and Greek from the Uni-versity of Georgia and a religious degree from a Kentucky seminary.

In the 1950s Koinonia found itself swept up in the frus-trations of angry white Southerners who faced inevitable, and perhaps enforced, integration. For two years, 1957-1958, the Christian fellowship of farmers lived through a siege of terror. Neighboring Georgians dynamited their once prosperous roadside store. An economic boycott wiped out their thriving poultry business. Machine-gun bullets tore their gasoline pump. Night riders shot into their homes. A group of children playing volleyball ducked bullets fired by occupants of a speeding car. Bullies threatened the families of Negro members. The Georgia sheriff who investigated each new incident, and there was one almost daily, never found a clue, much less a suspect.

In the midst of this violence, the Koinonians learned that President Eisenhower was visiting in Augusta. Dr. Jordan sent an urgent and detailed letter asking federal protection for his group. Eisenhower forwarded the letter to Attorney General William P. Rogers. Rogers sent it to Governor Griffin of Georgia. Governor Griffin promptly called a press conference, denounced Koinonia as "a cancer on Georgia's fair soil," hinted its members' possible arrest as Communists, accused the group of shooting at itself to get publicity, and called for its removal from the area.[5]

Paradoxically, President Eisenhower's Administration passed the first civil rights legislation since the Reconstruction. But significantly a director of the NAACP congratulated the then Democratic Senate Majority Leader Lyndon B. Johnson for "getting even this little bit from the Southerners." This legislation provided for the establishment of a Civil Rights Commission, a Civil Rights Division in the Justice Department, laws to strengthen enforcement of voting rights. However, the controversial Title III was eliminated; this would have given the Federal Government the right to seek preventive relief in all civil rights cases. President Eisenhower in his

[5] Martha Huntley in a study of *Koinonia* (unpublished thesis), 1962, Barnard College, New York.

1957 State of the Union message which proposed this legislation also called for a federal aid to education bill for school construction, "uncomplicated by desegregation riders."

In the months that followed, reporters pressed Mr. Eisenhower on details of the proposed legislation. Not only did the President decline to take a stand on the disputed items but often showed that he was confused over provisions of the bill itself. Walter Lippmann commented (Greensboro, N. C., *Daily News,* July 12, 1957): "Once again, as with the budget, the President has let it be known that he is not sure he is fully in favor of a major measure which has been put forward by his Administration."

During the last three years of the Eisenhower Administration, the Civil Rights Bill which had been passed in a Republican Administration proved no embarrassment to the segregationists of the South.

Obviously the Eisenhower Administration could not have provided a total solution for this crucial issue. But the Administration did not even try. It not only drifted, it gave aid and comfort to the enemies of the Civil Rights Bill which Republican spokesmen have claimed as their own.

In a story by White House reporter Don Oberdorfer appearing in the Charlotte *Observer* on January 14, 1960, President Eisenhower was described as throwing cold water on government plans to provide federal registrars where Negroes were being denied their right to vote.

The lead stated, "President Eisenhower threw cold water Wednesday on his own Civil Rights Commission's plan for federal registrars where Negroes are denied voting rights. . . . Ike's action was a major blow to chances for the plan on Capitol Hill, where it had been shaping up as an important part of a new civil rights package."

In the January 13, 1960, press conference, Oberdorfer had asked Eisenhower if he agreed with the commissioners that a law is needed to provide federal registrars when Negroes are denied the right to register or vote. Eisenhower answered, "I don't know—as a matter of fact, I don't even know whether it is constitutional. . . . Now, the way I feel about this civil rights: We have one bill that was put in last year in which extensive hearings have been heard and I should like to see Congress act decisively on this particular proposal."

There were men who knew that leadership, quick implementation, and reverence for the law could break the racial fever. The late Judge John J. Parker, chief Judge of the United States Court of Appeals of the Fourth Circuit, a Republican who had been denied confirmation to the United States Supreme Court by one vote, personally expressed himself on this issue. I do his memory no injustice to say that off the bench he was a segregationist. Born and raised on a farm in Union County, North Carolina, he was a Southerner to the core. But he was also a man of the law. He told me once, "I believe in two things—Jesus Christ and the Constitution of the United States."

In February of 1958 he asked me to send a memorandum to Luther Hodges urging the Governor by a nation-wide radio and television appearance to set a new pattern for the South. I put some rhetoric around the Judge's memorandum and sent it to Raleigh before the Governor was to go to a conference of Southern Governors. Parker asked Hodges to communicate three points:

1. The Supreme Court will not reverse itself;
2. The law must be obeyed;
3. We accept these realities and we ask men and women of good will to accept other realities. There are sections of the South where we can integrate the schools tomorrow without too much trouble; there are other sections where we can make some progress in ten or fifteen years.

But there are some sections of the South where we will not integrate the schools in our generation. It will have to be done by our children.

The common sense and moral tone of the Judge Parkers in the South did not prevail. The pattern was set instead by Senator Harry F. Byrd of Virginia who called for massive resistance, and the weapon was to be Interposition. The idea itself had been uncovered by an elderly country lawyer named William Olds. Interposition is the doctrine that a state has the right to interpose its sovereignty between the Federal Government and the state's citizens. Interposition's first important champion was James Jackson Kilpatrick, Jr., the young editor of the Richmond *News Leader,* a paper which greeted the Supreme Court ruling of 1954 with a conciliatory editorial, but soon changed over to hostility. A native of Oklahoma, Mr. Kilpatrick has succeeded in becoming somewhat more Virginian than Virginia. To Kilpatrick, Olds' disinterred paper was pure gold. He seized upon the idea and went energetically to work. The solemnity and grace of his editorials sold Interposition to the South.

The author of this book is a member of a minority and prides himself on being an "expert" on the phenomenon of the outsider becoming "more Virginian than Virginia." It has always fascinated me that two of the most ardent segregationists in the South are a Roman Catholic, Leander Perez, Sr., of Plaquemines Parish, Louisiana, and a Jew, Charles M. Bloch, a lawyer of Macon, Georgia, both of whom outProtestant the white Protestant segregationists.

When the Most Reverend Joseph Francis Rummel, Archbishop of New Orleans for twenty-seven years, excommunicated Leander Perez, Sr., and two others who had denounced the desegregation of the diocese's parochial schools, Mr. Perez told Claude Sitton, a New York *Times* reporter, on April

17, 1962; "I am a lifelong Catholic and will continue to be so, regardless of Communist infiltration and the influence of the National Council of Christians and Jews upon our church leaders." To which I add Mr. Perez could have at least said, "Except Charlie Bloch of Macon, Georgia."

Mr. Bloch, the well-known Jewish lawyer, led the Georgia delegation out of the Democratic National Convention in 1948 as a protest against the civil rights plank and he was subsequently a stalwart in the Dixiecrat movement. After the Supreme Court decision, Mr. Bloch became the vice-president of the Georgia States Rights Society. He published a book, *States Rights—the Law of the Land*, in which he said we must construe the clause in the Declaration of Independence that "all men are created equal" in the light of the times when it was promulgated; "Since at that time Negroes were not men but property, we are bound today to permit states to legislate about them as property." [6]

Let it be understood that Leander Perez and Charles Bloch are not alone in this attempt to prove themselves super-segregationists. For every Northern clergyman or student who joins the Freedom Riders or the sit-ins or picket lines in front of a restaurant in Mississippi or Alabama or North Carolina, one or more other influential Northerners take a place in the ranks of the segregationists. These are the Northern managers and superintendents of national concerns who have come into the South by the hundreds during the last twenty-five years. Notified of his transfer to a Southern post, the Northerner's wife buys a copy of *Gone with the Wind* and he gets himself a recipe for mint juleps. A few days after they are settled in their new Southern home, they write a letter to the editor: "We have just moved to your beautiful city from Scarsdale, New York, and we are well aware of the great agitation for

[6] Harry Golden, "The South Stalls its Future," *The Nation*, August 30, 1958, p. 185.

the integration of Negroes in the white public schools. This will never work. We know. . . ."

The point remains: the defiance that flooded the South did not well solely from Southern springs. The Northerners from Massachusetts who owned radio stations in Georgia complained about "outside agitators" and editors from Oklahoma discovered Interposition.

What erupted in the South and was wholly Southern was the leadership of the Negro protest, although for several years the protest was blamed on the nefarious NAACP whose headquarters is in New York City. Most of the states passed laws against the NAACP, the bête noire of the entire South. Thurgood Marshall loomed as a bogey man. I attended a meeting of leading citizens in Charlotte in 1957, where one lawyer rose to say, "If we do not do something quickly about that hospital situation, we'll have Thurgood Marshall on our neck." Even relatively liberal North Carolina toyed with a proposal in the state legislature to limit the activities of the NAACP. Luckily it was defeated by Charlotte's representative, State Senator Spencer Bell, who has since gone to the late Judge Parker's U.S. Fourth Circuit Court of Appeals. The U.S. Supreme Court finally overruled the lower courts of Arkansas, Florida, and Georgia in cases where the respective states had acted to seize the membership lists of the NAACP.

Then came the sit-in movement of Negro students in Greensboro, North Carolina, under the auspices of the Congress of Racial Equality, and CORE became the new cuss word. Folks began to look more tolerantly on the NAACP. When the Freedom Riders started coming and Martin Luther King gathered together thousands of protesting Negroes, the segregationists began to say, "O, for the good old days of the NAACP." After the young students in the Student Non-Violent Co-ordinating Committee (SNCC) staged their sit-ins, pray-ins, and kneel-ins, Southerners by now were ready to embrace the NAACP. Indeed they did. In my own city the name of Kelly Alexander, local head of the NAACP, had been anathema for a long time. Today Kelly Alexander attends meetings of the power structure. He has not changed his views, but the Southerners now dream about the days of the NAACP when all they had to do was file an answering brief in a court-house.

The NAACP was a coalition of whites and Negroes, in the beginning mostly Northern whites and liberals. But it was the Southern Negroes who eventually shook the South out of the magnolias. Just what the Southern Negro has done to the Old South is best revealed in Ralph McGill's classic story about the aged aunt living in an ante-bellum home in Union Point, Georgia. She is eighty-nine. There are magnolia trees about the place which are at least one hundred years old. In a talk with her Atlanta niece, the old lady asks: "Anne, what has got into the darkies? They seem so restless these days." If they are restless at Union Point, the ball game is over.

Indeed the social revolution of the American Negro, which burst out of the South to engulf the North, has made it impossible for almost any Negro to stay aloof except at the cost of ostracism by other Negroes as an "Uncle Tom." I have noticed that even those Negroes with a vested interest in segregation (owners of segregated cafés, restaurants, hotels, etc.) participate in the revolt. One of the wealthiest Negroes in North Carolina is John Wheeler who, because of his position as president of a large bank in Durham, has achieved fairly easy access to the white power structure of the city, yet has nevertheless been the most consistent supporter of the Negro and white organizations fighting racial segregation. Early in 1955 a high state official hinted that many Negro teachers would lose their jobs if the schools were integrated. A meeting of over seven hundred Negro teachers voted to "desegregate" without a single dissenting voice.

In 1954, a couple of months after The Decision, Governor
Hugh White of Mississippi called a meeting of ninety Negro
leaders in his state to ask their support of a "voluntary"
segregation plan in exchange for a state financial outlay to
bring Negro school facilities in Mississippi up to those enjoyed by white pupils. Of the Negro leaders present at the
meeting only one endorsed the plan; the others issued a joint
statement declaring that they were "unalterably opposed to
any effort of either white or Negro citizens to circumvent
the decision of the Supreme Court of the United States of
America outlawing segregation in public schools. 'I am
stunned,' said the Governor." [7]

The Southern Negro assumed leadership of the movement
principally because the white Southerner gave him the opportunity for leadership. The South insisted upon an absolute
Negro ghetto. While there were ghettos in the North, they
were not absolute. The Negro truck driver, teacher, and
singer in the North saw the ghetto patrolled by white authority: white policemen made their rounds, white teachers
taught black students, and often white doctors ministered to
Negro ills. In the South, the educated Negro doctor, lawyer,
teacher, clergyman, dentist, became the leader in the ghetto
because in the South there were not only Negro teachers but
also Negro principals and Negro superintendents of schools,
Negroes with authority which the Northern Negro rarely saw.
And because he had leaders in his ghetto, the Negro turned
to them when he wanted to escape his ghetto walls.

On December 1, 1955, in Montgomery, Alabama, a Negro
woman, Mrs. Rosa Parks, refused to give up her bus seat to a
white passenger. Mrs. Parks would not move because she was
physically tired after a day's work cleaning someone else's

[7] James Graham Cook, The Segregationists (New York, Appleton-Century-
Crofts, 1962), p. 307.

house. She was arrested. The Montgomery bus strike was on. Out of this crucible emerged the representative Negro leader, the Reverend Dr. Martin Luther King, Jr., who not only led the strike but infused the Negro movement with the philosophy of non-violence, an American adaptation of Gandhi's passive resistance: "If the streets must run with blood, let it be our blood and not that of our white brothers." Two sources, writes Dr. King, inspired this movement: "Christ furnished the spirit and motivation, while Gandhi furnished the method." [8]

In Montgomery, Alabama, they keep the home of Jefferson Davis as a museum. It is the "cradle of the Confederacy." And it was here that the Negroes won their strike. Not only were they sustained by the courts, but the Southern housewife sold out her segregationist husband and chauffered her Negro maid back and forth; no employer fired his Negro laborer who walked in order to hire a white laborer at higher wages.

Winning the Montgomery bus strike gave Negroes everywhere confidence they could win other protests, and by leading in that victory Martin Luther King became the pre-eminent leader of the cause of Southern Negroes. Fortunately, Dr. King came along when he did for, aided and abetted by circumstances and the moral abdication of the white Protestant clergy and the power structure, the issue had been left wholly to the malignant imagination of Southern politicians who, from the steps of every state capitol, kept promising that segregation and the segregated school system would persevere. They promised private schools with state subsidies, tuition grants, pupil assignment acts, local control, complicated legal steps for Negro parents, multiple forms to fill out for transfer to all-white schools, redistricting, interposition

[8] Martin Luther King, Jr., *Stride Toward Freedom* (New York, Harper Bros., 1960), p. 18.

and nullification; they set into motion a whole complex of cunning and cruel devices in an attempt to preserve an evil system.

But more than that, an atmosphere of fear and intimidation rolled in as the politicians made these promises. Southerners who spoke conciliatory words in 1955 were silent in 1958. They were silenced because they saw a few outspoken colleagues and neighbors dismissed from their pulpits, their classrooms, and their jobs in general. On May 2, 1955, Chester Travelstead, dean of the School of Education at the University of South Carolina, had written a letter to the editor of the local paper in which he said the Supreme Court ruling was "timely and morally sound." The board of trustees asked for his resignation. One of the college trustees told Travelstead, "A person should have enough common sense to know what he should and should not discuss. . . ." Nearly ten years later Dr. James W. Silver, history professor at the University of Mississippi, stated publicly that "Mississippi is a closed society where the white man does not dare speak out and where the search for truth has become a casualty."

This has been the great tragedy in the South since the Supreme Court decision in 1954, the tragedy of the white liberal. The clergyman needs his job and his congregation, the editor needs his job and his readers, the college professor needs his job and his classroom, but the private white liberal is the most helpless of all. The clergyman, the editor, and the college professor can occasionally sneak in a word above the battle, but the ordinary white liberal citizen is completely silenced. He cannot join the Negro community and he cannot separate himself (and his wife and children) from the surrounding society, his employer, his relatives, his customers, his friends, and his neighbors. Because that is what would happen to him. Indeed that is what has happened to a few hardy souls who could no longer contain themselves. The Negroes themselves have been intimidated. In the early days a few frightened Negroes took advertisements in South Carolina, Georgia, and Louisiana newspapers: "Notice the undersigned is NOT a member of the NAACP. . . ."

But eventually, one by one, the many legal devices invented by the several state legislatures came before the Supreme Court and were branded for what they were—transparent frauds. Even the white school children knew that they were frauds. And so the segregationists fell back on the fable of "state sovereignty," for fable it is. There hasn't been a "sovereign state" since 1789 when the last of the states surrendered its sovereignty by ratifying the Constitution. In 1821, in a case arising in Virginia, the Supreme Court ruled, "The Constitution and laws of a State so far as they are repugnant to the Constitution and laws of the United States are absolutely void." [9] The contempt which some of the Southern politicians have shown for what they call "the central government" involves only those areas of "states rights" concerned with the Negro. There are one hundred and thirteen other areas, however, in which the Federal Government "intrudes" upon the Southern states. Agricultural services alone totaled $5,895,000,-000 for the South in 1962.

To get some idea of the range and extent of federal grants, let us look at what Alabama, forty-ninth among the states in per capita income, receives. Excluding all payments *under one million dollars,* in 1962 the Federal Government gave Alabama alone (Report of the Secretary of the Treasury, Table 95, fiscal year 1962, page 801):

FOR SPECIAL MILK PROGRAM	$ 1,195,153;
FOR SCHOOL CONSTRUCTION	1,579,099;
FOR SCHOOL MAINTENANCE	5,368,962;
FOR HOSPITALS	3,265,303;

[9] June Purcell Guild, *The Myth of States Rights* (Richmond, Anti-Defamation League, 1958), p. 2.

FOR SANITATION	1,219,765;
FOR OLD AGE ASSISTANCE	55,317,235;
FOR PUBLIC HOUSING	6,293,084;
FOR VETERANS	5,309,517.

One day the governor of Alabama, George C. Wallace, stood in the doorway defying federal authorities to carry out a federal court order, and by coincidence three other Alabamans were applying for Area Redevelopment Administration funds which provide rural and urban areas with resources to stimulate employment. The Southern Senators have filibustered only when proposed legislation involved the Negro. They have remained silent about the principle when the legislation involved such "intrusions" upon "states' rights" as the use of federal funds for farm subsidies, pensions, and school lunches; or the building of roads, hospitals, airports, and industrial plants.

All the while James Meredith was trying to register at the University of Mississippi, Governor Ross Barnett kept asking the Attorney General (by telegram and telephone) why a court sitting in New Orleans had the right to tell a governor of Mississippi whom to admit to the state-supported university.

The Attorney General tried explaining to Ross Barnett that though he might not realize it, he was not only a citizen of Mississippi but also a citizen of the United States. At one point, Mr. Kennedy sent word to Governor Barnett that he was well aware of how the Governor felt about the precedent-breaking admission of a Negro, but student Meredith had a federal court order of admission and no one could defy the federal law. "Mississippi is part of the United States," said the Attorney General.

"I am not so sure now," replied Governor Barnett.

The Southern segregationists have many important allies. They muster not only the business and power structure but the state courts and school boards, the militia and police, the state legislature, the governor and the attorney general to deny justice to the Negro. Yet they whimper all the while that they are weak and defenseless. On May 18, 1961, John Siegenthaler, the representative of the President, was beaten unconscious in Montgomery, Alabama. Mr. Siegenthaler, an aide to the Attorney General, had seen a Negro girl pursued by a mob. He stopped his car and went to her rescue. After the beating he was left to lie on the sidewalk for half an hour.[10] No one was tried, nor was anyone arrested for this assault on an official of the United States Government. However, out of that incident grew a powerful injunction against the police force of Montgomery, enjoining them from failing to provide police protection to passengers in interstate commerce. But think of those who are not officials of the Government. As, for instance, the fifty-seven Negroes in the Itta Bena case in Mississippi. They had walked downtown to see the Sheriff at 10:30 in the evening and were arrested. To be fair, the police testified that they had told the group to disperse, that some members of the group did have bricks and bottles and bricks and bottles did come from the group. The point I want to make is that forty-five defendants over the age of 14 were tried and sentenced to six months to a year on the county farm in one afternoon in hearings that lasted a total of one hour and ten minutes.[11]

Probably the segregationists of the deep South in the 1950s and 1960s have been the biggest regional crybabies of all time. Can these men really be the descendants of the soldiers who followed Pickett? Louisiana for instance closed down the largest Negro college in the country, Southern University at Baton Rouge, following the students' street demonstrations. When

[10] Fuller, *op. cit.,* pp. 135-36.
[11] *United States v. Leflore County,* Civil Action, No. GC 6330, U.S. District Court for the Northern District of Mississippi.

the University reopened, it required all students to re-register and excluded many. The State Board of Education adopted a policy of not permitting students to return to the campus if they had taken part in the demonstrations. Alabama removed the president of the State College for Negroes, again after students took part in street demonstrations.

In November of 1962, Dr. H. Councill Trenholm, president of Alabama State College for thirty-five years, was given an unrequested year's leave of absence. A few months before, Dr. J. F. Drake, president of Alabama Agriculture and Mechanical College for over thirty years, was forced to retire. The then governor of Alabama, John Patterson, said of the forced retirement of Dr. Drake that it was urgent to get a college president who would require discipline and make students behave themselves.

Albany State College in Georgia suspended forty students indefinitely for taking part in anti-segregation prayer meetings, charging them with conduct detrimental to the college. These are but samplings of the punishment the segregationists inflict upon Negroes daily. The Negro in the South stood alone against the segregationist juggernaut. Of course he needed help from the Federal Government and from "outside" clergymen, laymen, and students. There is something bizarre in Alabama's accusation that a Department of Justice car drove Martin Luther King to a meeting, when the White Citizens Council is a legal arm of Alabama financially supported by taxes on all the state's citizens.

Such accusations are part of the segregationist's technique in isolating the Negro and those who support him. Fear settles in some Southern areas like a miasma. Say a word for integration in public or private and you are tarred with the same old brush "renegade," "nigger-lover," "scalawag." Say perhaps things might have been done differently, and pretty soon the telephones are alive with a rumor which has proved most effective throughout Alabama, Mississippi, and Louisiana: "There were two big black Cadillacs with New York license plates in front of his house all night." Because it is not particularly inflammatory, this gambit has had great success. I have even heard it as far north as North Carolina. It is always two Cadillacs, and of course they are both *big* and *black*—and supposedly filled with outside agitators, "Communists from New York." September 25, 1962, was one of the days of bitter trial at the University of Mississippi. Attorney General Robert Kennedy spoke with Mississippi's Governor Ross Barnett four or five times that day. James Meredith, the first Negro student to be admitted to the University, was on his way. The Attorney General wanted to make sure the local authorities could control the situation. During one of the conversations, Governor Barnett complained that Meredith and his party were coming to register *in two big, black Cadillacs*.

Southern strategy in the Civil War centered on making the war so hard the North would quit. Tactically, the Confederate generals hoped that by capturing Washington, D.C., they would get French and English recognition. But the Confederacy made an error in judgment, for the North was determined to win the war.

With all legal tactics exhausted Senator James Eastland of Mississippi was forthright in revealing the new strategy: "You'll remember the Confederate Army made a 'token capture' at Gettysburg. *Some* of Pickett's men reached the top of the ridge. But who won the battle? Since the Decision in 1954, we've had token integration in a few places, but the *South* has not been breached." [12]

Thus the segregationists' trump card! The Supreme Court decision which declared racial segregation unconstitutional is not the law of the land, but only the law of the case. In

[12] Cook, *op. cit.*, p. 5.

effect, the segregationists were saying to the Federal Government, "You will have to win state by state, county by county, public school by public school, voting registrar by voting registrar, and Negro by Negro," a challenge which the late President John F. Kennedy accepted.

CHAPTER SIX

"GET THE ROAD MAPS—AND GO"

Whooping rebel yells, the twenty delegates from Mississippi gave their votes for the Vice-Presidential nomination to John Fitzgerald Kennedy, the junior Senator from the Commonwealth of Massachusetts. It was Friday, August 17, 1956, and the Democratic National Convention was drawing to an exciting close. Its nominee for President, Adlai E. Stevenson, had urged the delegates to select by open balloting his running mate. The choice narrowed between two candidates —Senators Kennedy and Estes Kefauver.

The Southerners made Kennedy their favorite. Throughout the balloting, the South Carolina delegation kept up a steady, rhythmic chant, "We want Kennedy! We want Kennedy!" Senator Sam J. Ervin of North Carolina reported that his delegation, led by Governor Luther H. Hodges, cast seventeen and one-half votes for Kennedy. The delegates from Alabama, Georgia, Texas, and Virginia waved Confederate flags and cheered at this news. North Carolina, the most "regular" Democratic state in the Union, had given this young Massachusetts politician two thirds of its votes and this meant he might conceivably win the number two spot on the ticket.

The Southerners were cheering wildly for a graduate of Harvard University, a Roman Catholic, and an intellectual; they were cheering a New Englander who just the month before, in the pages of the *Atlantic Monthly*, had deplored the flight of the textile industry from Massachusetts to the South. And the Southerners could not have been unaware of the civil rights speech the young Senator had delivered on February 7, 1956, before the New York Democratic Club in which he said, "The Democratic party must not weasel on the issue. . . . President Truman was returned to the White House in 1948 despite a firm stand on civil rights that led even to a third party effort in the South. . . . We might alienate Southern support but the Supreme Court decision is the law of the land." [1]

The Southern delegates wanted Senator Kennedy as Vice-President not because he was for the racial *status quo*, but because his opponent for the nomination was the late Senator Estes Kefauver from Tennessee, a Southerner who, because of his own outspoken views on civil rights for the Negroes, was therefore a renegade. Of Kefauver, Senator Sam J. Ervin of North Carolina remarked, "I have never known him to stand with Southern Senators on any problem concerning the South." [2]

But the Northern and Midwestern states carried the day for Mr. Kefauver. Senator John F. Kennedy conceded. Perhaps the wild enthusiasm of the Southern delegates as he made his way to the platform signaled the rise of the Kennedy star. Certainly it signaled one of the more erratic patterns in racial politics and the attempt of the Southerners to maintain legally enforced segregation.

The test came during the Senate debate on the Civil Rights Act of 1957. Senator Kennedy took some hard knocks from

[1] The New York *Times*, February 8, 1956, p. 1.
[2] Charlotte *Observer*, Aug. 18, 1956, p. 1.

friends and enemies of civil rights. James M. Burns, in *John Kennedy, a Political Profile*, says:

> Unluckily for Kennedy, the very first vote on the bill threatened to throw him into a political embrace with Senator James Eastland, of Mississippi, the hated symbol of Southern racism. Under the regular procedure, the civil-rights bill passed by the House would go to the Senate Judiciary Committee, chaired by Eastland, before coming to the Senate floor. Knowing of the Mississippian's dexterity in bottling up such measures, liberals sought to invoke a little-used Senate rule that would let the bill bypass the committee.
>
> Kennedy would have none of it. The temporary advantage to be gained by bypassing Eastland's committee, he felt, was not worth a dangerous precedent that might come back to haunt liberals. He argued, too, that a discharge petition could be used to pry the bill out of Eastland's pocket, and he promised to vote for such a petition if one was needed. Morse strongly supported this view, but most liberal Democrats, including Humphrey and Symington, favored the bypass, which barely carried the Senate.
>
> "The most disgusting news I have read in a long time," a Long Island Negro wrote Kennedy on hearing of his position. . . .
>
> When it came to the substance of the bill, however, Kennedy was all militancy. The acid test was section 3, which authorized the attorney general to use injunctive power to enforce school desegregation and other civil rights, hence allowing greater use of civil sanctions instead of cumbersome criminal prosecution. The implications of section 3 were enormous; it might become the device by which a liberal President could push school integration, as well as voting rights, throughout the South. Well aware of these possibilities, the Southerners were seething, and the White

House itself had misgivings. One might expect, then, that the "moderate" Kennedy would shy from it. But no—Kennedy not only backed section 3 but took the floor to make his views clear.[3]

A year later Senator Kennedy began to lose his Southern support. He addressed a meeting in Jackson, Mississippi, in the fall of 1957, and told Southerners, "I accept the Supreme Court decision as the supreme law of the land . . . we must all agree on the necessity to uphold law and order in every part of the land." Doris Fleeson wrote in the St. Petersburg *Times*, October 24, 1957: "Sen. John F. Kennedy's romance with the South, one of the most provocative features of the 1956 Democratic convention, is the latest victim of Little Rock. . . . Since his return to Washington [from Mississippi] his mail, a part of it written more in sorrow than in anger, has indicated that he cannot expect from the South in 1960 the same support, which in coalition with big state delegations, almost put him over for the vice presidential nomination last year. . . ."

On June 23, 1960, the romance was shattered once and for all. Mr. Kennedy addressed the Liberal party of New York and said that he hoped to win the Democratic nomination for President without a single Southern vote in the convention. He also told his audience he regarded the civil rights issue as a moral question.

It is possible that some of the twenty Mississippi delegates who urged Kennedy's nomination in 1956 were politically active in Mississippi's most recent gubernatorial primary and election. The first Democratic primary on August 6, 1963, eliminated Charles Sullivan, a States rights advocate and forced J. P. Coleman, a former governor, and Paul Johnson,

[3] James M. Burns, *John Kennedy, a Political Profile* (New York, Harcourt Brace & Co., 1960), p. 201.

the lieutenant governor under Governor Ross Barnett, into a run-off primary. Paul Johnson campaigned on those several minutes he spent blocking United States Marshals from the University of Mississippi campus to register the Negro student James Meredith. Candidate Johnson also contended that Coleman had supported Kennedy in 1960 and intimated that since the President had offered Coleman a federal post his opponent was a "New Frontiersman" and not a true Southerner at all. One of Johnson's campaign posters showed the late Senator Theodore Bilbo's bed still in the governor's mansion at Jackson. Underneath was the caption "Kennedy slept here when Coleman was Governor. Make sure he doesn't sleep here again."

Coleman, on the other hand, swore he was a segregationist and that he held no brief for John F. Kennedy. But he didn't want federal troops in the state, he didn't want violence in the streets, and he didn't want new industry backing off from Mississippi. As the campaign neared its climax, it became in effect a referendum for or against the President of the United States.

The Saturday before the balloting, disfranchised Negroes held mock elections in their community centers and churches. Out of 27,721 mock ballots, 26,572 were for Coleman and 949 for Johnson. In the real run-off, however, Johnson carried the state two to one.

In the November election, Johnson faced Rubel Phillips, a Republican. Phillips campaigned by charging that Barnett and Johnson were undercover integrationists, that they had allowed Meredith to enroll in the University after conspiring with John F. Kennedy for a face-saving show of resistance.

To "prove" his point, Republican Phillips revealed portions of the telephone conversations Governor Ross Barnett and Lieutenant Governor Paul Johnson had held in Jackson, Mississippi, with Attorney General Robert F. Kennedy in

Washington. It was clear from the printed text that the conversations had been carefully edited. Omitted were a few highly important exchanges: On September 25, 1962, Governor Ross Barnett, on the campus of the University of Mississippi, opened his conversation with enthusiasm. Do you hear them cheering? he wanted to know. They are "cheering our side and booing Meredith."

Did Meredith get registered? asked Mr. Kennedy.

The Governor said No, that he and his officials would not let Meredith register because they were obeying the laws of Mississippi.

Mr. Kennedy asked, "Are you also citizens of the United States?" The final word from the Attorney General was that "the Federal Government will see to it that orders which are presently outstanding are maintained and enforced, whatever action that ultimately may require."

On the day of crisis and riot on the campus of the University, Governor Ross Barnett suddenly switched one of the conversations to foreign affairs and the politics of the European Common Market. He wanted the President to be informed how much he, Barnett, appreciated what the Kennedy administration was trying to do for the chicken farmers of Mississippi.

The Republican candidate Rubel Phillips also said a vote for him was an endorsement of Republican Senator Barry Goldwater's bid for the Presidency, who, said Phillips, "will appoint an Attorney General whose attitude will be more understanding to our problems." [4]

Phillips came as close to being governor as had Coleman, which is quite close for a Republican in Mississippi.

Southern candidates for state offices, Democratic and Republican, did not charge inept foreign policy formulations, they did not accuse the President of letting the economy

[4] *Newsweek,* October 14, 1963, p. 36.

stagnate, nor did they argue about "creeping socialism." They simply said that the Kennedys wanted to change the social order by ending racial segregation. There were Southern Republicans, as well as Southern Democrats, who thought this was a grievance heavy enough to win them election.

The hatred for John F. Kennedy among Southern politicians was not universal, but it was nevertheless intense and widespread and confined almost wholly to the race problem. It was at a desperate intensity just before he was assassinated.

Early in December, 1963, Samuel Lubell, political analyst, wrote from the deep South:

> Only nine days before President Kennedy's death I sampled a workers' precinct in Birmingham, Alabama, which in 1960 had given him a clear majority. In a day's ringing of doorbells I found just one Kennedy supporter left.
>
> All the other voters interviewed vowed they would go Republican or for an independent party in 1964—"Anyone as long as it isn't Kennedy." The bitter anger that saturated the precinct burst forth in comments such as, "He's cramming the nigger down our throats" or "If he's re-elected it will be the end of America."
>
> A construction manager from Baton Rouge, Louisiana, confessed, "I'd be satisfied to let them pass anything if they indicated they wouldn't be tough in enforcing it."
>
> Others said hopefully, "If Bobby Kennedy was out of there that would do it." [5]

And on November 17, the South's only "New Frontier" governor, Terry Sanford of North Carolina, sadly admitted that if the election were held at that moment Mr. Kennedy would probably lose the state. And North Carolina, remember, had gone twice for Adlai Stevenson.

[5] Charlotte *Observer*, Dec. 10, 1963, p. 3B.

Nor was the hatred simple political hatred. Indeed, the hatred was pervasive. Schoolteachers in Mississippi, Alabama, Louisiana, and Georgia must have been of one mind, judging from the tone of letters sent to the White House and to the Attorney General's office. Whole classrooms of children sent off letters in identical phraseology: "We had such a good relationship with the Negroes. They were so happy until you forced integration. Now there is only suspicion, hate, and fear. . . ."

The Attorney General answered the letters directed to him:

> . . . what the Federal Government has done in your state is to see that the orders of the Federal Courts are followed. Is this what upsets you? Do you think everybody in the United States should make his or her own determination as to what laws they are going to abide by, what Court decisions they are going to follow? . . . Are you aware that only about five per cent of the Negroes in your state are registered and can vote for Governor or even in national elections? . . . Do you and your fellow teenagers feel that this is the way you want your state run? . . .

It is instructive that in all the telephone conversations the President, the Attorney General, and Assistant Attorney General Burke Marshall made during the racial crises at the state universities, the governors and officials of Mississippi and Alabama raised the same arguments as the children.

President Kennedy was aware of the swelling resentment throughout the South. He and his aides were concerned lest it spread to the North, especially to the "Oh, no! Not next door!" moderates in suburbia. Undoubtedly he knew that this resentment endangered his chances for re-election. He admitted as much to A. Philip Randolph: "I know this whole thing could cost me the election but I have no intention of turning back now or ever."

The serious criticism came not from political enemies or segregationists whom the New Frontier had written off, but from Democratic liberals and Negroes who complained that President Kennedy had wasted two years before he ended housing segregation in government-financed units; and that when the President did end it by his celebrated promise of "a stroke of the pen" it was not half as strong as they hoped it would be. Northern liberals taunted Robert Kennedy with the fact that he let federal officials in Albany, Georgia, put Negroes on trial for conspiracy while Southern whites went about blowing up Negro homes with impunity. The novelist James Baldwin was particularly angry after meeting with the Attorney General, charging that Robert Kennedy was "insensible of and unresponsive" to the Negro's torment.

But the Administration's strategy was established before Mr. Baldwin divested himself of his bitterness. Both the President and the Attorney General posed one question to each individual or group of citizens, white or Negro, who came to them on behalf of civil rights: "What will you do to help us?"

Robert Kennedy put the question to James Baldwin and his accompanying Negro intellectuals just as he had put it a week before to forty Protestant, Catholic, and Jewish clergymen. I was at the Attorney General's home after he had appeared before the House Judiciary Committee to plead that the Kennedy Civil Rights proposals of 1963 be maintained to passable proportions. We discussed this criticism from Democratic liberals, from Clarence Mitchell, Washington director of the NAACP, from James Baldwin and his group, and Robert Kennedy said, "The President, Burke Marshall [Assistant Attorney General], and I know the risks and we are willing to shoulder them. These good people who criticize us have been accustomed to riding a burning issue; all they want is an issue, even at the expense of passable legislation that will improve matters."

But the people not fooled by the liberal and Negro critics of the President were those who had devoted their adult lives to keeping the Negro "in his place"—the Southern segregationists. They were not put off by the prospects of a slow passage of a watered-down Kennedy Civil Rights Bill. The segregationist politicians knew what was going on and it alarmed them. The Kennedy Administration alarmed them to a greater degree than the Roosevelt, Truman, or Eisenhower administrations ever had. President John F. Kennedy, the Attorney General and his civil rights staff were slowly but surely cutting the heart out of the racial *status quo* of the South. And they were doing it with the "watered-down" Civil Rights Act of 1957 and the equally compromised Civil Rights Act of 1960.

President Kennedy had accepted the challenge of the segregationists to fight the battle, county by county, school by school, and Negro by Negro. He was using laws which were there all the time—for over two and a half years of President Eisenhower's second term—but they were laws which had not been made into effective legal weapons.

When Robert F. Kennedy was confirmed as Attorney General, the chairman of the Senate Judiciary Committee, Senator James Eastland of Mississippi, congratulated him and with a wink said, "Your predecessor never brought a civil rights case in Mississippi." But the next day Robert Kennedy and the Civil Rights Division of the Department of Justice received their standing orders from the President: *"Get the road maps —and go."*

What generated Mr. Kennedy's enthusiasm was the Civil Rights Act of 1957, the first positive congressional measure passed in civil rights since 1875. This Act established a Commission on Civil Rights. It was an especially important act in beginning to redress voting inequities. It authorized the federal government to bring civil suits in its own name to obtain injunctive relief when any person was denied the ballot or when his right to vote was threatened. Until this Act was passed, injunctive relief was available only to individuals, many of whom were unable to bear the expense of long and complicated litigation. The Act requires the United States Government to provide the attorneys, make the decisions, pay the expenses of all lawsuits of cases involving the violation of voting rights of Negroes. The 1957 Act, in addition, gives federal district courts jurisdiction of such lawsuits, without requiring that all state remedies first be exhausted.

Thus for the first time the Department of Justice itself could sue in cases involving the denial of voting rights, and the suit could go before the federal district courts months sooner than had formerly been possible.[6]

The Civil Rights Act of 1960 provided the authority for federal judges to appoint voting referees to hear the application of persons claiming they had been denied the right to register and vote by state election officials. In addition to the voting referees section, other provisions of the bill:

1. Made it a Federal offense to use force or threats to obstruct any court order, the penalty for such violations being a fine of not more than $1,000 or imprisonment for one year or both;

2. Authorized the FBI to search for persons who flee across state lines to escape prosecution for hate bombing of any building or vehicle;

3. Required states to preserve voting records for 22 months and open them for inspection by the Attorney General;

[6] "Civil Rights and the South," *North Carolina Law Review*, Vol. 42, no. 1, Fall 1963, pp. 3-16.

4. Authorized the Armed Services to provide for the education of children of servicemen when local schools near a military post closed.[7]

Both acts had survived the ordeal of Senate debate and filibuster. The then Democratic Majority Leader, Senator Lyndon B. Johnson, had helped put through the Act of 1957; but the Civil Rights Act of 1960 was almost completely his own, for he had initially proposed it on January 20, 1959.

Liberals and the Negro leaders condemned each bill as too mild. The segregationist Senators were successful in their assault on Part III of the proposed law. Senator Sam J. Ervin of North Carolina spoke on July 8, 1957:

> I rise in opposition to the motion of the able and distinguished Majority Leader [to consider the Civil Rights Bill]. I do this because I know that the greatest blessing which could befall the United States at this particular time would be for further action on the Civil Rights Bill to be postponed until Congress reconvenes in January. . . .
>
> It is said, for example, that the bill is simply designed to secure voting rights for Negroes in Southern states. I am going to say this bluntly, and I will say it plainly, so that he who runs may read and not err in so doing: There is not a scintilla of truth in the oft-repeated assertion that the bill is simply designed to secure voting rights for Negroes in Southern states.
>
> The Attorney General under Part III of the proposed law, would be empowered to bring literally hundreds upon hundreds of different types of cases, in addition to cases to secure voting rights and to compel the integration of public schools.
>
> Mr. President, in every one of these cases the President would have the authority, under section 1993, of Title 42,

[7] *Congressional Digest*, Vol. 39, nos. 6-7, June-July, 1960, p. 162.

to call out the Army, the Navy or the militia to enforce the decrees entered in any one of these hundreds upon hundreds of cases.[8]

Senator Harry Byrd of Virginia declared:

I strongly suspect that the modern Thaddeus Stevens, now cloaked in the robes of the Chief Justice of the United States Supreme Court, has a thorough and complete knowledge of what could and would be done under the bill. And likewise I suspect that the NAACP, one of the principal beneficiaries of his official acts, has at least a working familiarity with the provisions of the bill. I suspect also that the ADA [Americans for Democratic Action—the "New Deal" wing of the Democratic party], the NAACP's gold dust twin, has at least guilty knowledge of what the bill proposes. . . . This whole iniquitous bill is a refutation of our entire American jurisprudence.[9]

Speaking on the Civil Rights Act of 1960, Senator Strom Thurmond of South Carolina said:

This proposal is extreme. It is punitive. It is flagrantly abusive. It is palpably and viciously anti-Southern. It would, in effect, treat the South as a conquered province to be ruled over, insofar as race relations are concerned, by a czar in the person of the Attorney General of the United States. . . .
    The uninformed so-called liberals refer to what they call the deteriorating race relations situation in the South and call for Federal law and Federal action to remedy the situation.
    Now, anyone who has been familiar with the South knows

[8] *U. S. News & World Report,* July 26, 1957, p. 97.
[9] *Vital Speeches of the Day,* Vol. XXIII, no. 20; Aug. 1, 1957, pp. 619-22.

that, left alone the racial situation actually was very harmonious, very peaceful. Prior to 1954, certainly, probably nowhere else in the world, where two such different races inhabit the same territory in large numbers, have race relations been so peaceful and harmonious. What deterioration has occurred since then has been, certainly, not an indication of any need of Federal action, but rather, the result of Federal action and Federal interference in the field of race relations—especially the Supreme Court's school desegregation decisions of 1954.

But even though the past four years have seen some grave developments in the South, it should be emphasized that there is no such state of conflict between the white Southerner and the Negro as the liberals seem to imagine. . . . Where in the South can one find what can properly be called a racial dispute? . . .[10]

When Robert F. Kennedy took over the Attorney General's office, for the first time in the sixty-year history of Jim Crow, the "happy" Negro of the South was going to get the chance to express his own views, as the lawyers and investigators of the Civil Rights Division of the Department of Justice began to study the road maps of the segregated voting districts of the deep South.

As a matter of courtesy, Deputy Attorney General Byron White called Senator James Eastland to tell him the Department of Justice was prepared to file several cases in the state of Mississippi on the investigations of voting records which had been initiated by his predecessor, Mr. Tyler.

"What's that for?" asked Senator Eastland.

"To enforce the law," replied Mr. White.

When Mr. White was appointed to the United States Supreme Court, he was succeeded by Nicholas De Belleville

[10] *The Congressional Digest*, Vol. 39, no. 1; January, 1960, pp. 11-17.

Katzenbach, former University of Chicago law professor, later in command at Oxford, Mississippi, amid tear gas and bayonets. "I've had enough war experience so that whatever fear I had was pretty well repressed," he says of the occasion. "The thing that went through my mind was the sense of failure—the great sense of failure. It was not particularly a sense of personal failure, but what we wanted to accomplish hadn't been accomplished." [11]

The goal the New Frontier had sought to accomplish, of course, was to show the world that in America's South law could triumph over custom, without violence.

It was Harris Wofford, the man who advised candidate John F. Kennedy to intervene on behalf of the imprisoned Martin Luther King, who recommended lawyer Burke Marshall as the chief of the Civil Rights Division of the Department of Justice. Helen Fuller describes the hesitancy of the Southern Senators about Marshall's appointment:

> The Senate Judiciary Committee met to confirm Marshall's appointment March 2, 1961. Senator Johnston of South Carolina questioned him closely about any civil rights organizations he might have belonged to. (Marshall had nothing more "suspicious" on his record than being a contributing member to the American Civil Liberties Union.)
>
> It was Eastland who got to the heart of the matter. He asked Marshall what his policy was going to be, bluntly, "Are you going to solicit complaints?"
>
> Marshall straightforwardly answered that "if statistics on registration and voting in particular areas showed a heavy imbalance against race, I think we would consider that sufficient enough to start an investigation."
>
> To tell the Chairman of the powerful Senate Judiciary Committee that the United States Department of Justice

[11] Chicago *American,* March 10, 1963, p. 12.

just might head for his state of Mississippi to see that
Negroes were permitted to vote may not have been a shot
heard around the world, but it sounded loud in that committee room that morning.

To teach Marshall his manners, Southern Senators delayed the confirmation for two weeks and seemed prepared
to filibuster longer when the Attorney General walked, un-
announced, into the third committee session on Marshall's
fitness and silently took a seat. A few embarrassed moments
later Marshall was approved.[12]

In the two and a half years the Civil Rights Act of 1957
was on the books, the Eisenhower Administration initiated
ten cases, six against registrars and four against private individuals. Of the voting cases, one had been settled, two had
been won, and one had been tried but undecided. Two of the
ten cases were filed on January 19, 1961, the last day of the
Eisenhower Administration. "It was apparent that little had
been done on the voting cases until Mr. Tyler came to head
the Civil Rights Division," said John Doar, Republican lawyer from Wisconsin. Mr. Doar, who by now knows every back
road in Mississippi, Alabama, Louisiana, and Georgia, told
me that it was Harold Tyler who said, "Let's litigate voting
cases in the South." Not only did Judge Tyler move the Eisenhower Administration in the voting cases, but I may add, he is
the one who brought John Doar to the Civil Rights Division.
Significantly, the Republican Harold Tyler was appointed a
Federal District Judge by the Democratic President John F.
Kennedy.

At the close of President Eisenhower's second term, there
were five lawyers working on the voting cases, which was the
basis for the establishment of the Civil Rights Division. After
the Kennedy inauguration and the arrival of Burke Marshall

12 Fuller, *op. cit.*, p. 119.

in March, 1961, the Attorney General hired five additional lawyers. In addition to the steady increase in staff, which is now up to twenty-four lawyers, Marshall initiated a summer program of eighteen college students who work the microfilm machines scanning voting records and looking for cheating. Among the American students are two Rhodes Scholars, Winston Churchill and John Kirby. Kirby was one of the first and now has worked in the Attorney General's office for three years, Churchill for two.

The late President Kennedy interpreted the Civil Rights Acts of 1957 and 1960 to mean that his Attorney General had the *responsibility*—not just the authority—to investigate and to bring legal action where citizens are denied the right to register and vote on account of race. When Robert Kennedy took office, Mr. Tyler's six cases had been filed. One of these had been settled and two others were almost settled. Attorney General Robert Kennedy himself successfully completed the other three. By December, 1961, Robert Kennedy could say in his civil rights report to the President that fourteen new cases had been processed that year, and that investigations were being made in sixty-one Southern counties.

Later, the Justice Department decided to take on an entire state, and the case of the *United States v. Mississippi* came into court. It is hard to imagine the detailed investigations such a case involves. Thousands of voting cases in scores of counties were looked into; records, going back for years, had to be tracked down and the Negro grievances recorded.

The Jim Crow record of voting denials was clear. Eleven of the Southern states were at the bottom of the list in voting registration. Here is a table [13] giving the percentage of the number of voters out of the total population and the rank that state occupied in the national presidential elections of 1956 and 1960.

[13] *The Texas Observer*, July 9, 1963.

States	per cent voting	Rank 1960	Rank 1956
North Carolina	53.53	38	38
Tennessee	50.26	40	40
Florida	50.00	41	39
Louisiana	44.78	43	42
Texas	41.77	44	43
Arkansas	41.13	45	41
Virginia	33.33	46	44
Georgia	32.85	47	45
Alabama	31.07	48	46
South Carolina	30.56	49	47
Mississippi	25.44	50	48

Please note that the Southern states are at the bottom. The two new states, Hawaii and Alaska, are among those states recording less than 55 per cent of their total voters: Hawaii with 48.10 and Alaska with 49.40. But compare Mississippi's 25.44 per cent of its potential voters going to the polls with leader Idaho's 80.64 per cent, or New York's, in twenty-sixth place, with 67 per cent.

President Kennedy and his Attorney General proceeded on the case involving complaints by Negroes of economic coercion brought to bear when they attempted to vote in Haywood County, Tennessee. The complaint, commenced during the Eisenhower Administration on September 13, 1960, charged that eighty defendants—merchants, landowners, bank and local officials, all named—intimidated, threatened, and coerced these Negro citizens to keep them from voting in federal elections. The alleged methods of intimidation included evictions of sharecroppers and tenant farmers, firings of employees, denials for loans by the banks, denial of credit by the merchants, and direct threats. In May, 1962, a federal court permanently enjoined the defendants from interfering with voting by Negroes.[14]

One of the two cases filed on the last day of the Eisenhower Administration was on behalf of a Louisiana Negro cotton farmer who allegedly could not get his cotton ginned, could not sell his soybean crop, and could not buy butane gas to run his farm machinery, because he had testified at a Civil Rights hearing.[15]

When the Negroes of the South saw that Mr. Kennedy and the Attorney General were behind their fight for equity and equality, they released a flood of complaints. Thousands upon thousands of letters flowed to the White House and the Department of Justice. For the first time in sixty years disfranchised Negroes of the South were signing their names to formal complaints and affidavits. However, the Attorney General and Burke Marshall do not wait for complaints. They have completed a thorough study of the voting record of every county in the South, and where statistics indicate that few Negroes are registered, their people go into the field to investigate the circumstances.

Formal complaints by Negroes have been sent also to Judge Daniel Holcombe Thomas of the Southern District of Alabama. The Judge had issued an injunction against the registrars. These Negro letter-writers were trying to get registered by the court under the referee provisions of the 1960 Act. They were asking the Judge to test their qualifications:

> My name is Evelyn Louise Turner. I am a housewife. I have a high school education. I have lived in Perry County, Alabama, all my life. I am twenty-six years old.
>
> I went to the Court House to register on December 17,

14 *United States v. Beaty,* 7 Race Rel. L. Rep. 484 (W.D. Tenn. May 2, 1962). See also *United States v. Beaty,* 288 F. 2d 653 (6th Cir. 1961).
15 *United States v. Deal,* 6 Race Rel. L. Rep. 474 (W.D. La. Feb. 3, 1961).

1960, at 10 A.M. They told me to wait and at 12:10 they told me the Board of Registrars wasn't registering. I went again . . . I am asking the Court to register me.

I was able to get a blank from the registrars and I filled it out to take the test to vote. Only seven were allowed to take the test out of fifty or sixty Negroes. We were failed on the test but they never told us why. Jessie Wayman Melton; Spratt, Alabama.

I, Robert Louis Hogue, am seventy-one years old. I have been to register three times, the first Monday in November, the first Monday in December, and the third Monday in December, 1962. Each time I went there at 10 o'clock and waited all day and each time they said the committee wasn't taking any more applications. I am a Negro. I finished the seventh grade. I am a farmer. I am asking the court to register me. Robert Louis Hogue; Marion, Alabama.

I went to the office to register three times in Perry County, Alabama. I am a farmer. I farm 100 acres of land owned by myself. I filled out a blank to register on November 19, 1962. I did not hear and went again on December 3, 1962. I waited more than a half day of my time. The committee said they would let me know. I never heard. Albert Stovall; Marion, Alabama.

On September 27, 1960, I went to New Orleans. I appeared before the Civil Rights Commission and testified as to my difficulties for voting. The next day, September 28, in the evening Mr. John Gilbert who is sheriff in East Carroll Parish came to my house and asked me to come out. I asked him to come in. He came up on the porch and told me that the ginners told him to tell me don't bring no more cotton to their gins. I asked him why, and he said, "Civil

Rights." Francis Joseph Atlas, East Carroll Parish, Louisiana.

In Louisiana, Mrs. Winnice J. Clement was accused of favoring Negro voters. Governor Robert Kennon ordered his Security Director, David Raymond, to investigate. The investigation showed that only two Negroes had tried to register since the charge was made. But she had turned down two dozen white men and women registrants. "I want to be fair to the Negroes, so I turned down the whites. They want the Negroes to interpret the Constitution, so I also asked the whites to interpret the Constitution." [16]

The rejections in Bienville Parish of Louisiana were particularly interesting. If a Negro filled out an application in fine handwriting, answering every question, he was failed on his answer to the question, "My color is . . ." The Attorney General's office has photostats of hundreds of rejected applications on which the answer was "dark," "brown," "colored," and "Negro," all of which were wrong. The correct answer was "black." If indeed a Negro wrote "black," the registrar turned him down for not knowing the name of the sheriff of an adjoining county.

In preparing the big case, *United States v. Mississippi,* Robert Kennedy established that Negroes were not voting in the state. This was not an easy task, since the State of Mississippi has made every effort to conceal the voting statistics. The government investigations showed plainly, however, that the percentage of Negroes registered to vote had declined steadily for the last seventy years. Nor could Mississippi say that fewer Negroes voted because fewer were literate, since the certifiable rate of illiteracy among Negroes has been decreasing steadily. In 1899 it was 53 per cent, by 1952 it was less than 9 per cent.

[16] *U. S. v. Louisiana,* Civil Action No. 2548, U. S. District Court, Eastern District of Louisiana, p. F-6.

Next, the Department of Justice secured the evidence with which it intends to prove that state officials had deliberately excluded Negroes from voting. The government's Mississippi brief cites such statements as those made by Senator Bilbo, during the 1946 campaign:

> Mississippi is white. We got the right to keep it that way and I care not what Tom Clark and Hugo Black say . . . I'm calling on every red-blooded American who believes in the superiority and integrity of the white race to get out and see that no nigger votes. Use all the power, the legal power, lawful power, and persuasion.

The Department of Justice presented records of the 1952 State Legislature which included a resolution requiring all voters to endorse the principles of the Democratic State Executive Committee including opposition to Negro employment legislation, opposition to anti-poll tax legislation, opposition to federal anti-lynching laws, advocacy of segregation of the races, and opposition to the repeal or modification of the segregation laws of the State. Any voter refusing to subscribe to these principles was turned away.

Next, scores of voting complaints were presented. Examples of the hundreds of cases include a Negro who was not permitted to vote until he got a poll tax exemption certificate. When he obtained one, an election official made him take an oath as to whether he believed in segregation and whether he was a member of the NAACP. He was told that his beliefs were against those of the Democratic party and therefore his vote was challenged and would not count. His white planter boss told him that any Negro on his place who tried to vote would be laid off. A white merchant told him that the "white people were going to run Tunica County and he could do without nigger business." The Negro never again tried to vote.

In Yalobusha County, a Negro testified that the Judge at

the polling place took his ballot away after he had marked it but before he could put it in the ballot box. He found a note on his business door which read, "You is gettin' to smart trin' to vote. Mr. Harris. Have youre name took off them Bookes— Real soon like—an straiten yore friens."

Many Mississippi Negroes tried pathetically to "bone up" for the literacy tests by hard study. One Negro youth testified that in June, 1962, he went with four other Negroes and tried to register: "He asked me who was the President of the United States and who was the Vice-President of the United States, who was the Secretary of State, who was the Secretary of Labor, and how was the President of the United States elected, and how was the Governor of Mississippi elected, and he wanted to know what was on the ballot, and after a little he says, 'Lewis, you go and brush up on your civics and come back' . . ." The witness was asked how many of the questions he had been able to answer.

"All of them, but one, to be sure."

"Which one was that?"

"He asked me what was on the ballot." [17]

Keeping Negroes from registering is much less sophisticated elsewhere. Many Negroes testified that they were simply not permitted to vote. Others were threatened directly or indirectly with bodily or economic harm.

One case presented in detail had to do with Carl Turnbow, a Negro in Holmes County, Mississippi, who tried to register after a registration drive conducted by the Student Nonviolent Co-ordinating Committee. Turnbow did not succeed in registering, but even so, a few nights after his futile attempt, he and his wife awakened to find their house on fire. It had been bombed. White men were still in the yard, and when Turnbow appeared they shot at him. He got down his gun and returned fire while his wife put out the flames.

[17] *U. S. v. Greene,* George County, Mississippi, 1962, pp. 25-29.

The Turnbows' house was uninsured. They lost all their furniture. Yet after the local sheriff had investigated, they, along with the young Negroes who had conducted the voter registration drive, were charged with bombing their own house.[18]

Lawyers and investigators under Burke Marshall documented over two thousand complaints, complete with sworn testimony and affidavits. One of these, from Ezell Singleton, Branton, Mississippi, went:

> I don't know exactly the date, but it was in June that I went up to the circuit clerk's office at Brandon, and I told her I wanted to register, and she told me to go upstairs and turn short to the left, and there was a man up there to take care of all the veterans. So I went up there, and I asked the gentleman in the office there, I told him I wanted to register, and he told me to sit down, and he talked with me awhile and then he asked me who sent me up there, and I told him I came on my own hook, and he got up from behind his desk, and started toward me, and I stood up, and he stopped, and he told me if I didn't want to get into serious trouble for me to get out of his office. So I did.

By 1963 the Civil Rights Division of the Attorney General's office had twenty-four full-time lawyers. Across the 1962 annual report of the Attorney General, President John Fitzgerald Kennedy wrote in ink: "Keep pushing the cases."

And Mr. Kennedy lived to see the wall beginning to crumble, even in the deep South. Here is an example: A voucher case, *United States v. Alabama*, Bullock County. The case was filed on January 19, 1961 and tried on March 28, 1961. The method used to disfranchise the Negroes was ingenious and effective. In order to be registered a prospective voter needed

[18] *United States v. Holmes County*, Civil Action No. 3417, U. S. District Court, Southern District of Mississippi.

to have someone vouch for him. The "voucher," however, had to be a registered voter, hence a white man, who could only "vouch" once.

On March 30, the day the trial ended, four Negroes were registered. Three of the Negroes had refused to "vouch" for others for fear of economic reprisal.

The court found "a pattern of racial discrimination" and granted an injunction against the voucher system on September 13, 1961. Let us examine the result as reported to the late Mr. Kennedy in mid-November, 1963:

REGISTRATION STATISTICS

	Persons of Voting Age	Persons Registered	Registered Per Cent
January 19, 1961			
White	2,387	2,291	96%
Negro	4,450	5	.1124%
April 1, 1961			
White	2,387	2,291	96%
Negro	4,450	4	.1124%
November 1, 1963			
White	2,387	2,380	99%
Negro	4,450	1,230	27.6%

Nearly one third of the cases and more than half of the pending investigations involved segregation in the public schools.

Since 1890, all public elementary and secondary schools in Mississippi have been segregated. Since 1890, however, there are more Negro children to educate than white children. The school census of 1960 counted 329,215 white children and 337,871 Negro children in Mississippi schools. Mississippi, naturally, has fewer Negro schools than white.

The average yearly salary of classroom teachers in 1961-1962 was $3,742.39 for whites and $3,236.75 for Negroes. In

1961, $173.42 instructional cost per child was spent for the white children, and $117.10 per child for the Negro children. In 1953, there were 42 one-teacher schools for the white and 1,077 one-teacher schools for the Negro. By 1962, however, this was greatly reduced. There were now only one one-teacher school for the white students and 47 for the Negro children.

The end of school segregation involves more than Constitutional principle. Mississippi has always admitted that public education for Negroes has been inferior to that for whites. In 1907 Governor James K. Vardaman said:

> Here is what I promised to do. I said if you elect me Governor and elect a legislature in sympathy with me that I would submit to the people of Mississippi an amendment to the State Constitution which would control the distribution of a public school fund so as to stop the useless expenditure in the black counties.
>
> Let's see whether I kept my promise. In my inaugural address, I devoted the greater part of it to that. The only time I ever got a chance to urge against Negro education as I wanted to without impairing the white schools was when a legislature passed a bill providing money to that Negro school in Holly Springs which was sent to me signed by the President of the Senate and the Speaker of the House. Did I sign it? No. I killed the bill and I killed the school . . .

And in 1950, Governor Wright told the Mississippi State Legislature:

> We face a serious problem in the matter of providing comparable educational opportunities for the two races of our state. As a matter of fact, the problem is composed of several phases. One of them deals with salary adjustments. A plan was proposed and submitted to the teachers this past summer. They voted it down. It is now necessary to prepare another plan . . .

I recommend that legislation be enacted providing for the equalization of teachers' salaries based upon qualifications, and removing any discrimination as between the races.

Second, I urge that a program be enacted providing for equal facilities between the races recognizing that children of both races are entitled to equal opportunities, but I will insist . . . that this program provide for segregated educational facilities . . .

"Keep pushing the cases" was having its effect in hundreds of Southern counties not yet visited by Burke Marshall, John Doar, and the other lawyers and investigators with the road maps.

By December 1, 1961, virtually every bus station, every railroad station, and every airport in the South had been desegregated. For the first time the Attorney General's office entered a brief seeking to forbid hospitals built with federal funds to discriminate racially against doctors or patients. The Department of Justice also brought a suit to require the desegregation of a school district financed with federal impacted area funds. Robert Kennedy said it made no sense for the United States to ask its citizens to serve their country in the armed forces and then put them in a place where their children would be discriminated against because of their race.[19]

On July 24, 1962, the Attorney General instituted the first proceeding of its kind under the Civil Rights Act of 1960, with the result that twenty-six Negroes of East Carroll Parish in northeast Louisiana were registered as voters by Federal Judge Edwin F. Hunter, Jr.[20]

[19] Speech by Robert F. Kennedy, October 28, 1962, to the American Jewish Congress.
[20] New Orleans *Times-Picayune*, July 25, 1962, p. 11. See also *United States v. Manning*, 206 F. Supp. 623-W.D. La. 1962.

On August 28, 1962, the Department of Justice filed a complaint in the United States District Court in Jackson, Mississippi. It asked the court to declare unconstitutional two sections of the Mississippi Constitution which require interpretation tests and "good moral character" requirements and made a similar request concerning seven state laws which set up other devices allegedly used to discriminate against prospective Negro voters.[21]

Not every Negro was aware of the way the President, the Attorney General, and Burke Marshall were proceeding, for not every Negro voted nor was every colored school child free from segregation. But it is safe to say every segregationist knew. The segregationists remembered Dr. Martin Luther King saying to his followers: "The Negro elected Kennedy. We must not hesitate to remind him of that." By 1963 segregationists had more than enough evidence to convince them that Kennedy never needed reminding. For if the Negroes thought of the 1960s as their crucible, John Fitzgerald Kennedy thought of the 1960s as America's.

On his inauguration day, when the campaign was over and the next campaign promises four years off, John F. Kennedy, joyfully watching the parade, turned at one point and told the then Vice-President, Lyndon B. Johnson, "Did you notice there were no Negroes marching with the Coast Guard unit?"

Actually, Negro students were not excluded from the Coast Guard Academy. But after Mr. Kennedy's memorandum of January 23, 1961, two days after his inauguration, the Coast Guard began an all-out recruiting drive to enroll Negroes. During 1963, two Negro officers, Lieutenant Bobby Wilks and Lieutenant Andrew Holleman, toured the country, visiting 199 schools, talking to 11,000 students and personally inter-

21 *United States v. Mississippi*, F. Supp. S.D. Miss. 1962.

viewing 561 Negro boys through the NAACP and the Urban
League in an attempt to enroll them in the Academy.[22]

Watching the inaugural parade that cold afternoon, John
F. Kennedy must have been turning over in his mind the
meeting he would probably have with Premier Nikita Khrush-
chev of the Soviet Union, the unprecedented trade bill he
would ask enacted, the possibilities of a *rapprochement* with
President Charles De Gaulle of France, and the plans he was
making for America's entry into the Space Age. Yet in the
front of his consciousness was the absence of Negro cadets in
the Coast Guard Academy contingent. Civil Rights for the
American Negro would be the big problem with which he
would wrestle every day during the less than three years he
would live.

At the first Cabinet meeting in January, 1961, President
Kennedy issued orders that positive action be taken immediately to promote equal opportunity for all persons employed
by the federal government. Mr. Kennedy said that it is up to
Congress, the people themselves, to legislate change but that
he intended to do everything possible to enforce the laws
already on the books. One of the first things the President
noted was that out of nine hundred lawyers employed by the
government in Washington, only ten were Negroes. The situation was changed within six months when there were seven
times that many. For the first time Negroes were serving as
district judges in continental United States, and the NAACP
lawyer Thurgood Marshall, who had won the big case of the
century, was appointed by Mr. Kennedy to the United States
Court of Appeals for the Second Circuit.

[22] Mr. Kennedy's Inauguration Day comment and subsequent action were
provided me by Lee C. White, Assistant Special Counsel to the President;
Recruiting information, Capt. W. K. Thompson, Jr., Chief Public Information, U. S. Coast Guard, Treasury Department.

It has been said that John F. Kennedy tried to find an answer, not to force a solution. His aim was to find the ways and means of granting every American the same fundamental and basic rights without producing a national convulsion. As soon as he had formulated his policies, he found he had also formulated his opposition. As the Department of Justice began its activities, the feeling against the President and his brother, the Attorney General, began to rise. For the President it was a meta-political opposition welling from those who somehow sensed that *this was it,* that they would soon be deprived of certain privileges and honors they had always enjoyed without any individual effort or struggle. It was a resentment, as close as I can gauge it, greater than the resentment the South mustered against President Harry Truman after he accepted the Civil Rights plank in the Democratic party platform of 1948.

Senator Strom Thurmond of South Carolina and other Dixiecrats were so outraged by the Truman platform they subtracted four Southern states from the Democratic column. But many segregationists still suspected Harry Truman of campaigning on a civil rights platform simply to get elected. Underneath, they thought (wrongly, it turned out) that he was one of them.

But John F. Kennedy and the Justice Department challenged the notion of the caste system itself. Had he lived to make the campaign in 1964, it would probably have been far more acrimonious and bitter than Truman's in 1948. I remember then hearing a Democratic County Committee leader in my state urge his membership, "To hell with the head of the ticket, let's just make sure we send our Representative back to Congress." When Alben Barkley, Mr. Truman's Vice-Presidential candidate, came to address a rally in Charlotte, the late Senator W. Kerr Scott, a liberal, took me aside and, pointing to the Democrats on the dais, said, "Half of those men are going to bolt the ticket." Called upon for his sentiments, Scott shouted into the microphone, "All I want to say is I am a Woodrow Wilson, Franklin D. Roosevelt, and Harry Truman Democrat."

Harry Truman almost lost North Carolina over his support for civil rights. (It had little to do with the result of course, but my readers will be interested to know of a story I investigated during the campaign—someone had started a rumor among the millworkers of the state that the Republican candidate, Thomas E. Dewey, was a Jew.)

The only contemporary Democrat who did not suffer critically for his sympathies with the Negro was Franklin D. Roosevelt. Republicans and Democratic conservatives complained taxes were too high, the unions too strong, and government expenditures too heavy. No one mounted a serious campaign over anything Roosevelt did for the Negroes.

President Roosevelt's Executive Order 8802, which created a Federal Fair Employment Practices Committee, known popularly as the FEPC, was the source of some political controversy. Roosevelt issued his unprecedented order on June 25, 1941, in the period of defense mobiliziation, to placate A. Philip Randolph, who had threatened to bring a hundred thousand Negroes to Washington to agitate for such a directive. The fact that Roosevelt released this executive order had a two-fold significance: one, Negroes now had demonstrated that they could function as an effective pressure group; two, the government gave notice to the country that Negro labor would be utilized in defense production.[23] It was hard, however, for the segregationists to challenge the fact that World War II demanded more and more manpower on the line and in the factories.

Instead, the segregationists brought their criticism to bear

[23] William Carl Berman, *The Politics of Civil Rights in the Truman Administration*, Villanova University, unpublished Ph.D. dissertation, p. 6.

against Eleanor Roosevelt. President Roosevelt received countless letters from Southern Democrats asking, "Why don't you
keep your wife home?" Undoubtedly he received similar
queries from northern Republicans but this only shows the
latter were ill-prepared for the proprieties of the twentieth
century; the Southerners felt betrayed when the First Lady
championed a Negro cause. The segregationists and the South
generally thought FDR conformed to their idea of the aristocrat. But they could not picture Eleanor as the cloistered, retiring belle of the mansion.

Only diehard segregationists hated President Eisenhower,
although he refused to compromise the federal courts on this
issue. After Eisenhower sent the 101st Airborne Division to
Little Rock, Arkansas, the feeling about his Administration
changed perceptibly throughout the South, but it did not
cool toward him personally. Even when Mr. Eisenhower himself had acted in the Little Rock crisis, the expressions of
hatred were directed at Chief Justice Earl Warren "who
started it all." The President's personal figure continued to
command great enthusiasm. Perhaps this was so because of
Mr. Eisenhower's philosophy that morality could not be legis-
lated; perhaps Southerners mistakenly interpreted this banal-
ity as a sure sign that Eisenhower understood their problem.

The South hated Kennedy because even as a candidate he
understood the proportions of the problem. In Minneapolis,
a month before election, in answer to the question, "What
legislation do you propose for the civil rights issue?" Kennedy
replied,

First, there is a good deal that can be done by the Executive branch without legislation. For example, the President
could sign an executive order ending discrimination in
housing tomorrow. Second, the President could compel all
companies which do business with the Government, and

after all, that is nearly every American company, to practice open, fair hiring of personnel without regard to race, creed, or color. . . . In addition, the Department of Justice can pursue the right to vote with far more vigor. The Vice-President's Commission on Contracts has been completely ineffective. It has not instituted one suit outside of the District of Columbia. So I would say that the greater opportunity is in the Executive branch without Congressional action [a point on which the late President was to change his mind]. The things I would ask the Congress to do are really twofold. First, to pass Title 3, which gives the Attorney General additional powers to institute suits to provide for constitutional rights. Secondly . . . provide technical assistance to school districts that are trying to desegregate.

Yet it was two years before Mr. Kennedy issued an Executive directive against discrimination in government housing. Political considerations stayed him. He had been a member of both the House and the Senate and he appreciated the *quid pro quo* of politics. He had other bills he wanted passed and could not afford to alienate Southern Democrats, and the bipartisan Republican support which would make them law.

This reasoning is explained by Helen Fuller in *Year of Trial*. Miss Fuller is not only an experienced journalist, but also a lawyer who served with the Department of Justice. She tells of the President's deep concern for the passage of the Trade Bill and his worry that any new civil rights proposals would have angered Southerners to the point where they would have deliberately stalled Administration policies in foreign affairs. The Housing Sub-Committees in both House and Senate were headed by Alabamans, Representative Alfred Rains and Senator John Sparkman, respectively. Both vehemently opposed an executive order on housing. Kennedy counted on Rains and Sparkman for support for the Trade Bill which indeed they gave, at the same time threatening to surrender their committee chairmanships in the event of a housing order from the White House.[24]

These were mild reactions compared to those, say, of Senator Richard Russell of Georgia or Senator John Stennis of Mississippi who voted against the Nuclear Test Ban Treaty, a gesture their apologists futilely said had nothing to do with their anger at President Kennedy's new civil rights proposals.

Anyone who doubts that Southern senators can react this irresponsibly has but to read the arguments some of these august legislators advanced against the admission of Hawaii to the Union in 1959.

Senator Strom Thurmond of South Carolina said: "What effect statehood would have on Hawaii's multiracial society and its oriental background, or what effect they would have on traditional American values and ideas, we do not know. But it seems obvious that some sort of adjustment would be necessary and the public is now in the process of learning just how painful that kind of adjustment can be. . . ." Senator A. Willis Robertson of Virginia said: "It would seem wise to at least allow more time for the amalgamation of this population into a unified group before giving it all the responsibility of statehood, including the selection of members of the Congress who will make laws for the entire United States." [25]

It is important to concentrate on these political decisions of the late President because we are a political society, and all the decisions which have made this society great and powerful have been political decisions. John F. Kennedy dealt with the race problem both politically and morally, but he dealt with it politically first.

[24] Fuller, *op. cit.*, pp. 37-42.
[25] *The Congressional Digest,* Vol. 38, no. 1, January, 1959, p. 21 f.

In October, 1961, President Kennedy sent Congress a proposal for the establishment of a new cabinet post, Secretary of the Department of Urban Affairs and Housing. Surprisingly, he told a press conference he intended to appoint Robert Weaver, a Negro and administrator of the Housing and Home Finance Agency, as his first Secretary.

In January, 1962, the House Rules Committee, composed of five Republicans, two anti-Administration Southerners, five non-Southern Democrats, and three pro-Administration Southerners, voted 9 to 6 to let the bill die in Committee. Kennedy next tried establishing the new agency under the powers conferred upon him by the Reorganization Act whereby the Chief Executive can send a "plan" for the creation of a new Department to the Congress and if neither house votes to reject it within sixty days, the agency is automatically established. Thus did Dwight D. Eisenhower create the Department of Health, Education and Welfare. The House of Representatives by the unexpected margin of 264 to 150 votes defeated the President's proposal.

Many were disappointed. Urban political leaders in particular blamed the bill's defeat on Kennedy's public announcement of wanting to appoint a Negro to the Cabinet. Everyone critical of Mr. Kennedy said he was playing politics.

Certainly this was true. That he played politics is one of his claims to greatness. He was playing politics in an attempt to get as much mileage out of his fight to end racial segregation as possible. Mr. Kennedy was aware that the House of Representatives is controlled to a dismaying degree by rural and small town legislators, although two thirds of our population live in cities. He was equally aware that his proposal for a Department of Urban Affairs and Housing would have rough going because of the disproportionate representation. But the President wanted to make a defeat for his proposal as costly as possible to the opposition. If they beat down a

Department of Urban Affairs, they would have to vote against the Negro too.

Afterward, Republican leaders suggested Mr. Kennedy appoint Robert Weaver to the post of Secretary of Health, Education and Welfare when Senator Abraham Ribicoff resigned. They promised to give Mr. Weaver a vote of confirmation to show they did not mean to oppose Mr. Weaver when they voted against the Department of Urban Affairs. To which Mr. Kennedy replied at his next news conference, "I see now that various people who opposed the Urban Department are ready to support Mr. Weaver for any cabinet position he wishes, Defense, State, Treasury, or anything else. While I'm sure he's grateful for those good wishes for a Cabinet position where there is no vacancy, I think he would have been, that this country would have been, better served to have voted for an Urban Department and permitted him to continue his service in that capacity."

Had Mr. Kennedy succeeded in establishing this Department, he planned to swear in Mr. Weaver as the first Negro cabinet officer in an unprecedented ceremony, a ceremony televised and photographed for every corner of the world.

The several Negro leaders who expressed their skepticism concerning Mr. Kennedy's designation of a Negro for a cabinet post not yet created proved only that Mr. Kennedy was far ahead of them. He was "using" the problem in hopes of advancing more than one solution.

Nothing impressed Negro leaders more, however, than their visit with the President after the protest March on Washington on August 28, 1963. Even such knowledgeable men as A. Philip Randolph and Roy Wilkins came to realize how much they had underestimated John F. Kennedy. After the March, Negro leaders bubbling with excitement, came to the White House and posed for the photographers with the President. It had been an awe-inspiring demonstration. Not only had two hundred and ten thousand people converged on Washington for a single day, but the demonstration had gone off without incident. A great mass of Negroes and whites had protested an evil, and had protested in "the inspiration of Christ and the method of Gandhi" as Dr. Martin Luther King would have it.

Mr. Kennedy shook hands with these happy, excited men, but he did not show any particular enthusiasm. He did not pat them on the back and tell them they had done a great job. Instead, when they assembled around a table filled with sandwiches, coffee, and milk, the President told them about the Civil Rights Bill he had before the Congress and that the people "on the hill" were the only ones who could really help now. He told the Negro leaders they faced hard work in their districts, cities, and states, and with pencil and paper Mr. Kennedy spelled it out for each man how to use his influence with labor unions, state political leaders, and even down to the local precinct officials. He gave each of them an assignment, warning them this was but a beginning. Negro leaders left the White House subdued in their realization that they were dealing not only with a President who was on their side but with a President who was determined that their side win.

Mr. Kennedy followed this same procedure with all the professional, religious, business, and labor groups he met in the White House. He never gave a pep talk about the evils of segregation; he always directed his attention to what could be done to end racial segregation, discrimination, and exploitation in the United States.

To the college presidents and educators Mr. Kennedy said it was not enough that they disapproved of segregation. They had to do something about it. He suggested an exchange of white college professors with Negro college professors and an exchange of students. Although only one relationship has reached the point of public announcement (between the University of Michigan and Tuskegee), four other Northern

schools that I am aware of are exploring similar relationships with Negro colleges of the South. An additional
Northern university is currently considering a working relationship with five different Negro colleges. I have the
names of those schools but I am somewhat reluctant to
disclose them at this time for fear that any public attention
may have some sort of adverse effect upon the negotiations
now going on. I can say, however, that one is from the big
three of the Ivy League, one is a Big Ten state university, two
are private institutions, and one is a state-supported university. In addition, the Office of Education is contemplating
adding a staff member who would work on relationships such
as these among other assignments.

It is safe, I think, to say that Mr. Kennedy's idea was
strong enough to have initiated considerable interest among
the educators of our country. I would expect that if these
early programs are productive a large number of northern
schools will want to move into the field.

Below is a list of the groups to whom Mr. Kennedy talked
civil rights in a forty-day period:

Leadership Group	Date	No. Attending
Governors	May 29, 1963	9
Hotel, Restaurant, and		
Theater Owners	June 4	120
Labor Leaders	June 13	215
Religious Leaders	June 17	250
Governors	June 18	8
Educators	June 19	250
Lawyers	June 21	250
Civil Rights Leaders	June 22	30
Women's Meeting	July 9	350
Business Council	July 11	70
Governors	July 12	6

Both the President and the Attorney General spoke at these meetings. The President said nothing could be done in Washington as effectively as what could be done community by community throughout the country. He warned that the schedule of civil rights would not be set by the Congress, by the President, by the public, but by the Negro community, and that it was the job of the clergy, business, labor, and professional leaders to insure that the transition from second-class citizenship to full-privileged citizenship would be as orderly as possible.

When a Southern clergyman asked the dramatic question about intermarriage, the President replied that the question before the country was not one of intermarriage but one of voting rights, jobs, and equal opportunities in education. He told the clergymen he had not asked them to desegregate their churches but to desegregate the public domain. He closed with the remark that they were a most fortunate group, that it was not often that people have had such a role to play in history.[26]

These informal conventions were influential. When Mr. Kennedy met with the top trade unionists, Walter Reuther, vice-president of the AFL-CIO, cut through the rhetoric with the crisp declaration: "If we really wanted to do something about it, the men gathered in this room right now could do more for civil rights in one month than the whole Government could in five years." Reuther, in fact, spearheaded the drive for $160,000 to post bail for the Negroes arrested in the Birmingham, Alabama, demonstrations.[27]

Up to a certain point, John F. Kennedy thought the power and prestige of the Presidency was enough to resolve the race

[26] Conversation with Rabbi Philip S. Bernstein of Rochester, New York, who attended the President's meeting with the clergy.
[27] A. H. Raskin, "Walter Reuther's Great Big Union," *Atlantic Monthly*, October, 1963, p. 92.

issue if coupled with the support of the courts. He was to sign three executive orders on civil rights: (1) Executive Order 10925, on March 7, 1961, establishing the President's Committee on Equal Employment Opportunity; (2) Executive Order 11063, on November 20, 1962, creating equal opportunity in housing; and (3) Executive Order 11114, on June 22, 1963, extending the authority of the President's Committee on Equal Employment Opportunity. But Mr. Kennedy was perhaps the first to realize that the Presidency was not enough for the simple reason that the courts themselves were not enough. The revolution which surges about us is waged for human dignity and equal opportunity and justice and the right to exercise free opinion. Down deep, however, this revolution has one locus: it is a war fought to see whether all of us will obey the law or only some of us. Revolutions are won only when everyone fights, when everyone becomes a participant.

The essential corruption of racial segregation is not that it is supported by lies but that people believe the lies. The segregationists will be disabused of their illusions not when the President says such beliefs are unworthy of Americans but when the Congress and the whole force of public opinion say these lies transgress not only reasonable decency but the law itself.

Several months after the inauguration of President Kennedy, I discussed with Edward R. Murrow, then the director of the United States Information Agency, the advisability of submitting an idea for a "Second Emancipation Proclamation" declaring an end to segregation on every level of American life on which the United States Government touched—property, contracts, installations, subsidies, grants, and loans. Mr. Murrow agreed to suggest it to Mr. Kennedy who said, "Let's see what you fellows come up with."

It was a pithy "declaration," not at all detailed, but something the folks could frame and put up on the wall. By the time Mr. Kennedy received it, however, he had come to the conclusion that the Congress and the people, as well as the President, must play appropriate roles in the civil rights struggle. It was a wise decision. While the folks might have had something for the wall, this did not open up the avenues of freedom.

I never heard directly from the President about the "declaration" but one of the President's friends might have been expressing Mr. Kennedy's own thoughts on the matter. When I asked him about it, he said: "Remember that even Abraham Lincoln found it necessary to add in his Emancipation Proclamation that it was an act of justice, warranted by the Constitution, *upon military necessity*." (My italics are on the words the President's friend had emphasized).

Mr. Kennedy readily admitted that he was controlled by events. To a Negro leader he said that the Negroes owed their heaviest debt to the dogs of Birmingham, Alabama, and to those who unleashed them, provoking a national crisis. Other events had been the assassination of Medgar Evers, an official of the Mississippi NAACP; the sniper murder of Willie Moore, the postman who thought he could bring good will to the deep South; the bombing of the Sixteenth Street Baptist Church in Birmingham, which claimed the lives of four little girls; and, earlier, the open defiance of federal court orders by Governor Ross Barnett of Mississippi and Governor George C. Wallace of Alabama.

The order of events, each augmenting the terror of the preceding event and promising an even more virulent succession, decided Mr. Kennedy's comprehensive policy. He resolved to make the Congress and the people participate in the struggle.

We Americans are violent before we are moral, and much

of our expressed morality is a sexual morality. Pushed to the moral act we can respond if that act is war against a foreign enemy but we are liable to lethargy if it is not.

Zeus chained Prometheus to the rock because Prometheus gave fire to man. Zeus was right and Prometheus wrong. Zeus wanted men strong enough not to need fire, and Prometheus, in the tragic view, made man weak. We Americans have a Prometheus complex. We want Prometheus off the rock but we will not give up the comfort of fire. If the President cannot solve the race problem, we want it to go away and stop annoying us.

But the constant pressures of the Negro made this a continuing public issue. Negroes took their cause to the streets before the general populace. They advanced. One of the reasons they advanced is because the late President John F. Kennedy focused the country's attention on the moral stakes for which the Negroes played.

Very early in his Presidential career, Mr. Kennedy outlined the moral possibilities of the race question. In return for his rights, the Negro offered no barter. This was the unusual truth the President had to tell the people. Speaking in Los Angeles on September 9, 1960, Mr. Kennedy said:

> When our next President takes office in January, he must be prepared to move forward in the field of human rights in three general areas: as a legislative leader, as Chief Executive, and as the center of the moral power of the United States . . . as a moral leader, the next President must play his role in interpreting the great moral and educational forces which are involved in our crusade for human rights. He must exert the great moral and educational force of his office to help bring equal access to public facilities from churches to lunch counters, and to support the right of every American to stand up for his rights, even if on

occasion he must sit down for them. For only the President, not the Senate and not the House and not the Supreme Court, in a real sense, only the President can create the understanding and tolerance necessary as the spokesman for all the American people, as the symbol of the moral imperative upon which any free society is based.

By June of 1963, Mr. Kennedy had realized that the moral imperative belonged not to him alone. Because it was a moral issue it had permeated every level of society. To the nation over the television networks, Mr. Kennedy said:

This is not a legal or legislative issue alone. . . . We are confronted primarily with a moral issue. It is as old as the scriptures and is as clear as the American Constitution. The heart of the question is whether all Americans are to be afforded equal rights and equal opportunities, whether we are going to treat our fellow Americans as we want to be treated. . . . This nation, for all its hopes and all its boasts will not be fully free until all its citizens are free. . . . We face, therefore, a moral crisis as a country and as a people. It cannot be met by repressive police action. It cannot be left to increased demonstrations in the streets. It cannot be quieted by token moves. . . . It is a time to act in the Congress, in your state and local legislative body, and above all, in all of our daily lives.

Eight days later, on June 19, 1963, the President concluded his message to Congress by asking for new civil rights legislation with:

I ask you to look into your hearts—not in search of charity, for the Negro neither wants nor needs condescension —but for the one plain, proud, and priceless quality that unites us all as Americans: a sense of justice. In this year of the Emancipation Centennial, justice requires us to insure the blessings of liberty for all Americans and their posterity—not merely for reasons of economic efficiency, world diplomacy and domestic tranquillity—but above all, because it is right.

It was in these ways that Mr. Kennedy lent the weight and prestige of his office to the Negro revolution. He acted decisively whenever the power of his office was challenged. Though he did not issue his Housing Directive until he was two years in office, he was barely in office when he found the solid ground he and the New Frontier needed to pursue to resolve inequities: "Get the road maps and go," he said about the Civil Rights Acts of 1957 and 1960; and after the first report on voting rights by the Department of Justice, he wrote confidently, "Keep pushing the cases."

Burke Marshall and his men were tramping the back roads and the back counties knocking on the doors of Negro sharecroppers asking, "Did you ever vote? Did you ever try to vote? Did you ever try to register? What happened?" They also asked about schools. In those cases where Mr. Marshall's men have challenged registration tests and standards, they wanted to be in a position to prove further racial discrimination. Such tests and standards are inherently unfair to Negroes because they had been afforded inferior educational opportunities. Thus the Attorney General's office was primarily interested in the kind of school the voter went to, which gave them the additional insight into the kind of school the voter's children go to.

But the job is not quite that simple. The challenge to Mr. Kennedy to implement the Constitution "Negro by Negro" is a complicated process. For every Negro interviewed, it was necessary to analyze the registration records of the white voters. In preparing their voting cases, the civil rights people of the Department of Justice must prove discrimination. They must show the registration card of a Negro who had been rejected and compare it with the registration card of a white citizen who had been allowed to vote. The results in the brief, *United States v. Mississippi,* are interesting. Hundreds of such "matching" instances have been recorded. For instance, in the brief involving Panola County, Mississippi, the registration cards of eight Negroes who had been rejected are in fairly good order, neat and well-written, but all were rejected. But here is a description of a few of the registration cards of white citizens who were allowed to vote:

Case A: Third grade education—Illiterate, could not read or understand question 20 about the duties of citizenship. She just signed the book .

Case B: No education—Illiterate, could not read question 20 about the duties of citizenship. He just signed his name, and nothing else.

Case C: Tenth grade education—He could not read section 30 ("There shall be no imprisonment for debt"). He read "That should be no. . . ." He could not read and did not know the meaning of "imprisonment" or "debt." The man helped him fill out his form.

Case D: Sixth grade education—Read question 20 except for the word "Constitutional." Did not know what it meant. Received form and "I signed what of them I knew, and them I didn't know I left blank, and then I signed a big book." [28]

If the segregationists of the South said it was a fight, Negro by Negro, school board by school board, voting registrar by voting registrar, so be it. Mr. Kennedy said the United States of America had met greater challenges in its history and had overcome them. The fight shifted from lawyers in morning coats arguing before the Supreme Court to lawyers with

[28] *United States v. Duke,* Civil Action No. D-C-53-61, United States District Court for the Northern District of Mississippi, 1963.

rumpled clothes and dusty shoes traveling along lonely roads.

This is not a dramatic process, certainly not dramatic enough to satisfy Negroes facing brutal policemen armed with prod sticks and dogs. It is a slow process. But it is an inexorable process. A political man, Mr. Kennedy thought in terms of voting rights. While the Negro needed additional legislation in housing, employment, and public accommodations, Mr. Kennedy felt voting rights was the key to the issue. The late President told Martin Luther King, "Once you get the ballot and the Negroes are educated to its use, all other things will fall in proper place." Medgar Evers, the murdered NAACP official of Mississippi, had said the same thing a year before: "If we could get the ballot we could weed out many of the injustices that Negroes suffer." [29]

When Mr. Kennedy was campaigning for the Presidency, he could have been expected to say as his opponent said and as most of the liberals said, that while in favor of civil rights he was opposed to "extremists," a phrase which, if it means anything, means let nature take its course lest the actions of men disturb it. But Mr. Kennedy did not resort to the hollow safety of sane but insipid phrases, even in the heat of a bitter campaign. He said he favored Freedom Riders and sit-in protests and he said this when no other national leader said it.

Mr. Kennedy inspired a moral tone which washed over the entire country. It influenced everyone, particularly those close to him. Three years later, Mr. Kennedy's Secretary of State Dean Rusk, a Southerner born in Georgia, made his point wholly understood before a Senate Commerce Committee during the hearings on the Civil Rights Bill: "If I were denied what our Negro citiezns are denied, I would demonstrate also." At this same hearing, Mr. Rusk said that foreign policy considerations were "secondary" to the fact that racial bias was wrong, but he added that failure to enact the President's

[29] Cook, *op. cit.,* pp. 95-96.

Civil Rights Bill would evoke world-wide questioning of "the real convictions of the American people." [30]

Mr. Kennedy's whole life gave him an understanding of discrimination and bigotry, because he came from a religion and a nationality which had known persecution. In a pamphlet on immigration written for the Anti-Defamation League of the B'nai B'rith, Mr. Kennedy wrote:

> By 1830 there were 150,000 Irish Catholics in New York City. Feeling against them was very strong and erupted from time to time in riots, the burning of churches and considerable bloodshed. The first appearance of this sentiment in national politics was the Presidential election of 1836, when Martin Van Buren was accused by his enemies of being a Catholic.
>
> The hatred of Irish and Catholic immigrants and more particularly of the Catholic Church, led to the founding of the Native-American or Know-Nothing Party in 1845. This party, whose whole platform consisted of three planks—vote only for native-born candidates, a long period of naturalization, and opposition to the Catholic Church—had the swiftest rise and swiftest fall of any major party in American history. . . .
>
> Yet it is a remarkable fact that in spite of . . . this agitation there was no official government response. . . . The sense of America as a refuge for oppressed and down-trodden people was never far from the consciousness of Americans.[31]

In private conversation the President expressed wonder at the vitality of the Negro civil rights movement. We may relate this wonder to the ideas he expressed in his little book on immigration. Mr. Kennedy was worried about America's future,

[30] *Facts on File*, Vol. XXIII, no. 1187, July 25, 1963, p. 269.
[31] John F. Kennedy, *A Nation of Immigrants* (New York, The Anti-Defamation League, 1963), p. 2.

this much we know. He was worried about the hard decisions yet to be made in our struggle wth the Communist world. And he was also worried that a more relaxed and affluent society may have lost much of its drive. The immigrant, on the other hand, has no choice. He must make good or remain forever alien.

When Mr. Kennedy publicly applauded the unorganized street demonstrations and approved the March on Washington, he may have related this vitality of the American Negro to the determination with which the Irish immigrant went about the task of making a better world for his children.

The immigrants from foreign lands provided America with a steady stream of vitality which helped make our country the richest nation on earth. This is not to say the immigrant was better than the native. On the contrary, his intense drive derived from his belief that he was not as good as the native.

The philosopher Eric Hoffer makes the point:

The discarded and rejected are often the raw material of a nation's future. The stone the builders reject becomes the cornerstone of a new world. A nation without dregs and malcontents is orderly, decent, peaceful and pleasant, but perhaps without the seed of things to come. It was not the irony of history that the undesired in the countries of Europe should have crossed an ocean to build a new world on this continent. Only they could do it.

The less satisfaction we derive from being ourselves, the greater is our desire to be like others. We are therefore more ready to imitate those who are different from us than those nearly like us, and those we admire than those we despise. The imitativeness of the oppressed (Negroes and Jews) is notable.

As to the blurring and camouflaging of the self, it is achieved solely by imitation—by becoming as like others as possible. The desire to belong is partly a desire to lose oneself.[32]

I witnessed this process as a boy on the Lower East Side of New York. It was during the years of unrestricted immigration to our shores. The immigrant came off the gangplank, looked into the faces of the Americans, and repeated the words that were said a few million times a day, in dozens of different languages, "Ah, when will I be like them?"

It is probably to the everlasting good fortune of America that after a whole generation of restricted immigration, we have been suddenly confronted with some nineteen millions of our very own people with that same intense drive to enter the open society of America and participate fully in all its assorted wonders. Like the immigrant, the American Negro is determined at all costs to succeed, and indeed, if he does not, like the immigrant, he, too, will regard himself as irrevocably lost. (The Negro population of the United States is 19,300,000, according to the latest reliable estimate. Knowledgeable Negro leaders, however, put the figure at closer to 23,000,000 which includes, they say, from 3 to 4 million Negroes who have *passed* into the white society.)

The Negroes say, "No white man can *think* 'black.'" They say this even of their closest white allies and they may be right. In his total commitment, Mr. Kennedy saw the social revolution of the American Negro as something more than a white man thinking "black." When Mr. Kennedy refused to frown publicly on the street demonstrations, and actually applauded the March on Washington, he saw in the Negro a charismatic symbol of a renewed vitality of the American civilization.

In his meeting with labor leaders on June 13, 1963, Mr.

[32] Eric Hoffer, *The True Believer* (New York, Harper & Bros., 1951), pp. 41-42.

Kennedy said that he did not agree with Negro leaders who urge "preferential" or "quota" employment for Negroes to help "close the gap." But the President acknowledged that *something will have to be done for the Negro* and in order to "reach" him, said Mr. Kennedy, the American 1960s will have to do it for all: for the poor, the unemployed, and the displaced, without regard to color, race, or creed. Mr. Kennedy said that we owe a debt of gratitude to the Negro "in the streets" for calling attention to the American Dream.[33]

[33] Author's conversation with Walter Reuther, Vice-President, AFL-CIO, Washington, D. C., August 28, 1963.

CHAPTER SEVEN

JUDGE WISDOM
AND LOUISIANA'S WALL

P RESIDENT KENNEDY'S concern was the speed with which Attorney General Robert F. Kennedy and Assistant Attorney General Burke Marshall could get their cases through the federal district courts into the circuit (appeals) courts. The challenge to implement existing federal court orders "Negro by Negro" was the key to the entire civil rights struggle until such time as the Congress approved additional civil rights legislation.

President Kennedy received a weekly report on the progress, and these reports assured him that he would win the struggle everywhere in the South by the end of 1968. The Administration's lawyers must complete their investigations, and prepare the complaints, affidavits, and exhibits for trial in the district court. While pursuing new investigations, they must prepare their briefs for the United States Court of Appeals, either as appellants or as appellees. And in the federal courts the cases are confronted with the American tradition of "comity."

"Comity," in a case where a state law is challenged, is the tradition of giving that state every possible opportunity to defend its position. The federal courts have always been careful about throwing out a state law or a city ordinance. In effect the federal judiciary says, it is your law, we will let you interpret it in your state courts before we decide whether it does or does not violate provisions of the United States Constitution.

All this takes time. Ending racial discrimination in a local situation is a slow, tortuous process. It may well be that leaders of Negro religious and social-action organizations are aware of this process but they have pressures upon them, great pressures, and the only way to relieve these pressures is to transfer them to the President or the Attorney General.

On July 31, 1956, long before John F. Kennedy was President, a federal court ruled racial discrimination in the public schools at Arlington County, Virginia, unlawful. The court called for desegregation. On the Monday following John F. Kennedy's assassination, seven and a half years later, those schools in Arlington were still segregated.

In 1956, the court issued an injunction against the Arlington School Board prohibiting further segregation. The School Board appealed this injunction and the appeal was heard in 1956. The injunction was affirmed. The School Board then sought a writ of certiorari. At the end of 1956, the United States Supreme Court denied the writ.

In 1957, the School Board was back in court asking a further suspension of the injunction. The district court refused. When the fall term began, seven Negro pupils applied for admission to the all-white schools in Arlington and were turned back. Their parents moved for relief in the federal district court. The court, after considering the School Board's defense, ordered these pupils admitted. The School Board appealed this decision. The Fourth Circuit Court affirmed the order to admit the Negroes. By now, it was 1958 and again the School Board asked the Supreme Court for a writ of certiorari which again

the Supreme Court denied on May 19. That September the
School Board initiated a "request for guidance" and its effective date for compliance with the first order to desegregate
was moved to February, 1959. So in January, the School Board
appealed this order and on January 28, 1959, the district court
denied the appeal. The Circuit Court also denied the appeal,
as did the Supreme Court.

This recitation of writs and appeals and denials is weary
reading and of course even wearier practice. It cannot help but
enervate the will and spirit of the plaintiffs. Even though a
last appeal was turned down, the School Board had still more
delaying tactics. Once the case was lost and all appeals exhausted, the School Board decided all students had to attend
schools in their residential areas. The Arlington School Board
then was able to claim it no longer had a policy of racial
segregation.

The Negroes had to return to court to charge that the School
Board had neither eliminated racial segregation nor intended
to. For the School Board had defined residential areas in such a
manner as to perpetuate school segregation. It had permitted
white children to transfer from Negro schools but no Negro
children to transfer from segregated to integrated schools. The
Circuit Court held that the racial minority transfer rule was
valid. When the United States Supreme Court ruled otherwise
regarding a different case, the Arlington Negroes went back
to court. Simon E. Sobeloff, Chief Judge of the United States
Court of Appeals for the Fourth Circuit, in the majority
opinion, ruled the Arlington transfer plan violated the Equal
Protection Clause of the Fourteenth Amendment.[1]

But the School Board had one more trump. It forbade

[1] United States Court of Appeals for the Fourth Circuit; No. 8708; Gloria
Brooks, an infant, by Ethel A. Brooks, her mother and next friend, appellants, versus County School Board of Arlington County, Virginia,
appellees. Argued September 24, 1963, decided Oct. 31, 1963, before
Sobeloff, Chief Judge, and Haynesworth and Boreman, Circuit Judges.

transfers of white students. Whether this is discriminatory or not is a question before a federal court at this writing in early January, 1964. The Negroes have argued that the School Board continues segregation by discriminatory attendance areas and the School Board contends the Negroes had not objected to these areas at public hearings.

This is one of the fronts: the battle the Justice Department and the Negro petitioners wage to get their cause past the district court and into the appeals court, and the battle to keep it before the court's attention. The years go by, yet there can be no other strategy.

The other front on which the Burke Marshall lawyers fight is that of the intense research which the Government must do to bring the cases to trial in the first place. Consider now the voting rights case of the *United States v. State of Louisiana.* The Government explained its case:

> The complaint seeks a judgment declaring the invalidity and enjoining the enforcement of the Louisiana voter qualification requirement which conditions registration for voting upon the ability of the citizen to understand and give a reasonable interpretation of any sections of the Constitution of the United States or the Constitution of Louisiana.

Appearing for the Government were Robert F. Kennedy, Burke Marshall, Louis Lacour, and John Doar. John Minor Wisdom, circuit court judge, and Herbert Christenberry and E. Gordon West, district judges, heard the case.

The Government argued that the Louisiana law which demanded that potential voters interpret either the Constitution of the United States or the Constitution of Louisiana was used to disfranchise Negroes.

In twenty parishes, the Government attorneys showed that where the interpretation test has been used, only 8.7 per cent of the adult Negroes are registered to vote. Yet 65.1

per cent of the adult white persons were on the voter rolls. Negroes highly qualified by literacy standards had been denied registration in many of these parishes for failure to interpret a section of the Constitution to the satisfaction of the registrar. Yet numerous white voters passed the interpretation test whose application cards indicate they were barely able to write their names.

Twenty-nine applications of Negro schoolteachers were rejected. On the other hand, the records of these parishes reflect that only one white schoolteacher had failed the test and this rejection came after the Government filed a discrimination suit against the registrar.

In Plaquemines Parish, from the time of the adoption of the interpretation test until March 12, 1962, over three thousand white persons and only seventy-four Negroes had applied for registration to vote. During this period 99 per cent of all white applications which presumably included an interpretation test were accepted while at least 44 per cent of all Negro applications were rejected.

In Plaquemines, unlike other parishes that had an interpretation test, the records are complete; both the provisions and answers are in writing. They show:

(a) White applicants received preferential treatment in the selection of sections to be interpreted. They were given easier test cards than were given to the Negroes. All but seven of the 1,586 white applicants passed in 1959. During the same year only 4 of the 20 Negroes who applied were registered.

(b) The Negroes were discriminated against also in the grading process. White applicants could answer "Only for emergency uses" or "never" or "always" in explaining the Constitutional provision guaranteeing the right of the people to keep and bear arms while a Negro, Kaywood J. Harvey, Jr., was rejected when he gave his interpretation of the provision, "all legislative powers herein granted shall be vested in a

Congress of the United States" as "all laws or powers given to anyone or group shall go through United States Congress."

(c) Furthermore, the registrar helped white persons with their interpretations. For example, on January 20, 1956, 26 of 56 white applicants got the same test card. All of their interpretations were almost identical to one another and to the answers on a model card used by the registrar for grading purposes. In addition, several white applicants mistakenly signed the registrar's model answer cards. A white lady who applied in 1962 had so much difficulty with the test (although she got an easy card) that the deputy registrar wrote out the interpretations for her and she copied them.

The Government had facts and statistics from every one of the parishes which they alleged practiced voter discrimination by race. In Feliciana Parish, a white woman, Mrs. Evelyn Dees testified that her examination consisted of the following: "And then he read it off—something about did I think everyone should go, you know, every human being should go to the same church, and I told him I thought they should go to the church of their choice," while the Reverend Thomas N. Phillips, a Negro, was rejected after interpreting the clause on illegal search and seizure as "To search you would have to get an authorized authority to read a warrant."

A Negro schoolteacher, Betty Lee, testified that she tried to register to vote in Ouachita Parish once in 1958. She failed the interpretation test. Mrs. Lee testified on cross-examination:

"Q. All right. Why haven't you been back?

"A. I haven't been back for the simple reason that I thought I interpreted it right the first time; and if I had interpreted it correct the first time, and she said it wasn't to her satisfaction, I know that if it was in a person, that if they just . . . I mean to say, that if they don't want it to be to their satisfaction, that I could inerpret something all day, and they could still say that it's not to their satisfaction."

The Government attorneys were able to compile statistics showing the discriminatory effect of the Interpretation Test in Louisiana. I have picked seven parishes at random out of the twenty-one involved in the suit:

Parish	Voting Age Population		Registered Voters			
	White	Negro	White	Negro	White	Negro
			Mar. 17, 1956		Dec. 31, 1960	
Bienville	5,617	4,077	5,328	587	5,175	25
E. Carroll	2,990	4,183	3,000	0	2,845	0
E. Feliciana	4,200	4,102	2,812	1,361	2,448	82
Plaquemines	8,633	2,897	4,741	49	7,160	47
Red River	3,294	2,181	3,575	1,512	3,429	27
West Carroll	6,171	1,389	5,660	292	5,182	70
W. Feliciana	1,632	2,235	1,272	0	1,303	0

The Court found for the Government in the most sweeping victory against racial discrimination since the enactment of the Civil Rights Act of 1957. Here are portions of Judge Wisdom's ruling:

A wall stands in Louisiana between registered voters and unregistered eligible Negro voters. The wall is the State constitutional requirement that an applicant for registration "understand and give a reasonable interpretation of any section" of the Constitutions of Louisiana and of the United States. It is not the only wall of its kind, but since the Supreme Court's demolishment of the white primary, the interpretation test has been the highest, best-guarded, most effective barrier to Negro voting in Louisiana . . .

We hold this wall built to bar Negroes from access to the franchise, must come down. The understanding clause or interpretation test is *not* a literacy requirement. It has no rational relation to measuring the ability of an elector to

read and write . . . considering the actual operation and inescapable effect of the law, it is evident that the test is a
sophisticated scheme to disfranchise Negroes. The test is unconstitutional as written and as administered . . .

. . . We do not have before us a test having a rational relation with the proper government objective of giving the
vote only to qualified persons. Despite assurances by state
officials at the meetings of the registrars that this test measures only "native intelligence," the truth of the matter is
that there is nothing in native intelligence that will enable
those untutored in constitutional law to give a reasonable
interpretation of a highly technical document containing
such legal concepts as, for example, venue, due process, the
requisites of a criminal indictment, appellate court jurisdiction and jurisdictional amount. Whatever name the State
elects to give to the test, it is not a test of intelligence or
citizenship when it enables a registrar to flunk eight Negro
school teachers while passing eight illiterate white persons . . .

Short of a government of philosopher-kings, and no one
has ever described Louisiana government in such terms,
there is just no correlation between an ability to interpret
any section of the Louisiana Constitution a registrar may
thrust at an applicant for registration and a legitimate State
interest in an informed electorate. . . . Our order forbids enforcement of the citizenship test until Negro applicants can
be judged by the same standards used in qualifying those
persons already registered. . . .

We summarize our holding. The Court holds that the interpretation test is unconstitutional because of its unlawful
purpose, operation, and inescapably discriminatory effect.
We enjoin its use in Louisiana. To make this decree effective
and to exorcise past discrimination, the Court enjoins the
use of the "citizenship" test in the parishes of Bienville,

Claiborne, De Soto, East Carroll, East Feliciana, Franklin, Jackson, La Salle, Lincoln, Morehouse, Ouachita, Plaquemines, Rapides, Red River, Richland, Saint Helena, Union, Webster, West Carroll, West Feliciana, and Winn as to persons of voting age who had the requisite residence in the parish before August 3, 1962. . . . We enjoin the use of the "citizenship" test in the named parishes until there has been a general re-registration of all voters in a named parish, or until it has been shown, to the satisfaction of the court, that the interpretation test has lost its discriminatory effect in the parish.

The briefs which explained the Government's case measured one foot high. The man-hours of investigation that went into this compilation took many months, and elections did indeed go by in which no Negroes voted or registered. The work on the part of the Attorney General's attorneys did not allay Negro impatience, but Judge Wisdom's decision is a great and far-reaching one and will enable Negroes to vote in twenty-one Louisiana parishes where they had found it almost impossible to do so before.[2]

The schools in Arlington, Virginia, will eventually be desegregated, but there are still a fantastic number of delaying tactics available to the School Board.

No President, no Administration can wipe out these delays, delays occasioned by preparation and the delays occasioned by

[2] *United States of America, Plaintiff, versus State of Louisiana:* Jimmie H. Davis, C. C. Aycock, J. Thomas Jewel, as members of the Board of Registration of the State of Louisiana: and Hugh E. Cutter, Jr., Director and Ex-officio Secretary of the Board of Registration of the State of Louisiana, Defendants. Civil Action No. 2548, Louis Lacour, United States Attorney, Burke Marshall, Assistant Attorney General, and John Doar, David Norman, Frank Dunbaugh, Attorneys, Department of Justice; Decision for the Government, John Minor Wisdom, United States Circuit Judge, Herbert W. Christenberry, United States District Judge; Dissenting, E. Gordon West, United States District Judge.

appeals and writs. Attorney General Robert F. Kennedy told his staff, "Go the last mile with the Southerners." No law requires such instruction, but it is part of the American tradition of the federal courts to "go the last mile" with the authorities of each of the states of the Union.

A Colorado Congressman wired Robert F. Kennedy, "One of my constituents has been in a Georgia jail for eighty-five days for taking part in a peaceful demonstration. Get him out"; the Attorney General replied, "You wouldn't want a national police force, would you?"

"Comity" no doubt encourages injustice such as that perpetrated by a magistrate in Danville, Virginia, who transferred the cases of dozens of Negro street demonstrators to far-off Norfolk. How can a Negro student who does not have his own carfare get his witnesses three hundred and fifty miles across the state so that he may be able to defend himself properly? The answer is he cannot.

Southern political leaders know the American Constitution precludes the abuse of power through an intricate system of legal balances. One of these balances, one of these safeguards, is this very process of delay, of appeals, writs, and requests, a safeguard which, I believe, neither the white liberals nor the Negro leaders would want to sacrifice. And for a brief moment we should think of the Arlington case and dozens like it in another context. We may recall how outraged some of these same people were when a government employee or a college professor, facing utter destruction, availed himself of these basic constitutional privileges and safeguards. The accused could demand that the FBI or his accuser or his government agency produce the research that proved his guilt. And when the accusers did not or were unable to, the defendant could go turned, or seek damages for the harm the process had inflicted to the courts to get his job back or have his conviction over-upon him.

It has been the United States Supreme Court in our time which has said that we cannot demand a fast freight when it suits our purposes and a slow freight when it does not. Everyone gets the same ride. By not trying to by-pass these legal processes, the Attorney General has done as much for civil rights as his preparation of the case against Louisiana's disfranchisement of its Negro citizens.

I remember that during the 1960 Presidential campaign Senator Hubert Humphrey of Minnesota asked me to join the civil rights committee on behalf of candidate John F. Kennedy. The first conference was held at the Park-Sheraton Hotel in New York City on October 11, 1960, and Mr. Kennedy told us about his hopes for signing an explicit directive on housing. His other proposals at the time sounded vague, but he was not vague when he outlined to the men and women in the room the work he expected of his Attorney General. He did not tell us at the time that if elected his appointee would be Robert Kennedy, his brother; he simply said his Attorney General would "hire a corps of lawyers and prepare cases against the disfranchisement of the Negroes in the South." After spending some time with the Attorney General, listening to him in private conversation, reading his speeches, statements, and telegrams and instructions to his staff, it dawns on me now why Mr. Kennedy took the political risk of appointing his own brother to this highly sensitive cabinet position. John F. Kennedy knew his brother. He knew how his brother would react when confronted with a palpable wrong.

I do not think that either the late President or the Attorney General was fully aware of the enormity of those wrongs when they took their oaths of office. But once they scented them out, they made haste to redress these wrongs. I think we can see this development in several speeches delivered by the Attorney General. In addition to the two important civil rights addresses by the late President, I am reprinting, in full, two of Robert

Kennedy's speeches, his first public address as Attorney General, delivered at the Law School of the University of Georgia in May, 1961, and his speech at the annual meeting of the Missouri Bar Association at Kansas City, Missouri, in late 1963.

President Lyndon B. Johnson, upon assuming the office, somehow sensed the extent and the meaning of this Kennedy commitment. As President John F. Kennedy, on his Inauguration Day in January, 1961, noticed there were no Negroes marching with the United States Coast Guard contingent, so President Lyndon B. Johnson's first appraisal of how to honor the work of his predecessor was also in terms of the Negro. On November 27, 1963, when the new President addressed a joint session of Congress, he urged:

> No memorial oration or eulogy could more eloquently honor President Kennedy's memory than the earliest possible passage of the civil rights bill for which he fought so long. We have talked long enough in the country about civil rights. We have talked for one hundred years or more. It is time now to write the next chapter—and to write it in the books of law. John Kennedy's death commands what his life conveyed—that America must move forward.

CHAPTER EIGHT

A FEW STOOD BUT MOST WITHDREW

No MODERN WAR ever received such unanimous support from the churches as the Civil War. Every church group and denomination in America (save for some dissident Episcopalians) urged the war but all the groups were split down the middle as to who should win. Southern churches championed the Confederacy, Northern churches the Union.

Nor has any internal struggle ever received such advocacy as the struggle of the Negro for his civil rights. Again the church is divided. The Southern fellowships believe the Negro should not disturb a way of life, the Northern fellowships believe that segregation is incompatible with American religious life and ethics.

At their General Conference held in Philadelphia in 1864, the Methodists sent a five-man deputation to Abraham Lincoln pledging anew all appropriate means to suppress the "cruel and wicked" rebellion. Lincoln replied, ". . . it may be fairly said that the Methodist Episcopal Church, not less devoted than the best, is by its greater numbers the most important of all." [1]

[1] William Warren Sweet, *The Story of Religions in America* (New York, Harper & Brothers, 1930), p. 461.

189

Benjamin M. Palmer of South Carolina, elected the first moderator of the Presbyterian Church in the Confederate States of America, declared in 1862, "We venture to assert that if men had drawn their conclusions only from the Bible, it would no more have entered into a human head to denounce slavery as a sin than to denounce monarchy, aristocracy or poverty." [2]

Before the Civil War, the church in America split itself in two over the central issue of race and thus ceded the possibility of exerting moral leadership. Morality was finally determined by political authority. During the Civil War, Abraham Lincoln, Chief Executive, leader of his party, Commander-in-Chief, was the moral authority who prevailed.

After the Supreme Court decision of May 17, 1954, the American church, the Protestant churches specifically, again split down the middle. In the 1960s, once again the President of the United States is the chief moral authority, the institution undivided by an internal difference. But that moral authority must be tempered by political considerations.

In 1861, when General John Charles Frémont issued a proclamation freeing the slaves in Missouri, and General Benjamin Butler declared all slaves within his lines were contraband of war, they were hailed by the church press in the North as the "day-stars of the nation." Lincoln countermanded these orders and one editorial in a church paper said, "Never had such a brave man such difficulties thrown in his path as Frémont . . . yet he had held to his way. . . . The people are incensed." Churchmen in the North could not comprehend the political difficulties Lincoln faced in freeing the slaves while at the same time trying to subjugate their masters. Nor could they understand the delicate situation Lincoln faced with the Border States who tolerated slavery and whose defection or lack of enthusiasm might damage the cause of the Union.

[2] *Ibid.*, p. 473.

In the 1960s, while John Fitzgerald Kennedy was contending with state officials who refused to obey federal court orders, while he contended with a Congress dominated in committee by a few arch-segregationist senators and representatives trying their best to delay the passage of a Civil Rights Bill with the threat of derailing an entire Administration program. The Reverend Dr. Eugene Carson Blake, chairman of the Commission on Religion and Race of the National Council of Churches; Father John LaFarge, S.J., of the Catholic Interracial Council; and Rabbi Joachim Prinz, President of the American Jewish Congress, in several individual articles and public statements urged the President to fulfill his promise to end segregation in government-financed housing. These clergymen were right and there is no doubt that Mr. Kennedy shared their sympathies, but he had no more moral unanimity from the churches of America than Abraham Lincoln had one hundred years before.

The Protestant minister or rabbi in the South who followed the moral impulse to speak out against racial segregation ran the likely risk of losing his pulpit.

In April, 1955, Mr. Joseph Sidney Rigell, in the pulpit of St. Paul's Presbyterian Church in Chester, South Carolina, urged his congregation to relax their rigid condemnation of the Supreme Court. Minister Rigell asked his membership to stand to show him their support. Only one rose, Mrs. Rigell. The minister sighed and told his congregation he could not let his wife stand alone. He left his pulpit, stood beside his wife for a moment and walked out. (Ministers who experience economic and other difficulties for taking positions they believe in keeping with their Church's stand on racial and social issues will receive help from a group recently organized, according to Dr. J. Randolph Taylor, pastor of the Church of the Pilgrims, Washington, D. C. Named a "Fellowship of Concern," the new organization will work within the Presbyterian Church, U. S. [Southern branch]. Its immediate aim will be to single out for help those clergymen who have suffered loss because of this stand on racial issues. So far, over one hundred twenty-five ministers and laymen have contributed twenty-five dollars each and signed a "statement of commitment" in order to join the group.)

The number of clergymen who lost pulpits because they supported the Supreme Court decision of May 17, 1954, is hard to determine. The number fired outright because of their "moderate" or "liberal" views are but a handful of those who found themselves out of work because they were "too controversial" or because they "devoted too much time to community affairs." One minister in the South, a personal friend of mine, condemned racial segregation one Sunday; the next Sunday his congregation let him out because "he wasn't visiting the sick as often as he should."

Only a minority of stewards, elders, deacons, and trustees of the South dared tell their minister forthrightly he was taking the wrong side. But there was one occasion when the Board failed to renew a minister's contract because "He is a stooge for the Supreme Court."

Some clergymen, of course, stood their moral ground and stayed on but they were few and far between. By and large, the Protestant clergy of the South abdicated its responsibility in this crisis. (I will discuss the Jews and the Roman Catholics further on in this chapter.) The mass of clergymen kept silent about the crisis and when these clergymen issued public statements they were cautionary and noncommittal statements. Since May of 1954, the sermons in most Southern churches have been concerned with the virtues of happiness and the evils of juvenile delinquency.

Let it be said, however, that the several Protestant denominations at the state and national levels, in synods, conventions, and conferences endorsed the ruling of the Supreme Court. This is also true of the rabbinical associations and all the Jewish social-action societies and fraternities. But a national declaration is one thing and a pale thing at that. It is in the local church that the commitment has real meaning. When a local minister or rabbi pays no attention to the state or national resolution, it becomes so much rhetoric. Which is exactly what happened in the South, all declarations of brotherhood notwithstanding.

Last August, some one hundred-odd members of the Presbyterian Church, U. S. (South) joined Negroes in the March on Washington at the very moment that eighteen officers of their church sent off a signed statement to the National Council of Churches saying they would not comply with the request to muster their congregants for the demonstrations. Thus the Presbyterian Church, U. S., was the only denomination whose regional leadership officially disassociated itself from the March on Washington. It was a significant disassociation. Not only do local Protestant churches of the South ignore the surging Negro revolution but in this one instance even a regional headquarters refused to accord nominal support. Fortunately, the one hundred and seven Presbyterian ministers were not deterred. They joined the Negroes in Washington and held a public service of prayer and penitence.

The refusal of the main Presbyterian Church of the South to support the March on Washington elicited a critical letter from Dr. John Randolph Taylor who wrote: "We as a church will have to pay a high price for withdrawal. If we do not identify ourselves with men's needs, how shall we ever be able to establish communication with men effectively enough to present the Gospel? Demonstrations will never of themselves solve the racial issue; only the Gospel of Jesus Christ can do that. But we do not bear witness to that Gospel in a vacuum.

We bear witness to men and must do so by being with them, not by withdrawing from them." [3]

I quote this letter of Dr. Taylor not to reinforce his plea, for he doesn't need me, but to show that astute members of the Southern ministry are aware of the price the Protestant Church will pay for its withdrawal. Had the Catholic clergy disassociated itself from the struggle of the Irish immigrant and workingman to unionize, then the Catholic Church in America would have been irreparably damaged in the 1890s, for the Irish workingman was the backbone of American Catholicism. There are many battles in which the neutral gets slaughtered.

Wherever the Southern clergyman is free from the layman's influence or patronage, wherever he is secure, there one finds valor and wisdom. Pfeiffer College, the Methodist school in Misenheimer, North Carolina, not long ago integrated the facilities and admitted its first Negro student. The College had just completed a building fund campaign with more than $850,000 in pledges. When some of these donors learned a Negro was living in a Pfeiffer dormitory, however, they reneged on $150,000. It cost little Pfeiffer College $150,000 to enroll one Negro student, a sum it could ill afford to lose. Yet no official of the college has expressed regret over this loss nor did any official of the college consider changing the policy of integration.[4]

But this integrity is isolated in the South. The South has more churches per capita than any other area of the country. In many areas of the South, church attendance is not only a social but an economic imperative. I am sure the ministry is numerically one of the South's important professions, probably

[3] "Some Presbyterians Marched, Some Revolted," *Presbyterian Survey,* October 1963, p. 48.
[4] Conversation with Dr. J. Lem Stokes, II, president of Pfeiffer College, February 26, 1963.

as articulate and influential a segment of the population as,
say, teachers in a Northern suburb are. Where, however,
these teachers are for better education or better schools or
more advanced teaching techniques, these ministers are not for
better ethics or for equity or for the solution of civil disturb-
ances. These ministers are not even for the *status quo* of
"gradualism." They are completely withdrawn from one of the
most turbulent social struggles of the century. It is as though
the course and career of this struggle dare not be mentioned
from the pulpit or in public.

And the question is: why did the local clergy and the local
Protestant Church of the South withdraw? Why did neither
church nor churchman see that the struggle would envelop
them just as it enveloped John F. Kennedy and Lyndon B.
Johnson and all America?

The rise of a Southern middle class in the last forty years
not only secularized many of the urban churches and dampened
their influence but also robbed the minister of his classical
function. It may be said the South is no longer the "Bible
Belt." Southerners spend a lot of time in church, they are
punctual in their attendance, but for the last twenty years a
casual observer cannot sit through most of the crowded Protestant services without thinking of George Bernard Shaw's comment that Christianity would be a marvelous philosophy if
only the folks would try it. This "secularization" is even reflected in the work of the itinerant tent evangelists.

Forty years ago, the hymn-singing evangelist who staged the
"tent meetin'" revival asked the convert for a sacrifice to prove
good faith. A man was redeemed because he gave up smoking or
drinking or consorting with painted women. The sawdust trail
was a trail of personal abnegation. Today the revivalist simply
asks the sinners to believe, believe, and the Berlin wall will
come down, television will abjure violence, the Chinese Communists will become missionaries, and anxiety will only be

another name for a headache. Today, the secretaries do not have to forswear sin with commercial men nor does the advertising salesman have to abjure beating his wife. Redemption is a tranquilizing experience, no longer a conflict between body and spirit.

Forty years ago the Baptist, Methodist, or even the Presbyterian who rose in the world might have joined the Episcopal Church which throughout the South has always been the aristocrat's church. But material wealth is so much more easily come by since 1940 that many of the Methodists, Baptists, and Presbyterians have turned their own church into an Episcopal Church, insisting on a much more formal religious service, on more elaborate vestments for their clergymen, on a more imposing edifice for their place of worship.

The middle-class parishioners remade their church in their own image. One consequence of their efforts has been to rob the minister of his authority. He no longer made more money than the members of his congregation, he made less. He no longer accounted to the officers for a charity financed by men of great wealth, he accounted to fuel-oil distributors who had once been mechanics and to contractors who had once been carpenters.

As the middle-class proliferated, their need for self-expression also grew. Lacking the talent or inclination for politics, traditionally the province for the rich man's personal ambition, the well-off layman found he could fulfill his hunger for expression by managing his church. He along with others like him gave the church money, and then they formed a church committee and decided jointly how they would spend it. Eventually, too, this committee began to oversee the content of the Sunday sermon since they wanted their church to reflect them, not their minister who was now but an agent.

When the race issue began intruding on Southern life, the

middle-class deacons, stewards, elders, and trustees told their clergymen, "Stick to religion."

As a result, the Protestant Church throughout the South is rarely the champion of the unpopular cause, not even the unpopular cause remote from the racial crucible. The church conforms in almost all respects to the prevailing beliefs and sentiments of the overpowering majority. What makes this so cruel a situation is that belief in the efficacy of religion, if not belief in its substantive truths, is widespread. The South has been called a myth and much of the South's interior dialogue is in terms of myths, particularly religious myths. To these everyone but the devil and the Communists presumably subscribe. Thus when the Reverend Edward Cahill of the Charlotte Unitarian Church ran for the school board, he seemed a sure bet until several letters in the newspapers pointed out Unitarians do not believe in the divinity of Jesus. The votes of a few hundred Unitarians, ten Jews, and that of the organizer for the Textile Workers Union were all Cahill finally received.

All political candidates in the South proclaim their belief *in* religion—Christian religion, as they call it. In all political advertisements, the candidate's most important boast is that "He is steward of the Second Methodist Church," or "He has been a member of the First Baptist Church for forty-three years." "He teaches a Sunday school class" is the most effective of all.

But in the South, religion does not instruct the middle-class, the middle-class instructs religion. The new uses to which people put religion are manifold. Mr. W. W. Taylor, a former member of the North Carolina House of Representatives, appeared before a legislative committee in March of 1959. He came as a representative of small businessmen who opposed passage of a seventy-five-cent minimum wage law for the state.

Said Mr. Taylor, "Jesus Christ would be out of place if He returned to earth where employers were told what they could pay their employees." Clearly, he implied that Jesus would have opposed a minimum wage of seventy-five cents an hour.

There are a surprising number of clergymen who insist there is a Biblical injunction against integration. The Reverend John R. Richardson of Atlanta, Georgia, in one of his sermons, declared, "Segregation does not constitute a stigma to either the white or black races. It is merely a social separation that helps protect the racial integrity of both groups of American citizens. . . . The Bible favored a social separation of the races to promote racial purity." This was a sermon delivered not in 1890 but in 1954.

The Northside Missionary Baptist Church in Glenville, Georgia, requested the Georgia Baptist Convention not to use any monies it had contributed in any desegregated enterprise. Said the Northside Church members, "We sincerely believe it is not the will of our Heavenly Father for different races of people to intermarry and produce a mixed and mongrel race. . . . This action is taken not because of any hatred for any race, because of color, but because social and school mixing produces mixed marriages." [5]

The Episcopal Reverend James Dees, whom I discussed in Chapter One, is also president of the segregationist North Carolina Defenders of States Rights, Inc. Dees has also served on the editorial board of the *Citizens Council*, the official segregationist newspaper published by Bill Simmons somewhere in darkest Mississippi. "Of one thing we are certain," says Dees, "the races of the earth are not equal. They are not equal mentally, morally, nor are they the same in any number of ways physically. And when you mix a lower with a higher, then you drag down the higher." (Fortunately or unfortunately,

[5] James Wesberry, "Court Decision Rocks Georgia," *Christian Century*, August 18, 1954, p. 988.

as the case may be, the Episcopalians caught up with the Reverend Dees. Late in 1963 he left his Episcopal parish and organized a church of his own, announcing, "I have had all that I can stand of [the Episcopal Church's] social, economic, and political program of socialism, pseudo-brotherhood, appeasement of Communists, so-called civil rights, and of its rejection of much that I consider to be fundamental to the Biblical faith." Dees' new church goes by the name Anglican and is an independent Episcopal congregation. Its membership will be culled from those who worshipped with the Reverend Dees in his Statesville, North Carolina, parish.)

James Sellers in *The South and Christian Ethics* says, "Segregation must be discussed for what it is: a religion, a theology. It is in fact the unrepentant Southern kingdom of God, offering the same comfortable false piety to white Southerners today that the institution of slavery did a hundred years ago. It is *temptation,* just as slavery was. It is the invitation for the Southerner to build himself a proud world. . . ." [6]

Mr. Sellers is at once profoundly right and at the same time profoundly wrong. While people may believe intensely in a series of credos, that belief does not make of the credos a religion. A religion usually insists upon a total ethic, even if that ethic is symbolized by simple dietary observances, the Jews avoiding pork and shellfish, the Catholics meat on Friday. Christianity, for example, changed men's natures by insisting they be merciful, and while men are not perfectly merciful, they are more merciful than if there had been no Christianity.

Nor can we say segregation is a religion in the perverted sense that Communism is a religion. Communism provides what is essential to a religion, an expectation. It promises that once the State owns the material means of production, men will be good and earth will be a paradise. Segregation has

[6] James Sellers, *The South and Christian Ethics* (New York, Association Press, 1962), pp. 115-22.

neither an ethic nor even an expectation, at least neither an ethic nor an expectation *sui generis.*

But I introduce these objections not to cavil with Mr. Sellers. His observation that segregation is a theology is right in that it is an adequate and satisfying *substitution* for hundreds of thousands of people. It replaces the traditional theology. Segregation resembles a religion because of the intensity of belief it commands and musters from its adherents. But segregation is not a religion. It is a heresy, and as divisive a heresy to American Christianity and Constitutional America as the Albigensian heresy was to Roman Catholicism in the thirteenth century. The courage and valor of some Protestant clergymen comes from this realization.

Since the late 1940s the famous evangelist Billy Graham insisted on integration at all his meetings and revivals. Graham had been asked to go to Little Rock, Arkansas, during the crisis in that city, and to Birmingham, Alabama, at the time of the street riots in 1963. But Graham conducts his revivals only at the invitation of the local Protestant churches, a fact which was not fully explained in the press. Thomas F. Pettigrew tells of the time Billy Graham was urged to allay the racial tensions in Little Rock:

All the segregationists ministers were opposed to his visit. . . . To some, the reason appeared to be that Graham's comments on race would destroy his influence as an evangelist: "He would slant his sermons toward integration and that would destroy his religious effectiveness to the people. Besides, most people in this town are Baptists and they just couldn't possibly go to services that were unsegregated, so all in all I just think it would stir things up and worsen things." [7]

[7] Thomas F. Pettigrew and Ernest Q. Campbell, *Christians In Racial Crisis* (Washington, D. C., Public Affairs Press, 1959), p. 3.

The most interesting division in Southern Protestantism is within the Methodist Church, which is the only denomination with a completely segregated hierarchy. Negroes occupy the Central Jurisdiction of the Methodist Church, totally segregated with its own bishops; a church within a church. The Reverend Dr. Philip Wogman, a Methodist clergyman, discussed this division in *Christian Century* calling this racially divided structure ". . . more deeply entrenched in the sociology of America's largest denomination than it was twenty-five years ago. At the same time the moral dilemma has widened for Methodist thought on race relations as a problem of Christian social ethics, generally keeping pace with that of the rest of Christendom." [8]

The Methodist Bishop and Cabinet of the Mississippi Methodist Conference issued a statement:

We each declare anew our support of the doctrine and historic positions of the Methodist Church.

Tensions of many kinds are in the world today, among them is that of race relations. The Ninth Amendment to the Constitution of The Methodist Church places racial relationships on a voluntary basis. By the provisions of this amendment integration is not forced upon any part of our Church.

Our Conference has a great program in evangelism, education, missions, and other areas. Let us move on to do the work of the Church, loving mercy, doing justly, and walking humbly with our Lord, pressing toward the mark of the prize of high calling of God in Christ Jesus.[9]

This is a curious position for Methodists to take, completely at odds with Methodist history. It is not too exaggerated

[8] Philip Wogman, "Focus on the Central Jurisdiction," *Christian Century*, October 23, 1963, pp. 1296-1298.
[9] *The Mississippi Methodist Advocate*, Jackson, Miss., January 16, 1963, p. 2.

to say the Methodists started out in England as an early CIO-NAACP of the Anglican Church. Methodists argued that the church had to concern itself with the whole man and it was Wesley himself who said it was the duty of the church to comfort and help the poor and homeless. The Methodists, led by William Wilberforce, Granville Sharp, and Thomas Clarkson abolished slavery in the British Empire. Thomas Paine, who first waged war against the slave trade, failed when he made slavery a political issue. In his pamphlets Paine urged, "No king but liberty and equality." Wilberforce, Sharp, and Clarkson succeeded because they made slavery a moral issue. The British at the time had large investments in the West Indies where the economy was based on Negro slavery, and the English Cabinet argued that slave ships trained the nucleus of the British fleet. But Wilberforce convinced Parliament that no Christian could believe in slavery. (Wilberforce died in 1833, a month before Parliament outlawed slavery.)

The Methodist "Social Creed" of 1908 included such goals as a living wage in every industry, abolition of child labor, and "the recognition of the Golden Rule as the Supreme Law of society and the sure remedy for all social ills." In the same year, when thirty-three Protestant denominations formed the Federal Council of Churches of Christ in America and drew up their statement of social principles, they copied almost verbatim the Methodist Social Creed.

But segregation is more than a bone in the throat of Southern Protestantism; it is a partial paralysis of the brain center. It often produces different muscular and nervous responses. The Reverend Charles Jones of the Presbyterian Church of Chapel Hill, North Carolina (University of North Carolina), let student ushers seat Negro members on an integrated basis in the pews early in 1952. Forty members of his church resigned and brought formal charges against the Reverend Jones. They charged him with neglect of the sick, with failing to properly ordain his elders, and with using an unorthodox hymnal. Jones was "tried" first before his session, composed of the church elders. The session supported Jones, but the forty dissidents placed their charges before Presbytery, composed of an elder and the minister of each of the churches in the district. The Reverend Jones was defended throughout his ordeal by Frank P. Graham, elder in his church and former president of the University of North Carolina, but the Presbytery found against him. The clergyman then appealed to the synod, a state-wide group. The synod turned the affair back over to the Presbytery.

While the unhappy subject of race was never even mentioned in the charges against the Reverend Jones, or in his statements of defense, it certainly was crucial to the case.

After four years of church litigation, the Reverend Jones felt he had had enough and resigned his pulpit He founded the Community Church in Chapel Hill on an integrated basis. This church flourishes today. While these charges passed from session to Presbytery to synod, the dissidents betook themselves to the local Episcopal Church. But David Yates, who was rector, told them immediately he had every intention of integrating, too. The dissidents returned to the Presbyterian Church of Chapel Hill only to find that the minister who had replaced Charles Jones now had colored worshipers in his pews.

There is no question that Charles Jones won his fight. The dissidents were unable to face the inevitable, for Chapel Hill which houses thousands of students is a sophisticated, progressive community, populated by girls and boys and faculty members from all over the United States and from many foreign countries. But not only did the Reverend Jones lose his job, the segregationists lost their privilege.[10]

Too frequently the dissidents win their fight, often convulsing their church. During World War II, Southern sympathy

[10] Conversation with Dr. Frank P. Graham, December 25, 1963.

swelled for Toyohiko Kagawa, the Japanese Christian who had built nearly two hundred and fifty Protestant churches in Japan between 1911 and 1940. In the bad days of the war, Southern church publications found comfort in the knowledge that a civilized Christian influence might temper Japanese militarism, because Kagawa had converted nearly a hundred thousand Japanese.

Kagawa visited the South after the war and in 1950 spoke to over a thousand people at the First Methodist Church in Charlotte. Kagawa told his audience he was shocked by the signs proclaiming one facility for colored and another for whites. He delivered three such sermons but the Southern press rarely quoted him. Instead they described the large crowds, and what the ladies wore, and who was having the tea and reception afterward. At one civic club luncheon, shocked Southern businessmen listened unbelievingly as Kagawa told them they could win against the class-conscious Communists only with Christian socialism. "Without God," he said, "there can be no democracy and without Christian socialism there can be no happiness." After that, there was never any publicity about the great Japanese Christian and only the New York *Times* carried his obituary in 1960.[11]

The Protestant segregationist directs as much of his venom toward the National Council of Churches as he does toward the Freedom Riders, the sit-ins, and the Northern "agitators." In race relations, the National Council has been the most active of all Protestant organizations. The Council dispatches speakers to every Southern area, it sets up study groups, it publishes and disseminates probably the best material on the subject. On August 25, 1963, the Council, through its Commission on Religion and Race, underwrote a full-page advertisement in the New York *Times*, setting forth its position on school desegrega-

11 Facts from the Charlotte *Observer*, October 20, 1960; quotes from the author.

tion, housing discrimination, and Negro employment, stating:
"We believe that the August 28 March on Washington under
the unified and responsible leadership, assuring a demonstration free of violence, will dramatize the urgency of the civil
rights legislation now before the Congress."

Despite the National Council's considerable influence it is
still a difficult task to reach the Protestant segregationist of the
deep South; even in the Border states the local Protestant
church rarely participates in any racial progress.

It is instead the United States Attorney General and his staff
and the Negroes with their writs, their demonstrations, their
protests, and their unbelievable patience who insure progress.
Time and time again, the district judge tells Negro complain-
ants, "You have not exhausted all the remedies open to you,"
and time and time again the Negro spends another eighteen
months going through state courts, finally to appear before the
district judge again with the truth: "I've done it. I've exhausted
all the remedies, but I'm not exhausted."

Carson McCullers, the Southern novelist, wrote to editor
Ralph McGill:

> All of us seek a time and a way to communicate something
> of the sense of loneliness and solitude that is in us—the hu-
> man heart is a lonely hunter—but the search of us Southern-
> ers is more anguished. There is a special guilt in us, a seeking
> for something had and lost. It is a consciousness of guilt not
> fully knowable or communicable. Southerners are the more
> lonely and spiritually estranged, I think, because we have
> lived so long in an artificial social system that we insisted was
> natural and right and just—when all along we knew it wasn't.
> The fact that we bolstered it with laws and developed a secu-
> lar liturgy and sacraments for it is evidence of how little we
> believed our own deceits.[12]

12 McGill, *op. cit.*, p. 217.

Dr. T. B. Maston, professor of ethics at Southwestern Baptist Theological Seminary and a member of the Advisory Council for Southern Baptist Work with Negroes, spells it out for us:

> As [Gunnar] Myrdal so pungently has said, "America is free to choose whether the Negro shall remain her liability or become her opportunity." It now seems, more than a decade after Myrdal wrote, that time is fast running out. The world awaits the decision of America.[13]

If anything, the dilemma of the Jewish clergy in the South is more excruciating than the Protestant. Where some Protestant clergymen definitely believe in what they say pro or contra, and say it, the rabbi is frustrated. It is, without qualification, impossible to find a rabbi who does not hold segregationists in contempt and who does not hold in contempt those of his congregation who insist on his silence.

Sociologist Albert Vorspan, writing in *American Judaism*, says that "white groups—Jews included—are no longer the leaders of the civil rights fight. Negroes are. Those Negro organizations which in the 1940's clung desperately to Jewish labor and white liberal leadership today find these old allies an embarrassment in many instances, virtually the enemy in a few cases. Negroes have seized control of their own destinies." [14]

The Jew missed an opportunity, an opportunity to give the sort of help he himself has had to ask all through these long bitter centuries. The Jew missed this opportunity not because he lacked sympathy for the Negro and his cause, but because the Jew feared his own security depended upon conforming with the habits, attitudes, and prejudices of the surrounding society. Like their Protestant counterparts the Jewish middle-class congregants told their clergymen, "Stick to religion."

13 Thomas Bufford Maston, *Segregation and Desegregation: A Christian Approach* (New York: The Macmillan Co., 1959), p. 5.
14 Albert Vorspan, "The Negro Victory and the Jewish Failure," *American Judaism*, Fall, 1963, p. 7.

Long before the Supreme Court delivered its desegregation decision, there were many Jews of the South deeply worried by the activities of the ultra-liberal American Jewish Congress which filed an *amicus curiae* brief on behalf of the NAACP in the original school segregation cases. Some of these Southern leaders told Dr. Israel Goldstein, the then president of the organization, that they might cut back their allocation unless the Jewish Congress curtailed its "racial activities."

The more conservative American Jewish Committee, under the leadership of Irving Engel of New York City, made every attempt to establish a strong liberal stand on the race issue. In 1959, Mr. Engel convened a meeting of several Southern chapters in New Orleans and invited Rabbi Charles Mantinband of Hattiesburg, Mississippi, the most outspoken integrationist of all the Southern rabbis, to speak. Mr. Engel also invited me, but none of us cleared the air. A delegate from Memphis confirmed our fears when he rose and said, "You Jews from Brooklyn should keep your long noses out of our Southern way of life."

A year later, in 1960, the Central Conference of American Reform Rabbis held a closed session over which the late Rabbi Emil Leipziger presided. The rabbis did not show to advantage. They were almost as hysterical as the lay members of the American Jewish Committee. But their hysteria, of course, had a source different from the sources which fed Protestant hysteria. While Protestants imposed a silence on their clergymen because they feared the Negro, Jews imposed a silence on their rabbis because they feared white Protestants. Only the Negro was without fear, and the Negro was more threatened and deprived than whites, Jew or Protestant.

There are rich Protestant churches in the South and poor ones; churches which sing the hymns of Handel and Bach and churches which sing "The Old Rugged Cross" and "The Little Brown Church in the Wildwood." The vast number of Protestant poor find their way into the Fundamentalist sects—Will Herberg called them the sects of the disinherited—but both rich and poor fear the Negro invasion. If the Negro invades the primitive sects, the disinherited white will want to move into the rich man's church. Jews do not have sufficient numbers to support a rich man's temple and a poor man's temple, nor are they worried about the colored man's invasion. There are few Jewish wage earners in the Southern towns; most of the Jews are self-employed. They are almost wholly an entrepreneurial class. I remember visiting with my rabbi and two officers of the Temple one night when I mentioned that a new Jewish family had come to town. The officers whipped out their notebooks and asked his name, the size of his family, his wife's age, and finally, "What does he do?" I said the newcomer was the CIO organizer in the area and the two officers immediately closed their notebooks and said no more. For all they cared, he might just as well have been a Grand Inquisitor.

Protestants are watching the social revolution of the Negro knowing its success will affect their economic, political, and social structures: the politician fearing loss of power; the employer fearing that the end of discrimination will ultimately bring unionization; the worker fearing he will be displaced; the farmer fearing that the Negro will marry his sister; but the Jew has no such worries.

The Jew is already virtually unemployable. Therefore, he is a professional man, or a merchant, or a Northern manufacturer's representative. The Jewish factory owner cannot fear unionization because he is already unionized. The Jewish factory owner is unionized because he feels himself doubly exposed, both an employer *and* a Jew. Neither he nor his fellow Jews would dare expose themselves to parading Christian pickets. (The experience of the rubber and chemical workers indicates that the Jewish employer joins his Gentile opposite number in resisting unionization only when his employees are safely Negro.)

The textile union some years ago asked me to sound out the management of the Lowenstein people about mediating a strike in their Rock Hill, South Carolina, plant. The workers had lost the strike and to save face, the union indicated it was ready to settle for a five-cent increase. This didn't fool the Lowensteins. Their lawyer asked, "Why can't the union organize our competitors instead of badgering us all the time?"

But the unions know enough to attack at the weakest point. A Mr. Cooper can walk out of his mill in Henderson, North Carolina, and spend the next year watching one thousand strikers picket while they sing "Onward, Christian Soldiers," but a Mr. Goldberg dare not watch singing Gentile pickets line up at the relief wagon.

Lowenstein and Cone, two of the largest textile complexes in the South, have been unionized for years because their ownership is Jewish, while Firestone, Cannon, and Stevens, their giant competitors, have never had to sign a union agreement. In Gastonia, North Carolina, the largest mill city in the world, only the mills operated by the Gurney and Goldburg families who are Jewish have submitted to a collective bargaining agreement. The Negro, too, understands that the Jew is the weak point in the white power structure of the South. By instinct, the Negro launched his strongest demonstrations in Birmingham, Atlanta, Richmond, and Savannah, against the Jewish-owned department store. Tragicomically, Jews clutch my arm to tell me Negroes are anti-Semitic.

There is indeed considerable anti-Semitism among urban Negroes, an attempt, perhaps to use another minority group as a substitute target for the hostilities they feel toward the more powerful white Gentiles. Mr. Roi Ottley points out: ". . . the Northern Negro comes into contact with discriminatory white men at four vital points—as fellow worker, as landlord, as merchant, as employer. In the latter three particularly the white man with whom he deals is likely to be a Jew. The anti-Semitism of the Negro can be understood partly, therefore, as simply an expression of anti-white feeling." [15]

Two of our leading historians of the minority groups in America write that "Negro anti-Semitism is partly a sign that Negroes share an attitude that is prevalent in our culture . . . partly an attempt by Negroes to make their own status seem better by expressing prejudice against another minority group." [16]

It should be noted, on the other hand, and I base this on my own considerable communication with Negroes, that most realize Jews are probably, on the average, less prejudiced against them than are other whites; that Jews are more often willing to trade with Negroes, hire them, rent to them; and that Jews in the North give a great deal of support in money and social-action experience to organizations dedicated to ending racial segregation.

In my own city the leading Jewish manufacturer sought for years to become a member of the Board of Directors of the Community Chest. In Charlotte this board has represented the top social level of what is called "the power structure." And there was rejoicing in the Jewish community when Mr. Isidore Witcoff (not his real name) was finally elected. I met him right after his first meeting but Mr. Witcoff looked terribly dejected. He said wearily, "They handed out the solicitation cards and the louse gave me all the Jewish names."

But the Negro wants to be *the Negro* on the board. All new-

15 Roi Ottley, *New World A-Coming* (New York, Houghton Mifflin Company, 1943), pp. 122-36.
16 George Eaton Simpson and J. Milton Yinger, *Racial and Cultural Minorities* (New York, Harper & Bros., 1953), pp. 196-97.

comers to the American open society fought against a specific identification in sociological or political terms. Immediately upon achieving citizenship, the Irish, Poles, Jews, Italians, Hungarians, and Czechs wanted to be known as either Republicans, Democrats, or Socialists. The Negroes are also interested in our political parties, but that's a mere detail as far as they are concerned. Roy Wilkins says the NAACP "will fight Democrats and Republicans" who oppose the late Mr. Kennedy's civil rights proposals of 1963. Mr. A. Philip Randolph, the father of the social revolution of the American Negro, and for thirty years a powerful force in organized labor, has never referred to "Labor and the Negro railroad workers in my union." He has always said, "Labor *and the Negroes.*" Bayard Rustin, deputy director of the March on Washington, has called for a political coalition of "Labor, liberals, *and the Negro.*"

The Negro calls attention to himself at every level of our national life and he calls with clarity and vitality.

There is no reason for the Jew of the South to fear the Negro insurgent politically. Except in isolated instances, the Jew does not participate vigorously in Southern political life. His withdrawal is due neither to indifference nor insufficient patriotism. Jews make adequate political impact through their support and contributions to candidates, contributions far beyond the proportion contributed by their Gentile counterparts. The Jew ordinarily refuses to enter political life in the South because the terms are hard. If he runs for the city council, he must run as "our Jew" or if he runs for the school board he must run as "the Jewish member." This the Jew refuses to do. He wants participation as a Tar Heel, a Virginian, a Southerner, a privilege which the surrounding society usually refuses. A liberal newspaperman in one of these Southern cities spoke with reverence of the leading Jewish merchant in his town who supported every public charity for over half a century. Said this newspaperman nonchalantly, ". . . all the Goldstein boys married *American* girls."

One of the paradoxes of Southern life is that the white Protestant welcomes the Jew, as a Jew, in his civic and communal organizations, the specific condition the Jew dislikes and often will not accept, while the white Protestant denies the Negro participation on the same basis which is often precisely what the Negro wants.

Nor is there danger of the Negro intruding upon the religious, communal, or social life of the Jew. The Jew himself is socially segregated from the mainstream of Southern social life. Conceivably, the Jew could achieve social communication with Gentiles below his economic level but he tries only for the top strata of the social establishment and, when rebuffed, retires into his own religious and social groups, piling one activity atop the other. One has but to look at the statistics concerning Jewish-Gentile mixed marriages in the South to see this. Most of these unions involve a Jewish male and a Gentile female. But the Jewish merchant does not marry the sister of his Christian competitor; he marries his sales girl. The Jewish lawyer does not marry, nor even meet, the daughter of a Christian colleague; he marries his secretary whose father is perhaps a barber. Social life between Jews and Gentiles in the South has a definite limit. Between five and six o'clock each evening, after the last sale is recorded and the last client quieted, the shades are drawn and the Jew goes one way and the Gentile another. While the Jewish bourgeois wages a frustrating psychological war against Gentile separatism, the young Jewish intellectual reconciles his science-oriented skepticism with the longing to impart a sense of Jewishness to his children, a development sweeping American communities which may well change the tenor of Jewish life in this country.

If the local Protestant Church of the South has a sorry record in the social revolution, the Jewish fellowships in the South have an even sorrier record.

But nothing helps. The bitter irony of it is that demagogues throughout the South "accuse" the Jew of inspiring the whole Negro movement. Leander Perez, Sr., of Plaquemines Parish, Louisiana, publicly says, "The Jews are leading the Negroes. They'll resent it and I say they are unadulterated damn liars because I do resent any Goddamn Jew trying to destroy our country and our rights and that's what they are doing, and they are using the Negro for it." [17]

The Southern Jews failed the Negro for the overly complicated but obvious reason that Jews failed to understand that anti-Semitism has nothing to do with racial segregation or anything else. If the American Jewish Congress never filed one *amicus curiae* brief, if Irving Engel never tried to commit his entire conservative organization to the Negro, if the Anti-Defamation League never committed itself to the cause of civil rights, the anti-Semite would never have missed a beat. All the anti-Semite needs is Jews, not liberals, not racists, not patriots, not scientists, not fools, not villains, only Jews.

No one expected the Jews of the South to become crusaders. It would have accomplished little and, besides, the Negroes never solicited crusaders. The Jewish fault was in bringing their lay influence to bear in silencing the rabbinate and, to some extent, silencing their national organizations. Southern Jews have been particularly disturbed by the presence of Northern rabbis among Freedom Riders. Rabbi Kurt Flascher in *Jewish Currents* of May, 1963, describes the pressure the Jews of Albany, Georgia, brought to bear upon him and Rabbi Israel Dresner when these two clergymen demonstrated with Negroes. The Albany Jews telephoned all the rabbinical organizations claiming that the presence of Northern rabbis placed Southern Jews in a difficult position.

[17] Reese Cleghorn, "The Segs," *Esquire*, January, 1964, p. 72.

In Montgomery, Alabama, in 1956, Rabbi Seymour Atlas, of Agudath Temple, took part in a radio program during Brotherhood Week. A Roman Catholic priest and the Reverend Ralph Abernathy, a Negro, were the other participants. *Life* magazine reported the program and included a picture of the three clergymen who were reviewing the progress of the Montgomery bus strike.

The Temple's board of trustees were, to put it mildly, distressed. They were annoyed at *Life,* at the Reverend Abernathy, and particularly annoyed at Rabbi Atlas. They demanded that he ask *Life* for a retraction. Rabbi Atlas explained that *Life* didn't make retractions except when its reporters were in error, which in this case they weren't and that he had willingly participated in the program. The trustees ordered the rabbi to make no further statements outside the temple and to stop inviting Negro clergymen to the weekly Hebrew class. To compound the ugly situation, a week later Rabbi Atlas sent off to the newspaper, as is the usual custom of all clergymen in the South, the title of his weekly sermon, which he called "Social Integration." The rabbi wanted to discuss the successful integration of the Arab minority with the Jewish majority in Israel. The trustees had had enough. They accepted Rabbi Atlas' resignation and voted to ask the next rabbi for a contractual pledge not to discuss segregation "in any manner, shape, or form"; almost the same wording was used by the 1917 Alabama legislature in proscribing the manufacture of whiskey "on land, under the sea, or in the air." [18]

Charles Mantinband of Hattiesburg, an outspoken rabbi and a popular one, found it terribly hard to keep fighting on two fronts. It was hard enough contending with the segregationists but doubly hard contending with members of his

[18] Harry Golden, "A Rabbi in Montgomery," *Congress Weekly,* May 13, 1957, p. 109.

congregation who circulated round-robin letters condemning
the "mischief-making" rabbi. A national foundation contributed twenty-five hundred dollars to the Hattiesburg Temple
honoring Rabbi Mantinband's "sane approach and wisdom in
dealing with the racial issue." The board of directors grew
panicky. They were afraid to accept the money, fearing re-
prisals. But their panic was inspired by more than twenty-five
hundred dollars. It was in part inspired by the Jewish drive
for middle-class status and the desire to reflect the culture of
the majority; in part inspired by the historical Jewish fear
that when the Gentiles are in trouble, the Jews catch hell; and
in part inspired by the hope not to be troubled by forces no
community can control.

But Rabbi Mantinband was not alone. Rabbi Marvin Rez-
nikoff of the Liberal Synagogue, Baton Rouge, Louisiana, not
only helped integrate his Ministerial Alliance but actually de-
fied the legislators in the Louisiana capitol. Rabbi Robert
Kahn of Temple Emanuel of Houston, Texas, was the author
of the Race Relations Message of the Central Conference of
American Rabbis, and in Jackson, Mississippi, Rabbi Percy
Nussbaum of Congregation Beth Israel was consistent in his
heroic stand for justice, both in and out of his pulpit.

Having considered the agonies of Protestants and Jews, both
of whom have varying degrees of religious autonomy, we discover a curious truth: at one level, true autonomous democracy may not be democracy at all. And at another level
religion, with policy determined by a rigid hierarchy, may be
a more democratic and equalitarian religion than any other.

Roman Catholicism, too, has suffered the ravages of the
rising middle class which has diminished the importance of
the priest. Catholics feel much the same fears as Protestants
and Jews and there are probably as many Catholic segregationists in proportion to their numbers as there are Protestants. Many of the Catholics I know in the South are much

closer politically to the Protestant Senator from Virginia, Harry Byrd, than to the Catholic Attorney General, Robert Kennedy. But Roman Catholics comply with desegregation orders of their church, and their compliance is directed solely by the way their church is organized.

In seven of the old Confederate states the Southern Catholics desegregated their parochial schools and churches immediately after the Supreme Court decision. In some instances, they had desegregated a year before the Court read its ruling; some of them, two years before. They accomplished this because the moral direction came from the top, from the bishop of the diocese, and obedience is one of the cardinal Catholic virtues.

This is not to say the bishop makes his flock integrationists. Significantly there has been little, if any, integration in Catholic institutions in Mississippi and Alabama. In these states, the rigidity of the surrounding society is so firm not even the bishop, or for that matter, the pope, can so quickly obliterate hardened attitudes re-enforced by law and custom.

But if there is any "give" to the society, any flexibility, any interior debate, the bishop can and does surprise many of his parishioners. When Archbishop Francis Rummel of New Orleans desegregated his school system, there were devout Catholics who expressed immediate outrage. "No such orders had come from Rome," they shouted. "We are a monolithic structure."

Ah, but a monolithic structure they soon found they were not. They sent a petition to the Holy See complaining they did not want to desegregate. The Vatican dismissed this petition and in effect told these segregationists, "The Bishop is the boss and now you have the wishes of the Holy Father, if ever you doubted he wanted integration."

By September of 1963, the New Orleans Archdiocese Office of Education announced a record enrollment of 74,283 pupils

in parochial schools, an increase of 1,000 over 1962's enrollment. Last year 200 Negro children attended Catholic parochial schools previously all-white.

The Catholic schools of New Orleans integrated because
there was leadership which said it must integrate and integrate now. There was bitterness over this decision: the Archbishop had to excommunicate three parishioners, but there
was no vacuum which the white supremacists could fill with
their confusion and nonsense about states rights.

The problems of integration, of racial imbalance, overwhelm
us when there is no leadership, when there is no responsible
chain of command from the top to the bottom. When such a
chain exists, when such responsibility to Christian and democratic principles as integration and equity is exercised, the
problems are helped toward solution and grievances redressed.

Newton Grove in Sampson County, North Carolina, is a
small agricultural village where the pace is slow and deliberate in all things. There were two Catholic churches in this
little Southern village—The Church of the Holy Redeemer
for whites, and St. Benedict's for Negroes. They were situated
one hundred yards apart, on the same tract of land wholly
owned by the Roman Catholic Church. The bishop of the
North Carolina diocese is Vincent S. Waters, born in Virginia.
Ten years ago he decided upon a racial merger of these two
parishes. This decision provoked more excitement in Newton
Grove than the decision the Confederacy made at Appomattox
Courthouse. No one in Newton Grove protested Appomattox,
but they protested Bishop Waters' decree.

Newton Grove Catholics drew up petitions which demanded
that the Bishop grant them an audience. The Bishop gave his
parishioners a simple reply: "After the order I have issued
is obeyed, I will be glad to talk to you about it."

The two parishes merged on May 31, 1953. It was a perfect
spring day, and the Bishop drove to Newton Grove from

Raleigh to celebrate the first of three masses for both whites and Negroes in the Church of the Holy Redeemer. Twenty-five white men, surly and arrogant, waited near the rectory demanding to see the Bishop. But the Bishop was already about his holy offices, having been escorted into the church by two deputy sheriffs and a cordon of young priests. The mob pushed onto the porch of the rectory, spurred by their own anger and the screams of their women. A young priest, Father George Lynch, barred the doorway. The men turned back. Hearing of this disorder, the Bishop promised to grant these men an audience, but he would see them one at a time, a gambit that effectively dissipated their collective anger.

The near-riot was the last expression of Catholic fury in Newton Grove. True, some of these parishioners drove as far as sixty miles to hear mass and make confession. And on sub-sequent Sundays, only eighty-four white and Negro Catholics attended mass out of four hundred communicants. Within a year, however, Monsignor James McSweeney, Bishop Waters' Chancellor, reported Newton Grove was "back to normal." Ten years later, Monsignor McSweeney said all the communicants had returned to the parish (save those who had moved away for economic reasons; as in all Southern farm areas, there has been considerable migration from Newton Grove and the number of parishioners has dropped by one hundred since 1953).

The reaction to his integration order led Bishop Waters to issue a pastoral letter on June 12, 1953, read in all Catholic churches under his jurisdiction (which includes all of North Carolina except Belmont Abbey College in Belmont). Said the Bishop:

In the future so there can be no misunderstanding on the part of anyone, let me state here as emphatically as I can: there is no segregation of races to be tolerated in the diocese of Raleigh. The pastors are charged with the carrying out of this teaching and shall tolerate nothing to the contrary. Otherwise, all special churches for Negroes shall be abolished immediately as lending weight to the false notion that the Catholic Church, the Mystical Body of Christ, is divided. Equal rights are accorded, therefore, to every race and nationality, as is proper, in any Catholic Church, and within the church building itself, everyone is given the privilege to sit or kneel wherever he desires and to approach the sacraments without regard to race or nationality. This doctrine is to be fully explained to each convert who enters the church from henceforth in the diocese of Raleigh.

The Bishop also said: "As a Southerner, I am not unmindful of the forces of this virus of prejudice among some persons . . . and I revolt against our children being infected with it."

Dr. Carl E. Gaddy, Sr., retired Baptist preacher from Micron, North Carolina, in a letter to the Open Forum of the Raleigh *News and Observer* commented, "As I see it, there are but two things the good folks in the Catholic Church around Newton Grove can do, worship with the Negroes or go to hell."

The "good folks around Newton Grove" chose not to "go to hell."

The old ratio of three white Catholics to two Negro Catholics still prevails. The total Catholic population is 273, including 142 children. The breakdown between whites and Negroes? "We don't record it that way," the Monsignor told me recently.

Bishop Waters integrated Newton Grove a year before the Supreme Court decision of May 17, 1954. He set a pattern for Catholic institutions of the South. In Arkansas, Tennessee, Virginia, and Texas, Catholics grumbled about integrated churches, but never again was there anything resembling the mild disturbance in Newton Grove that pleasant Sunday in 1953.

The Catholic diocese of North Carolina was not the only one to anticipate the Supreme Court decision. Back in 1947 Belmont Abbey College took the chance of violating city and state ordinances by conducting a week-long conference of white and Negro students from various North Carolina colleges. It was probably the first time in North Carolina that Negroes roomed with whites and ate in the same dining halls. In June of 1952, the abbot of the college announced that henceforth Belmont Abbey, a four-year liberal arts college, would accept Negro students regardless of consequences. Today the College is integrated and so is its sister college, Sacred Heart, and so is the grammar school. Belmont Abbey now has seventy Negroes in a total enrollment of two hundred and fifty.

Let us remember, however, that Southern Catholics had another advantage, in addition to the acknowledged leadership from their church superiors.

Most of the Catholics who have come South in the last thirty years belong to the managerial class. They are salesmen, regional or branch managers of national concerns, advertising men. The local power structure identifies them immediately as one of their own. Furthermore, Catholics, for one reason or another, achieved an immunity from suspicion during the postwar era. No one accused a Catholic of subversion. If the Catholic Bishop desegregated his churches and schools, the Red-hunters had to look the other way. A charge of Communism leveled against a Catholic priest was nothing short of ridiculous. As Glazer and Moynihan comment in *Beyond the Melting Pot,* "Fordham men were checking up on Harvard men when Senator Joe McCarthy was dictating our foreign policy." I admit that in the pursuit of my own ends I have always felt a larger security because of my close friendships with Bishop Vincent S. Waters, Father Cuthbert Allen of Belmont Abbey, and the labor priest Father Maurice Sheen of York, South Carolina.

This is neither here nor there in understanding the great racial crisis of the South. The Catholics have proved themselves strong in dealing with the racial problem. They have proved themselves not only stronger but more flexible than either the Protestants or the Jews, although on such policies as birth control or child adoption policies Catholics as a whole are often illiberal in contrast to Jews and Protestants.

The simple secret is that the priest is not afraid of losing his job. The simple secret is that the priest knows the dogmas of his church, and knows that if he interprets them liberally his church will back him up, that Rome itself will support him, for Rome has no fear of any action that will enlarge the influence and reputation of the church.

The lesson here is that the ordinary Catholic was no more an integrationist in New Orleans, Georgia, or North Carolina than the ordinary Protestant, but all the Catholic schools were totally integrated where only a small portion of the public schools had token integration. The Catholic clergy did not back away from the problem. The Protestant clergy did back away from the Negro, and the rabbinate, while not backing away from the Negro, backed away from the Protestant.

And it was, in the long run, a Catholic to whom liberal America listened. They listened to President John F. Kennedy not because he had the power and history of the Roman Catholic Church behind him, but because he had the Constitution, the courts, and the electorate behind him. Certainly, liberal America quickly adjusted to Lyndon B. Johnson. Nevertheless there is a certain symbolic significance in the fact that our second Emancipator President was our first Catholic President just as there is a certain significance in the fact that our agnostic President, Abraham Lincoln, made of the Civil War one of the unique spiritual and religious quests in the history of mankind.

Kennedy, no less than Lincoln, found the office of the Presidency not only the office of the Chief Executive, the Commander-in-Chief, and the leader of the party, but also the office of the "national church." For though the President is a secular figure, he also, no matter what his personal faith, reflects Americans' concern with matters religious.

As Carl Degler so remarkably insists in *Out of Our Past,* we are a secular but not an antireligious society. "Our Presidents invoke the Deity and offer Thanksgiving prayer, our armies and legislatures maintain chaplains, and the state and federal governments encourage religion through the remission of taxes." [19]

Defending the New Deal, Franklin D. Roosevelt said, "The New Deal is as old as Christian ethics, for basically its ethics are the same . . . it recognizes that man is indeed his brother's keeper, insists that the laborer is worthy of his hire, demands that justice shall rule the mighty as well as the weak." [20]

Dwight D. Eisenhower opened every Cabinet session with a prayer and attended church services punctually and with attendant publicity. All Presidents commend Jews on Rosh Hashana and Yom Kippur and wish the Greek Orthodox Church a merry Christmas on January 6.

There is an American Church, a mass of church-going Americans, who understand neither the Ten Commandments nor the Constitution but who are sure both are interchangeable. We have had Presidents who felt the same way. But both our Emancipator Presidents saw that the American Church had divided itself into two sects: one sect claiming the race issue was a social and economic question and the other that it was a moral question that had only one resolution. One sect

[19] Degler, *op. cit.,* p. 97.
[20] *Ibid.,* p. 349.

is populated by industrial and urban parishioners and the
other by agrarian worshipers.

As early as the Civil War and definitely because of it, the
Northern churches realized they had to adapt themselves to
the new needs of the urban complex. By the turn of the century, this was the positive policy of every church above the
Mason-Dixon line. Much the same thing happened within
the Catholic Church. In 1891, Pope Leo XIII, spurred on by
the urgings of James Cardinal Gibbons of Baltimore, issued
his *Rerum Novarum* aligning the Catholic Church with the
"dignity of labor," the "equality of rich and poor," and the
"moral obligation of employers to pay fair wages."

The Social Gospel that washed over the North never made
a ripple in the South, however, an agricultural and rural area
with none of the urban problems.

Because the American Church is divided does not mean
either half is ineffective or that the Southern Church is in-
humane. This American Church faced the crisis of the Depression and the rigors of World War II with unity, but it cannot
resolve, by instruction or example to its parishioners, the
racial problem.

It was left to President Kennedy as it was left to President
Lincoln to invest this political issue with spirituality. And
neither Lincoln nor Kennedy challenged the churches. Both
Presidents left the churches alone.

At one point, Lincoln's War Department authorized the
provost marshals of the Union Army to depose Confederate
ministers, preachers, and priests. The Northern churches began inundating the South with volunteer preachers to occupy
these empty pulpits. Lincoln immediately stopped this trans-
gression, writing to the commanding general in St. Louis in
January, 1863, that, "It will not do for the United States to
appoint Trustees, Supervisors, or other agents for the
Churches," and in May, 1864, to the military commander at

Memphis, "I am told that . . . the military put one set of men out and another set of men into the building. This, if true, is most extraordinary. I say again, if there be no military need of the building leave it alone, neither putting one set in or out of it, except on finding someone preaching or practicing treason, in which case lay hands on him, just as if he were doing the same thing in any other building, or in the street or highway."

John F. Kennedy never made any public appeal to the churches for support. In fact, when he was an aspiring candidate he told reporters once that he put the Constitution ahead of his religious faith which, in 1960, produced a noticeable annoyance in the Catholic press of America. Mr. Kennedy went to the church issue once when he told Protestant ministers in Houston, Texas, that as a Catholic he had every right to be President and that no Protestant had anything to fear from a Catholic in the White House.

Mr. Kennedy's appeals on behalf of his Civil Rights Bill of 1963 and on behalf of the Negro were always made to citizens, not to churchgoers. But they were always ethical appeals. No religious man could ever misunderstand what the President asked.

His address to the General Assembly of the United Nations on September 20, 1963, had more of a religious than a patriotic fervor: "I hope that not only our nation but all other multi-racial societies will meet these standards of fairness and justice. We are opposed to apartheid and all forms of human oppression. We do not advocate the rights of black Africans in order to drive out white Africans. Our concern is the right of all men for equal protection under the law—and since human rights are indivisible, this body cannot stand aside when those rights are abused and neglected by any member state."

Lincoln's argument was that slavery was wrong and Kennedy's that segregation was wrong, and this is different from the political argument that slavery and segregation are illegal.

CHAPTER NINE

WHY THE RESISTANCE?

THE ADMISSION of James H. Meredith to the University of Mississippi cost an estimated $406,508: $292,769 was for overtime pay and travel expenses of the 541 United States Marshals; $67,723 was for supplies and equipment; $23,469 for communications; and $22,547 for miscellaneous—including $11,668 for repairs to vehicles damaged during the rioting on the University campus September 30, 1962. It cost the Department of Justice nearly one half million dollars to register one Negro student in what is, at best, a second-rate college.

During 1963 more than twenty thousand demonstrators, Negro and white, were arrested. Ten persons died under circumstances directly related to racial protests. Thirty-five known bombings occurred during the year.

What is behind all this?

When England discussed the slave question at the end of the eighteenth century, Prime Minister Pitt proposed to the French government that the two nations unite in abolishing Negro slavery. Three hundred thousand persons gave up using sugar in their tea as a protest against the sugar plantations in the West Indies, the slave trade's stronghold.

225

France was not enthusiastic. The French peasant himself was a virtual slave. When a man is poor, he has no enthusiasm for "liberating" another.

The Englishman was poor too, almost as poor as the peasant of France; but the Englishman had been caught up in a great religious revival. The poor Englishman helped abolish the slave trade.

Pertinent to our story is the fact that the arguments in France and in England in the early 1800s as well as those in the United States in the 1850s were the same arguments. It was the argument that said, "The Negroes are happy," "We understand them," "They are really children in heart and mind," and, "If the outsiders would only leave us alone, all would be well."

These are the arguments used by the segregationist in the 1960s. It is reasonable to assume that racial segregation is really a psychological extension of Negro slavery, since no new arguments have been raised against its abolition.

The segregationist says of Chief Justice Earl Warren, "He is trying to destroy our way of life." A century ago, the State of Georgia put a price on the head of abolitionist William Lloyd Garrison, because, said the legislature, "He is trying to destroy our way of life."

The white supremacist hates Justice Earl Warren and he has hated Harry Truman, and he hated John F. Kennedy absolutely. Curiously, there was never any serious hatred against President Eisenhower.

But the outrage felt against a mild civil rights man like Truman and against a civil rights President like John F. Kennedy involved more than race. Partly the hatred was inspired because both were liberal Democrats. Southerners who may have been moderates on race had an opportunity to express their feelings against Truman and Kennedy and remain loyal Southerners to boot. They could express opposition to the

New Deal, the Fair Deal, and the New Frontier, which to them was the all-important opposition.

But with Eisenhower, the Southern racial moderate had no such worries. There are many Southern doctors, for instance, who are among the strong supporters of the White Citizens Councils. These doctors are not really worried about the race issue, but they support the racists because of the "socialized medicine" proposals introduced first by Mr. Truman and again by Mr. Kennedy. Much the same can be said of the entire sophisticated business community in the South. These men give moral and financial support to the segregationists because it is the more convenient way to wage war against any new social legislation. Alone, the doctors, mill owners, and real estate men would not be enough. They can muster personally very little passion where race is concerned, and their political goals are diffused. But joined with the great mass of the people who resist recognition of the Negro as an equal, indeed a phalanx moves against reason.

From what springs of hatred or pride or ignorance comes the intense resistance?

I am not speaking here of the sniper who killed the NAACP organizer, Medgar Evers, by felling him with a rifle shot from behind; I am speaking of the decent men on the Birmingham School Board who to this moment still deny Medgar Evers' children the right to attend a public school of their choice. I am speaking not of the psychopaths who bomb Negro churches; I am speaking of the respectable preachers who will not conduct an integrated service. I am speaking not of the red necks running amuck in a riot; I am speaking of governors and state attorneys general thoroughly conversant with law and the Constitution of the United States. I am speaking of the people who work at desks, sell rolled steel or cars or advertising space, of the people who teach, form little theater groups, and support community concert series.

These are the people who so desperately resist equal rights for the Negro that they cannot even acknowledge changes transpiring about them and throughout the world, changes inconceivable ten years ago, omnipresent changes which affect not only income and housing and travel and schooling but the quality of life itself. Why can they not sense this quality, feel it, perhaps even rejoice in it?

Sadly they cannot. They pretend the tenor of life is as it was in 1923 or 1903 or 1883. The strength of their protest is so strong that as they live longer, grow richer, know more luxury, more and more harshly and more and more contemptuously do they treat the law and the Negro.

This phenomenon of resistance has intrigued me for the last twenty-two years. I have known Southern liberals, men who have supported the New Deal, the Tennessee Valley Authority, the reforms of Franklin D. Roosevelt, the work of the United Nations, foreign aid, the Atlantic Alliance, the Korean police action, but when history faces them with the race issue, they pound the table with their fist and "nigger" is all they can think.

One is aware conditions are bad in the North. Regarding housing, employment, and schools, the Northern cities of New York, Chicago, Philadelphia, and Detroit sit on smoldering volcanoes because of *de facto* segregation. But there is this difference: every elected official of the North, every community leader declares himself against racial segregation and discrimination of every kind. And this declaration and impulse shames the majority and often makes some of them change their discriminatory policies. The man who moves from an apartment house because a colored family occupies one of its units will not confess his aversion to colored people though he knows that is why he moves. He will give instead a hypocritical answer to the question why is he moving and this is a good sign. To be ashamed is to start on the way to respectability and honor. But the first ten Southerners even in the liberal city of Charlotte in the liberal state of North Carolina will echo their leaders and public officials and declare, "He isn't ready," "This is not the time to do it," and further South, this man on the street will be prompt to say the Negro was happy until Northern agitators put a bug in his ear and that it is only a Communist who would want to change the Southern way of life. And this man on the street in Charlotte or Birmingham or Decatur is an ordinary man, ordinary in that he is no psychopath, no night rider, just a man with a mortgage to pay off, children to educate, and a wife he loves.

On occasion, however, this ordinary man is ferocity itself. In Southside, Virginia, Mr. W. was a prominent preacher and farmer. He owned a hundred-and-fifty-acre farm. Every year, Mr. W. borrowed money for his operating expenses and repaid it after he sold his crops. Before 1954, the ordinary man paid little attention to Mr. W. Southside thought he was just another Negro preacher who worked hard hoeing. Mr. W. decided, however, to run for one of the three seats on the County Board of Supervisors, the county's governing body. The day after this preacher had announced his candidacy, his creditors demanded the eight thousand dollars he had borrowed. These creditors, ordinary men all, had lent money on demand notes, taking Mr. W.'s oral promise that he would begin repayment after he sold his crops. There is no other way for bankers or creditors to lend planting money and collect interest in Southside than this. But these creditors lend money to Negroes only on demand notes so they can harass any colored man who steps out of line, and they are as effective and murderous in this harassment as snipers harassing stragglers of an invading army. They brought economic disaster upon Mr. W.[1]

These ordinary men on the subject of race relations some-

[1] *Report on Voting Restrictions in Virginia,* Civil Rights Commission, W. Hale Thompson, April 27, 1958.

times stop speaking the same language. Consider the lengthy conversation between the United States Attorney General Robert F. Kennedy and Governor George C. Wallace of Alabama which took place in Montgomery on April 25, 1963.

The Attorney General made the trip to the Alabama capital and his first statement to Wallace was: "I hope, Governor, all of these matters concerning the federal court orders could be handled at the local level and the problem worked out by state officials and those involved in the political life and business of this state without outside influences at all." The Attorney General explained that his federal responsibilities centered neither on segregation nor integration but on the obligation to enforce the law and see that federal court orders were obeyed.

Following is a résumé of a conversation between two Americans who were able to communicate nothing at all to each other.

The Governor said that since Mr. Kennedy was his guest, the Attorney General could select what matters they would discuss.

Integration at the University of Alabama, said the Attorney General. He had to enforce the law which ordered that Negroes be admitted to the student body and he was sure the Governor would do no less than enforce the law.

Governor Wallace confessed he had a different interpretation of the law and he would enforce the law as he saw it.

"In the case of a federal court order," said the Attorney General, "no one needed further interpretation."

No, said Wallace. It was up to the Governor of the state to maintain peace and protect the safety, health and morals of the people. "You can't have peace in Alabama and an integrated school system." Governor Wallace went on to point out that Alabama had more peace and law than Washington, D.C.

Mr. Kennedy agreed that Washington, D.C. had problems and, for that matter, so did Boston and Chicago.

Well they did not have that problem in Alabama, said the Governor, pressing what he thought was an advantage. They had safety and peace and good will in Alabama and there was no place in Montgomery or Birmingham where a body could not walk at night in perfect safety.

At which point, Mr. Kennedy and Governor Wallace agreed they could solve nothing through further conversation.

The decent, ordinary everyday Southerner has a low boiling point on the subject of civil rights. In 1946, the Alabama Legislature passed the Boswell Amendment to the State Constitution, which made legal the arbitrary outlawing of Negro votes. When Joe Gelders, a professor at the University of Alabama, told a meeting that this amendment was a violation of civil rights, he was kidnaped, brutally flogged, and left for dead on a lonely road.[2]

But, of course, any journalist could make an encyclopedia of horror stories. My purpose is to reveal only the intense depths of resistance the ordinary man musters against the Negro encroachment. In Danville, Virginia, the library trustees closed the library rather than integrate it. A group of citizens formed an association for the purpose of operating a private library (for whites only), each contributing ten dollars a year in dues. This association managed to obtain a rent-free building and had every intention of operating this private library if the city council would pass a bill enabling them to buy the books of the former public library at a token fee. The association collapsed when the city council could find no constitutional means to pass such a bill. When another group of white citizens circulated a petition to have the library reopened on an integrated basis, the city officials quickly pointed out that several names were duplicated on

[2] Robert S. Allen, *Our Fair City* (New York, Vanguard Press, 1947), p. 121.

the lists. The city fathers of Danville, a town in mid-twentieth century America, accused their citizens of practicing fraud. Said the city fathers, "We do not have that many citizens who want the library reopened." [3]

In Albany, Georgia, the city fathers also closed the library before they would integrate it. When they reopened it finally, they did so by implementing my own Golden Vertical Plan wherein Negroes and whites stand but never sit. Ten years ago, when I prepared this plan, I thought it was a joke. Negroes and whites in the South stand together in line at the banks, at the car wash, at the draft board with no acrimony. So I said the solution is to take the seats out of the schools. But I never meant "solution" literally. The Kress Department Stores took all the stools out of their snack bars and thereby avoided the inconvenience of the sit-ins. Albany, Georgia, has a library now because no one has to sit down with a Negro; everybody can read standing up.

Black Monday for Little Rock, Arkansas, was September 23, 1957. One thousand whites gathered early outside Central High School, scheduled for desegregation. They cursed, shoved, tore their hair, and wept when they learned the nine Negro students had been taken in through a side entrance. Not many in the crowd had even seen the Negroes approach. A diversion occurred when several people turned suddenly on newspapermen and photographers, knocking one of them down, pushing, shoving, and hitting the others. A police patrol broke through to remove the newsmen. Then the mob turned its attention to some Negro journalists. They jumped on the back of one of these reporters and knocked him to the ground, mauling and kicking him. The cry "the niggers are in our school" saved him. "Let's go get those niggers," screamed these ordinary people. To the white students peering

[3] Dorothy Miller, *The Story of Danville, Virginia* (Atlanta, Georgia, Student Non-violent Coordinating Committee, 1963).

out of the windows they urged, "Come on out. Don't stay there."

Meanwhile, fearful parents having heard of violence began to arrive at the school to get their children. The mob continued to push at the police barriers. There was grave concern lest the police themselves go under in the rush. Finally, it was agreed that the Negro students should be removed.

James Jackson Kilpatrick, editor of the important Richmond *News Leader*, editorialized that "Closing the public schools in Prince Edward County did not violate the U.S. Supreme Court's 1954 desegregation decision, and Negroes themselves are to blame for the fact that Negro children had no formal education for four years."

Mr. Kilpatrick elaborated on these same views on November 14, 1963, in an address at Hampden-Sydney College, a private institution for men located in Prince Edward County. He said that the 1954 decision stated only that no child could be denied admission to public schools because of his race.

"Exercising their prerogatives, and operating at every point through the processes of republican government," Kilpatrick went on, "the people [of Prince Edward County] closed all their public schools. They thereby achieved a status of complete obedience to the Supreme Court's decree. The county no longer was denying admission to any child to any public school, for there were no public schools."

Referring to the private segregated school system for white children, Kilpatrick said the Negro parents of the county had exactly the same opportunity.[4]

A group of Negro leaders called on the late Senator Willis Smith of North Carolina to discuss the prospects of employment in textile plants in their state. Senator Smith said there is only one solution: "Why don't you Negroes build some textile plants of your own?"

[4] *Southern School News*, Nashville, December, 1963, p. 5.

Ralph McGill, publisher of the *Atlanta Constitution*, recalls a discussion he and the late President Kennedy held. They talked about the great hatred for the Attorney General and the President himself which came from some sections in the South. President Kennedy said he knew the historical reason for this hatred but, he told McGill, he could not comprehend why 160 million Americans feared so simple a thing as respecting the civil rights of a mere 19 million. Men, continued the President, are so rational about everything else that it puzzled him they could reach such frenzied heights because a relatively few people wanted an equal share in national life.

The ordinary man, we have unfortunately learned, is a fierce and frightening prospect when he says no to orderly process, no to reason, and no to justice. These are perilous days for the ordinary man. A sense of mutiny which menaces all inspires the frustrated among us. This sense of mutiny is not endemic but it finds pockets of American life where it flourishes. There are forces alive in this world, as dangerous as tornadoes and cyclones, over which no one can promise control, and this is a terrifying and frustrating realization for some. Frightened of the twister, they run to the subterranean storm cellars where they brood and curse and blame. These are the Americans who are against for the sake of being against, the Americans who are frightened and want to make us fearful, who feel they are superfluous and want to make us useless too. All they need for their revenge is a cause. The cause can be a petition to impeach Chief Justice Earl Warren or a campaign to get the United States out of the UN and the UN out of the United States. It does not matter what the focus for this emotion is as long as the energies that emotion feeds can hurt and deprive other spirits. No cause better presents itself to the man looking for blind, unreasoning anger and bitterness than segregation and white supremacy.

For he can ravage and deny not only progress but people, and more than people—law.

The South is no stranger to this invading hate. Certainly this sense of mutiny encourages the resistance of the Southerner, the segregationist, the Negrophobe.

This is one reason for the resistance, but not the only reason.

The Southern politician gained seniority in Congress and in the state legislatures by disfranchising the Negro on behalf of racial solidarity. But the politician had to give fair value. He gave the poor man white supremacy, which at bottom, God save us, is first a sense of mastery and second, and more important, a sense of snobbery.

America made citizens out of immigrants within a generation, surely one of the greatest acts of generosity, of courage, of patriotism in history. America did this despite prejudice and fear and intense xenophobia. Every stranger was a threat—a threat to a job, a threat to policy, a threat to everyday living. Agitation never ceased. Close the gates, keep them out, make the country safe. It was an agitation that over several decades made some strange bedfellows. Many recent immigrants, part of the labor movement, were themselves desperate advocates of restricted immigration. Booker T. Washington, the Negro leader, warned America that further immigration from southern Europe would create a problem for the South more difficult and dangerous than the problem of the Negro.[5]

Congressman Thomas Abercrombie of Alabama, to his eternal discredit, said of the Southern and Eastern Europeans, "The color of thousands of them differs materially from that of the Anglo-Saxon." [6]

[5] John Higham, *Strangers in the Land* (New Brunswick, Rutgers University Press, 1955), p. 169.
[6] *Ibid.*, p. 168.

John Higham quotes the testimony of Texas Congressman Martin Dies, Sr., before a House committee to show that the Southern assault on the new immigration blended race feelings with Anglo-Saxon nationalism:

> Mr. Dies: As the little turtle, when the egg hatches on the sea shore instinctively makes for the water, so these beaten races of earth instinctively turn to the head of the government as the great father. . . . I would quarantine this Nation against people of any government in Europe incapable of self-government for any reason, as I would against the bubonic plague. . . . I will admit the old immigration of the English, Irish, Germans, Scandinavians and Swedes, the light-haired, blue-eyed Anglo-Saxons, or Celts—I mean the nations I have enumerated—
>
> The chairman: Pure Caucasians?
>
> Mr. Dies: Yes; they were great in their own country and great in our country.

And Higham goes on to show that although racial nativism tugged at men everywhere in the United States, during the prewar years it never established a really firm grip on public opinion outside the South and the West Coast. Those were its strongholds; the aroused and pervasive race-feeling of those areas touched the East and Midwest only to a limited degree. A spirit of confidence, sustained by the march of progressive reform, remained widespread throughout the era, and in the Northeast progressivism tended to inhibit racial anxieties. As long as Northeastern progressives took to heart their optimistic faith in environmental reform, they held the Anglo-Saxon tradition in check. But this was not true of the South or of the Far West. There, without anguish and with no apparent sense of inconsistency, reform-thinking accommodated itself to race-thinking; progressivism was for whites only.[7]

[7] *Ibid.*, p. 174.

It is no coincidence that white supremacy and the nativist movements blossomed together in the 1890s. But these movements never really took root in the North. The North's accelerated pace of industrialization diluted xenophobia by assimilating the immigrants into the labor force, the sweat shops, the railroad gangs. Just as the immigrants joined the laborers, so they joined the political life of their communities because the politicians cultivated their votes. Only the turmoil of World War I and its aftermath of suspicion and fear of subversion was strong enough finally to compel a law restricting immigration.

The South, ravaged by the Civil War, was unprepared for industrialization. Consequently, few immigrants made their way into the poor and labor-surplus South. In place of industrial wealth, the South substituted racial segregation. Treating the Negroes as inferior, white Southerners affirmed that despite their poverty they belonged to the elite.

By decreeing the Negro a sub-citizen, the Southerner's white society had one advantage over the Northerner's money society; the Southerner's wealth could never be displaced—his society was always stable whether the price of cotton rose or fell, whether panic swept the market place or not.

The Southerner had status, a status shared by the rich and poor men alike. It was a status the segregationist passed along to his heirs, unshakably his forever.

America had handed the ordinary Southerner a gift signed by the United States Supreme Court first in 1883 when it made it clear that the South would have a free hand in determining the civil rights of Negroes, and again in 1896, *Plessy v. Ferguson,* which declared the separation of the races was compatible with American democracy. This gift, supposedly given in perpetuity, let the Southerner detach himself from the tumult, confusion, and competition of twentieth-century life. The gift was a promise that the Southerner need never worry overmuch about wages, hours, or unions; about merit, education, or progress. He was not only fashion and family, he was virtue, too. His neighbors, the Supreme Court, history, and he himself had pronounced that he was superior.

But the United States Supreme Court was an Indian giver. It wanted the gift back. For the Negro decided he no longer need surrender himself and his aspirations, and this decision put the segregationist in agony. The encroaching, ever-demanding Negro threatened to displace the white supremacist and change his life.

The segregationist must, however, rationalize his passion. Hatred demands provocation, at least normal people believe they need provocation and will even manufacture provocation if need be. Men hate those who make them suffer, who insult them, who do them grievous wrong. To hate someone who has never done you a wrong, whom you do not even know, requires perverse imagination.

Now anti-Semitism has outlived most of the social revolutions of the world, because the anti-Semite is able to create for himself the illusion that the Jew wants to "take over." The anti-Semite has made the term "Jew" synonymous with "shrewd," "wily," "powerful," and so when he smashes a retail shop owned by a Jew or beats up a Jew in a dark alley he imagines he pits himself against a formidable enemy. "Behind Churchill and Roosevelt, stands the Jew," said Adolf Hitler.

And the Negro of the South is a formidable enemy to the segregationist. But the segregationist cannot at one and the same time call a sixty-year-old Negro, "boy," and describe all Negroes as lazy, shiftless, and childlike and still convince himself the Negro is shrewd and wants to "take over." This is implausible not only to the world, but to himself. So the segregationist fears the Negro's sex. He fears the Negro will marry his sister; that the Negro is so sexually powerful he will overwhelm whole groups of white women.

Yet when the segregationist discusses his phobia, he rarely if ever includes the female Negro. He fears her not at all. She will not seduce him, at least not permanently. The racial issue centers on the phalanx of "big, buck niggers." The segregationist is conveniently ignorant that tuberculosis is a frequent killer of the Southern Negro, a fact which indicates that there are a few skinny emaciated Negroes. For the segregationist, every Negro is a "big, buck nigger."

Behind the whole crisis we find a metaphorical necessity causing a war as bitter as the foolish beautiful Helen caused between Greece and Troy. Men died for the "ideal" of Helen's beauty as indeed they die for the "ideal" of a sexually pure society. For say what the segregationist will about natural selection, the segregated society is an artificial society. In artificial societies the imagination runs riotously romantic.

Once the segregationist created the menace of the oversexed Negro, it followed that Southern woman was in special danger. Being in special danger gave her a special role in a special place and in a special time. She became a psychological virgin, not in her own mind, but in the mind of her champions. She was a vessel of purity in need of constant protection by self-elected Knight Templars.

Lo! the age of chivalry was reborn. Chivalry to the Southerner, to paraphrase Edward Gibbon, has been and still is nothing more complex than the worship of the Jewish God commingled with the worship of the white lady.

Chivalry spread through the South for the same reasons it spread through pre-Renaissance France, Italy, England, and Spain, although instead of inspiring Petrarchian sonnets and Provençal ballads it inspired lynch mobs. Chivalry is the poetic adjunct to a social order wherein the upper-class males enjoy free sexual privilege with the women of a lower social order. The upper-class lady becomes in these areas an ornament, denied her classical role of love object and bed companion; she becomes first a substitute for poetry before a subject for caress and endearment.

I have heard Southerners say, "I never knew white girls did that until I was eighteen years old." I've heard the same words repeated often, only that the age differs all the way from twelve to twenty-two.

> She was the South's Palladium, this Southern woman—the shield-bearing Athena gleaming whitely in the clouds, the standard for its rallying, the mystic symbol of its nationality in face of the foe. She was the lily-pure maid of Astolat and the hunting goddess of the Boeotian hill. And she was the pitiful Mother of God. Merely to mention her was to send strong men into tears—or shouts. There was hardly a sermon that did not begin and end with tributes in her honor, hardly a brave speech that did not open and close with the clashing of shields and the flourishing of swords for her glory. At the last, I verily believe, the ranks of the Confederacy went rolling into battle in the misty conviction that it was wholly for her they fought.[8]

Wilma Dykeman and her husband James Stokely toured the South in the early fifties. In their book *Neither Black Nor White,* they record some interesting interviews:

> A Negro school teacher: "I'll tell you something that happened in one city in East Texas recently. Some of the leaders of one of the civic boys' club organizations met to discuss whether or not they should integrate the various branches of their club. In the office where they happened to be meeting a Negro boy was working. He was not in the discussion, no business there at all as far as these men were concerned, but he overheard all the argument. Didn't speak a word until after a while one of the white men said: 'Well,

8 Cash, *op. cit.,* p. 86.

one thing we're not going to have nigras marrying our daughters!' Then the boy said, 'Now wait a minute, mister. You mean Negroes aren't going to be marrying your wife's daughters. We've been marrying your daughters for a long time.' "

The white aristocrat could keep his wife on a pedestal in the parlor because he had a black woman in the kitchen and backroom, and the individual exceptions only made the rule more respectable. That such an arrangement degraded everyone concerned was no topic for polite conversation. One white Southerner stated the situation thus: "With segregation you've got miscegenation and lots of it; with integration you'd have intermarriage and less of it. One is inequality and hypocrisy; the other is equality and honesty." [9]

Probably America's best reporter of the generation said it flatly:

Segregation equals sex. Or perhaps one should say merely that sex is the basic reason for segregation. The strictures that forbid whites and Negroes to eat together, drink together, play together, talk together, are at bottom the result of white fear that such intimacies will lead to a breakdown in sexual barriers, and the involvement of blacks with white women. A dozen times I have heard whites say, "Of course I want full equality for Negroes—but under segregation." . . . Indeed, the issue is so distorted that, in the South, almost anyone who takes a strong line against segregation is sure to be accused of "advocating mixed sexual relations." But to most Negroes, intermarriage is not a vital preoccupation; it is an issue as remote as the Himalayas. What the overwhelming mass want is not a chance to marry a white

[9] Wilma Dykeman and James Stokely, *Neither Black nor White* (New York, Rinehart & Co., 1957), pp. 86, 121.

woman, but equal treatment and justice in the realms of economics, politics, and law, and opportunity to educate brown children decently. . . ." [10]

Gunnar Myrdal in *An American Dilemma* gave the underlying reason for segregation in the South as the psychological fear of Negro male retaliation for the white man's sexual relations with Negro women for the past two centuries.

When Theodore Roosevelt was criticized for having invited Booker T. Washington to the White House, he said that he had nothing but contempt for those Southerners who shrieked in public about miscegenation but leered as they talked, in private, about their colored mistresses and the colored children of white men they knew.[11]

"Do you want your sister to marry a Negro?" is not a simple question. It is the mark of an obsessed man, for no Southerner can imagine "yes" for an answer. A question which admits only "no" is no question at all. It is a code passed between guilty men over a guilty subject.

John Howard Griffin, a white Texan newspaperman, wondered what it was really like to be a Negro. He underwent a series of medical treatments that changed his color temporarily to black, shaved his head, and traveled from November 6 to December 14, 1959, through Mississippi and Alabama, Louisiana and Georgia. His book, *Black Like Me*, recounts his experiences.

In nearly every instance where he successfully thumbed a ride with a white man, questions from the driver inevitably revolved around sex. The white man kept asking the "colored" boy, "Tell me, did you ever have a white woman?" The Negro usually answers that he's not crazy enough to court a lynching.

10 John Gunther, *Inside U.S.A.* (New York, Harper & Bros., 1947), p. 694.
11 Edward Wagenknecht, *The Seven Worlds of Theodore Roosevelt* (New York, Longmans, Green and Co., 1958), pp. 230-36.

At this point the white man would get angry, "You're lying, you've thought about it, haven't you?"[12]

Not every Southern woman is as retiring and naive as her husband or brother or protector believes. A century ago, Mary Boykin Chesnut of Charleston, S.C., wrote:

> Under slavery, we live surrounded by prostitutes, yet an abandoned woman is sent out of any decnt house. Who thinks any worse of a Negro or mulatto woman for being a thing we can't name? God forgive us, but ours is a monstrous system, a wrong and an iniquity! Like the patriarchs of old, our men live all in one house with their wives and their concubines; and the mulattoes one sees in every family partly resemble the white children. Any lady is ready to tell you who is the father of all the mulatto children in everybody's household but her own. Those, she seems to think, drop from the clouds.[13]

As late as 1951 Mark Ingram, forty-four-year-old Negro sharecropper and father of nine children, was charged with assault with intent to commit rape by a seventeen-year-old white girl. The case was tried twice in Caswell County, North Carolina, half of whose population is Negro. The girl admitted that Ingram didn't come within "sixty-five to seventy feet" of her, but he leered at her. A magistrate convicted Ingram of simple assault and sentenced him to two years on a road gang.

The case was appealed to Caswell Superior Court in November, 1951. Like the magistrate before him, Superior Court Judge J. A. Rousseau dismissed the charge of assault with intent to commit rape, leaving only the charge of simple assault.

[12] John Howard Griffin, *Black Like Me* (New York, Signet Books, 1961), p. 78.
[13] Mary Boykin Chesnut, *A Diary from Dixie* (Boston, Houghton Mifflin Company, 1949), pp. 21-22.

The defendant's strongest point was his declaration to officers, supported on the witness stand by the plaintiff, that
he did not touch the girl at any time. How could a man
assault a woman without touching her? Both the judge, a
solemn jurist with seventeen years' experience on the superior
court bench, and Solicitor R. J. Scott, a dignified legal veteran
who rarely raised his voice, stressed that it was not necessary
for the defendant to have been in striking distance. It was
not necessary that he be close enough to lay his hands on the
girl. No one has the right by a show of violence to place a
person in fear.

I cite this case to show that the woman, the white woman,
is a goddess to the segregationist. Her words and her fears
every moment convince him. And he is always at pains to
protect her from the ravages of the ordinary world. He is
ordinary and will confess it; she is not, and never so accuse her.

This enables the Southerner to move through two worlds,
one populated by ordinary creatures and one populated by his
wife. He need never commit himself socially with the people
he meets unless he commits his wife.

I have known Jewish merchants in the South with a record
of business success and civic works, who have lived in their
community for over a quarter of a century in good fellowship
with their fellow Gentile businessmen but who have never
met the wives. Occasionally the wife of a Gentile merchant
will call for her husband and the husband will notice that
Mr. Goldberg is standing outside his store; he will say to
his wife, "That's Mr. Goldberg whom I always speak to you
about"; she will wave graciously and nod her head in recognition. Only occasionally is there an introduction and never
does she entertain the Jewish merchant in her home. When
Mr. Goldberg finds himself in the home of the banker, civic
leader, or fellow merchant at a meeting of the Retail Men's
Association or the Credit Bureau or the "Watch Pinetops

Grow" Committee, the wife remains upstairs. When the meeting is over she will come down and graciously shake hands with all the departing guests. She will be part of the meeting itself only when those attending are part of the accepted social circle. She will be gracious and pleasant to Mr. Goldberg and even to a Negro visitor to her home because she thinks of it in terms of communal affairs, civic betterment. But the wives of Goldberg and the Negro cannot be admitted under any such rationalization and remain forever remote.

Frederic Morrow, a Negro White House aide during the Eisenhower Administration, tells of a touching incident:

> I received an invitation from the Reverend Doctor Elson, pastor of the New York Presbyterian Church, which the President attends, to be present at a special pre-Inaugural service to be held in the church. It was scheduled for nine o'clock, and I asked my fiancée, Catherine Boswell, who was visiting relatives in the city, to be ready at eight, since all the guests had been asked to arrive there by eight thirty. . . The center portion of the large auditorium was roped off for members of the President's family, friends and staff. An usher met us and scrutinized our admittance cards for a long time. . . . In a very cool and impersonal manner, we were ushered to a rear seat across the aisle from the roped-off section.
>
> I looked about me and saw the faces of several colleagues —men with whom I work every day. They ignored me or looked over my head, with no sign of recognition. This often occurred when these men were accompanied by their wives. Perhaps they feel they may have to introduce me as a colleague, or perhaps they are embarrassed to speak to me before a group of people for fear it might indicate some kind of personal relationship. I didn't know, but afterward I never trusted them again.[14]

14 Morrow, *op. cit.*, pp. 118-19.

During the 1954 Congressional campaign the late Speaker of the House, Sam Rayburn, came to Charlotte. It was necessary to invite the six or seven Negro political leaders—those Negroes who bring out the vote in each of the black-slum areas of the county. I was speech writer for one of the political leaders at the time and attended a few soul-searching meetings. The boys were terribly worried: what if the Negroes bring their wives? For three sessions, the Democratic chieftains argued about this. Finally they asked would I undertake the job of telling the Negroes diplomatically that the invitations were for them only? I turned them down. They settled the matter by "reserved" seating arrangements. When the Negroes arrived they found themselves seated at separate tables.

At the inauguration of Governor Donald Russell of South Carolina in 1963, it was rumored that some Negroes had attended the reception after the inaugural ceremony. A group of legislators made a special trip to the governor and protested against this outrage. They went away satisfied and happier than when they came. The governor informed them that no part of the reception had taken place *indoors*.

There have been events at which the men and women of the white power structure have found it necessary to sit down with Negroes at the same table but in these instances the whites maintain the *status quo* by seeing to it that the service is on paper plates and without a tablecloth. The tablecloth is crucial. If Negroes for one necessary reason or another do enter the house, the wife will always explain she did not have a tablecloth on the table.

Chivalry always comes to the same demented, erratic end. Don Quixote signaled the end of chivalry when instead of charging dragons which he could not find, he tilted at windmills, and the Southern segregationist keeps table linens clean. Don Quixote believed he was a knight errant because the windmill tossed him, and the segregationist believes he is part of the elite because he eats on occasion with paper utensils.

And it is the man with table linen and silver and crystal stemware in his home who is crucial to this terrible issue. Sex is real enough in the imagination of the poor white but can it be that vivid in the mind and imagination of the banker, the lawyer, and the real estate man? Does he believe his wife and helpmate, who shops in supermarkets and leaves the gas tank empty usually is a goddess who needs his shield? He has no fears the Negro will marry his sister nor does the Negro threaten him with social oblivion. Yet it is he who initiated the whole fight to keep the Negroes out of the schools; it was this man who set up and incorporated White Citizens Councils; he who thought up the countless legal restraints to keep Negroes from the polling places.

And he did it to maintain a caste system.

Once the poor white and the tenant farmer and the one-mule tobacco grower realize they are no longer superior by virtue of a white skin, they will seek their own self-esteem and proof of individual worth in areas other than Negrophobia. The poor white will join labor unions, and the tenant farmer will vote for a "creeping socialist," for more farm subsidies, medical and hospital insurance, more social security and federally financed education.

The wife of the poor white will say to the employer, "My husband is a doffer in a mill and he gets $1.45 an hour and a doffer in a mill in Pennsylvania gets $2.00 an hour; and we've been willing to work for this wage because it was worth 55 cents an hour to us to tell the Negro to go to the back of the bus and to stay out of our schools, restaurants, movies, cafés; but now we can't say that, the law says we cannot say it; so give us that 55 cents an hour we've got coming."

The average weekly wage of the industrial worker of the South is $64.32 based on the figures of 1960 for 40.9 hours a week. The average industrial wage in the North is $98.42 for the same number of hours, a difference of $34.10. If you multiplied some two and three-quarter million industrial workers in the South by $34.10 a week you will see that racial segregation and the maintenance of a caste system has a lot more to it than putting a tablecloth on the table or circulating the myth about your sister marrying a Negro.

There's no greater example of this need to maintain a caste system than the city which thus far has given the most fierce resistance to the end of racial segregation, the city of Birmingham, Alabama.

Birmingham is sixty, perhaps seventy, years old. It has no "War Between the States" tradition whatsoever. Indeed, Birmingham has no links with the myths surrounding the antebellum South of dueling pistols, crinolines, and darkies singing spirituals under the big magnolias. Birmingham has no memories of the plantation society.

Birmingham became a city because its surrounding hills were rich in iron ore and coal. The white and Negro sharecroppers and tenant farmers came to the city to work in the steel mills and nearby mines. But since the Negro came from the agricultural society, he knew "his place" in the new industrialization and his place was to provide a psychological status for the working-class white.

When John L. Lewis came down to Birmingham to organize the miners, the whites agreed to the unionization on the gentleman's agreement that racial segregation would be maintained. The absentee owners were willing to go along with this arrangement because the white steel and coal workers of Alabama were willing to take less pay than the men doing the same jobs in Illinois, Minnesota, or West Virginia. Thus the poor white made a bargain which held sway among the industrial workers of the South: "I'll take from thirty to ninety cents an hour less if you keep the Negro in his place."

Birmingham is not upholding the Confederate tradition. It is upholding the traditions of a caste system which regulate the movements of everyone. The poor white stays in his place because the Negro stays in his.

Earlier we saw the Populists challenge caste in the 1890s. They lost then. Now the Negro challenges the system. And if the Negro wins, so will the poor white.

The segregationist talks in terms of tradition and culture and customs and honor, but the dynamitings at Birmingham give his speech the lie. Negroes do not displace white men in Birmingham. Really displaced in Birmingham is the conviction of pitiable poor white people that they have status. They are not so sure now.

Do not insist that this is a hard fact to face. It is not. There are steelworkers all over the world who have pride and conscience and lack Negroes to whom they can feel superior. It is true that most men need leadership to convince themselves they ought to be fair. One is hard pressed coaxing them sometimes. But it can be done. By law or perhaps even humor.

The Reverend James Reynolds called me once from the Charlotte bus station. He came by appointment but he had been delayed. I told him to go to the leading hotel where I had an account and we would get together in the morning.

Early the next morning, the hotel manager called me. "Harry," he said, "what color is Reverend Reynolds?"

"I never met him," I replied. "You have him there, what color do you think he is?"

"The consensus here is that he is a Negro."

I knew Reynolds had intended to spend two nights in Charlotte so I had to think fast. "I don't think that can be right," I said. "Reverend Reynolds is a Hindu who has converted to Christianity, that's why he isn't wearing a turban." I told the hotel manager that this was his lucky day, not only does he have a Hindu in his hotel but a Hindu who is a Methodist to boot.

When the Virginia-born Negro clergyman visited me later that morning he was profuse in his praise for North Carolina enlightenment and good will. "Wasn't it nice of the hotel manager to send me a bowl of fruit this morning?"

CHAPTER TEN

"WE SHALL OVERCOME"

"**L**ET THE NEGROES first prove themselves," argued the segregationist leader of North Carolina, Dr. I. Beverly Lake, with whom I debated at North Carolina State College. Dr. Lake, a former assistant state attorney general, represented North Carolina in the *Brown v. Board of Education* case which went to the Supreme Court. As I write, Dr. Lake (Doctor of Juridical Science) is again a serious candidate for governor.

Not every segregationist is as specious or subtle as Dr. Lake. Most segregationists who consent to a debate start right off with statistics showing how badly integration has affected Washington, D.C. The standards of the public schools have fallen and crime in the city is out of proportion allegedly because of the large integrated Negro population.

But what proof of themselves can Negroes muster when they and Dr. Lake and other segregationists know that until recently there was little danger throughout the South that any show of white violence against Negroes would bring legal reprisal or punishment?

In Brundidge, Alabama, in 1951, an armed band of whites

shot a Negro field worker. The mob acted on the suspicion the Negro had kidnaped a white woman. Actually, the Negro was the victim of a perverted rumor. He had carried the white woman's baby son to a doctor's office after the woman's car had been in a minor accident.

In many places in the South, white violence against Negroes is considered a virtue. It is hard to prove oneself in the face of unequal and cruel treatment.

Throughout the South and, to some extent, in areas in the North, law enforcement officers have no strict tradition of rendering justice to Negroes who have committed crimes against other Negroes. "They're big laughing children," said a McMinnville, Tennessee, judge recently as he gave a warning to a Negro guilty of repeated offenses against other Negroes.

Many Southerners believe Negroes should suffer corporal punishment. Negroes who resist arrest, who "get uppity," who are surly, who complain about their treatment, who refuse to obey orders, or who attempt to escape, are likely to receive immediate, corporal punishment, a whipping or a beating in violation of ethical penal practices and in violation of the laws of the state. When the wife of one Negro suspect refused to prosecute her husband, the white policeman said, "The next time he raises hell down there I am not going to arrest him but just work him over myself. That is the only way we can handle some of these troublemakers because if we don't see the fighting or trouble ourselves, the others will never prosecute. . . ."

There are perhaps several hundred Negro police officers now in Southern cities. They do their job, and their presence on the police force has had a beneficial effect according to most of the reports, but still these policemen work under a handicap. Other Negroes taunt them with the question, "Why don't you arrest whites?"

While I have no disposition to modify or wave away the statistical evidence about Negro crime, there are still certain factors about which most whites are ignorant. My home city of Charlotte, one of the most liberal in the South, arrests many Negroes each year for infractions and violations which beget only a warning for whites.

But there are other problems beyond the power of the police to modify. Not long ago in Charlotte, a man entered a bar and stepped on the newly polished shoes of another. The man with the shined shoes was demented. He had a long history of antisocial aberrancies. This time he drew a shiv from his coat and stuck it between the ribs of a man innocent of hostility who was trying to apologize. Multiply this madman by a thousand and you will realize a significant amount of Negro crime is committed by persons who should have been institutionalized long ago and for whom there is no room or institutional space.

It is hard enough for the South to provide adequate facilities for demented whites; for the demented Negro there is usually one institution in each state which cannot even keep up with the demands made by one large city, let alone the demands by one third to one half of the state, the approximate population ratio between Negroes and whites.

Considering that we never gave a thought to the needs of the healthy, ambitious, intelligent Negro, it is obvious that we would be absolutely callous and indifferent to the sick and deranged Negro.

There are areas in the South where respectable Negroes live in fear not only of the white man but of the itinerant Negro criminal, for the law is slow and bored when it has to test crime or civil suits involving two Negroes.

Southern courts have handed out thousands of two-year sentences to Negroes convicted of murder. The murder was that of another Negro and the court found the whole thing rather humorous and, moreover, did not want to crowd Negro jails at the taxpayers' expense.

Full integration of the schools in the South will probably lower the educational standards temporarily. But to demand that segregation be maintained on the grounds of Negro inadequacy is to argue that the *results* of racial segregation be the reason for perpetuating it.

Similar arguments have been advanced against all unpopular minorities through all history. It is an argument easily made invalid once equality is granted. Once whites and Negroes are treated alike, once Negro policemen can arrest white criminals, once Negro children can share the same teaching methods and use the same materials and equipment whites do, and once Negroes share equitably in the employment market, then statistics become proportional.

Count Mirabeau championed the Jews who sought first-class citizenship in post-Revolutionary France. There were many who argued the Jews had been too long in the ghettos; that they were parochial, knowing only how to read their own religious books; that they qualified only as peddlers. How could they make a fair contribution to France?

Mirabeau wanted Jewish equality not only as a principle of justice but for a practical advantage as well. He had seen enfranchised Jews in Holland and other countries who indeed had made contributions and he wanted as much for France. He contended that the true contributors to the state are those who share full economic, political, and cultural equality. Proof of individual worth is something each of us must earn by individual effort, he said, but "it is impossible to compete successfully with the rest of the population unless a man can live in freedom."

Injustice is a repetitious process. Injustice inflicts the same punishment and deprivations in the same way generation after generation. For the moment this injustice is practiced in the form of "tokenism." Many of the Southern moderates are proud of their accomplishment of token integration, particularly in such states as Virginia, North Carolina, South Carolina, Georgia, and Florida. Tokenism is the restriction established by a society which, in order to test its powers of resistance, takes a small dose of poison, or maybe even a few germs, but not too much for fear it would die. In Europe this was called *numerus clausus*. According to the *Universal Jewish Encyclopedia* (Vol. 8, p. 251), the idea was first introduced at the University of Padua and spread throughout Europe after the middle of the nineteenth century at the time when Jewish students were seeking academic degrees. Token integration is probably the most dehumanizing of all aspects of racial prejudice.

But Mirabeau's successful argument once and for all ended any claims to logical or social validity of the plea, "Let the Negroes prove themselves first."

Mr. Kennedy's logic did not deviate at all from Mirabeau's when he called Congressional leaders together in 1963 to discuss his new civil rights proposals. The late President told these men that the Negro, more than any other minority, needed legislation every step of the way.

Mr. Kennedy proved himself acutely aware of the fact that the Negro moving within our country has no hope of subterfuge or pretense. He cannot change his name to alter his origins, nor can he change his religion, nor can he move from cities to isolated areas. The Negro needs legislation every step of his way because he is born not only into a desperate economic and social complex, but he must struggle against a psychological complex which entraps and demeans every American, white and Negro. We cannot help recognizing a black man, and there are many whose recognition triggers terror, let alone contempt or condescension. This is a conditioned psychological response that only reason dissipates, but there are many who are unreasoning.

Of course the Southern politician has no intention of changing his thinking or the thinking of generations yet unborn. This politician's first reaction to the civil rights proposals of 1963 was that the "public accommodations" section would restrict the property rights of businessmen. Where the villains and the heretics once ran into the church for sanctuary, now they run onto "private property"—than which nothing is more sacrosanct.

The "public accommodations" section of the civil rights proposals makes no more an infringement upon private property than the legislation which requires a businessman to buy a license for his store or restaurant, and the legislation which forces him to admit public health authorities to inspect his place of business, and the legislation which demands he get a building permit if he wants to make an addition. The federal and state governments moreover specify the minimum wage this businessman must pay his employees and they limit the hours he can work them. Both the state and federal governments require a businessman to collect and remit taxes from both employees and customers, and government agents reserve the right to inspect an employer's books. In many states, local laws tell the businessman when he can stay open and when he must close, to whom he may sell liquor and to whom he may not.

Perhaps such laws are infringements on the rights of "private property." Perhaps they should be repealed. I know of no one, however, likely to undertake such a campaign. A law requiring the businessman to be color blind as to the complexion of his customers seems no more an infringement on his freedom of action than any legislation passed to benefit the public weal.

Nor is the Civil Rights Bill inhibiting legislation. It is, in fact, a form of legislation which seeks to create a balance in our national life.

James M. Dabbs, president of the Southern Regional Council, has said that the enfranchised, the integrated Negro may bring to the white Southerner a quality of balance, a wholeness the South has lacked in the past. Mr. Dabbs is a descendant of the Southern plantation society of South Carolina, a society which derived its necessary tension from a sense of guilt rather than from the internal struggles other societies count upon to make them strong.

Mr. Dabbs speaks of a wholeness to life, and here is the Negro and his NAACP who put the meaning of the Constitution to its clearest test; here is the Negro who has infused Christianity with a new vigor; here is the Negro who reactivates all the old American traditions, including civil disobedience.

The Congress of Racial Equality has an operating code for civil disobedience. Every member carries the card:

Don't strike back or curse if abused;
Don't laugh out;
Don't hold conversations with floor workers;
Don't block entrances to the stores and aisles;
Show yourself courteous and friendly at all times;
Sit straight and always face the counter;
Remember love and non-violence;
May God bless you.

When Martin Luther King called for Christian support for the Montgomery bus strike, the significance of one of his early sermons was not lost on the Christian scholars of America. From a small Negro church in the deep South came an amazing sermon on the meaning of Walter Rauschenbusch's injunction, "The chief purpose for the Christian Church is the salvation of individuals." There are Christian seminaries not too far from Charlotte where students have never heard of Paul Tillich let alone the Social Gospel of Walter Rauschenbusch. I do not mean that Martin Luther King is going to revive the Social Gospel of Christian America single-handed, but he is going to help.

Against this idea of health and wholeness the segregationist struggles unreasoningly. He has not even stopped to consider that if tomorrow he gave the Negro everything he demands, the Negro will have only gained his right to participate in America with his hands finally untied.

Once the Negro achieves his goals and eliminates all the legal obstacles to the right to vote, attend school, and compete with his skills in the labor market on a fair basis, only then will he be starting from scratch.

The immediate victor, the real victor, will be the white Southerner. He will be the victor first because a great burden will be lifted from him. The white Southerner will be able to go about his own business for the first time in nearly a century.

Though many Negroes today consider Booker T. Washington an Uncle Tom, I entertain no such disrespect for the memory of this great man. It is true that Booker T. Washington accepted racial segregation as a necessary part of Negro life in the America of the 1890s, but he did so with one grave warning to the white society of the South. He said, "Remember if you keep us in the gutter you will have to get down in the gutter to hold us."

The white Southerner will be able to move back into what was once the most politically creative society in the western hemisphere, the society that produced Washington, Jefferson, Mason, Pinckney, and hosts of other great minds. Men today, such as Senator J. William Fulbright of Arkansas and Senator Richard Russell of Georgia and Senator Lister Hill of Ala-

bama, men unusually qualified, have enslaved themselves all
these years because they had to worry whether Negroes are
moving from the back of the bus to the front and thereby
enraging constituents. These white politicians with the superior minds have been enslaved and handicapped no less than
the Negroes.

The human resources the South will gain are enormous.
North Carolina in the past twenty-four years has spent
$694,842 to educate Negro students in out-of-state colleges.
A Negro qualified for these funds if the subjects he wanted
to study were offered at a white college in North Carolina
but not at a Negro college. The state paid a Negro graduate
student $200 a quarter or $300 a semester to help his education along elsewhere. This $694,842 in twenty-four years is
rather a puny amount. I mention it only because few Tar
Heels have ever even heard of it.

The great paradox here is that the Southerner thinks of
himself as a fiscal conservative. He wants the budget balanced,
and in recent years he hangs the picture of Senator Harry
Byrd of Virginia in the space once occupied by William
Jennings Bryan.

Yet this fiscal conservative, with the lowest per capita earnings in the land, has wasted his meager resources in trying to
maintain facilities and whole systems in duplicate, for "white"
and for "colored," down to the two sets of unnecessary plumbing fixtures for the segregated toilets in the courthouse. The
waste of money has been so fantastic that much of it has been
hidden from view. If the Southern segregationist shows any
shame at all about maintaining the racial *status quo*, it is in
hiding some of the ridiculous costs of racial segregation.

The victory of the white Southerner will be so overwhelming
he will eventually agree with Dr. Albert Dent, president of
the Negro Dillard University in New Orleans, who said that
one day in retrospect the white Southerner will look back

upon the Supreme Court decisions of the 1950s as the beginning of his own emancipation.

The white Southerner will finally ask his own sister that question and she will laugh right in his face. She has been wise to him all along. The Negro seeks not white women but simply the right to be master of his own house, a role the South has been at pains to keep him from fulfilling. The Negro culture has been a matriarchy. The wages of the female domestic have been fairly steady, while the Negro male has been victimized as soon as the financial stability of the community was in the slightest danger. The Negro male is therefore an itinerant more or less, and he, like the children, are dependent on the money his wife and daughters bring home.

There are, of course, Negro psychopaths. There are authentic cases of rape by a Negro man upon a white woman. But if the law was as vigilant with white psychopaths who ravish Negro women, the Negro would often be shown more sinned against than sinning.

True, there will be intermarriage. But there has been some intermarriage under even the strict laws of the segregated Southern society, and marriage is nobody's business but the husband's and wife's. The obstacles to it in our society are very great. Even among people under the most favorable conditions, same race, religion, background, income, and education, marriage is often a gamble. For the foreseeable future, intermarriage between white and Negro will probably continue to be restricted to those who are self-sustaining by career in the arts or sciences or to *émigrés* abroad. These are the people who are not seriously disturbed by the inevitable alienation from their own socio-religious groups.

The German poet, Heinrich Heine, warned his fellow Jews in the middle of the nineteenth century, "We must be twice as good to get half as much."

This will be the hard truth the Negroes will have to face.

The Negro's entry into the open society as a political and economic equal will not bring him automatic ease and relaxation but automatic hard work and struggle. The Negro for the next two decades will be poorly educated, poorly informed, poorly trained, even if everything John F. Kennedy and he ask is granted tomorrow by an indulgent Congress. The Negro will have to be three times as good to get one third as much. By instinct, Negroes know that the way to reduce these odds is by education, and it is for the prospects of equal education he has made his boldest, strongest, and most sustained moves.

Eric Hoffer, the philosopher, has correctly stated that the ghetto was as much a fortress as it was a prison. Once out of the fortress, a man stands alone. When the ghetto walls of Europe crumbled, the Jews were dismayed to discover that the emancipation did not solve the problem of prejudice and discrimination. A great anguish followed, which resulted in mass conversions into the religions of the majority. Indeed, at least one third of the Jewish population of Berlin made this escape, an escape which is obviously impossible for the Negro, impossible even for those victims of self-hatred who would seek such escape. So many Negroes will be dismayed when final emancipation comes and there is no one to help them but themselves. For instance, there are places in our country from which I am excluded because I am a Jew. There are thousands of such residential areas, resort hotels, country clubs, fraternities, and luncheon and civic clubs for business and professional groups. And this discrimination is not wholly social. It effectively eliminates Jewish "competition" for patients and clients as well as the opportunity for many jobs which require complete social integration in the community, such as branch managers, regional sales executives, and so forth. But because this exclusion is not sanctioned by law and public opinion, I doubt whether it has seriously prevented the Jews in America from achieving middle-class status based almost entirely on their individual talent, character and ambition.

Mr. Kennedy's significance in the Negro's advance was not so much that he helped him along as that he understood his revolution was important and that it must succeed, not only in the cause of justice for the Negro but, more important, for the welfare of America.

Some of the Negroes themselves have failed to see this. I once asked Roy Wilkins of the NAACP about the humorless approach of Negro intellectuals to the civil rights problem and wisely Mr. Wilkins said, "When we Negroes produce an Albert Einstein, we will be able to laugh at ourselves too."

When James Baldwin told a Negro audience in December, 1963, "Let us not be so pious as now to say that President Kennedy was a great civil-rights fighter," he missed this whole point.[1] But Mr. Baldwin is not the only Negro intellectual who has been cynical about the racial activities of the late President, which reminds me of a story about the French Captain Alfred Dreyfus.

The Dreyfus Affair in France shocked the entire world at the turn of the century. The one Jewish member of the French General Staff was accused of treason despite the insurmountable evidence that he had been framed. The Captain himself was rather an unpleasant fellow who often tried the patience of Emile Zola and Georges Clemenceau, his most ardent champions. Clemenceau once said of the reactionary Dreyfus that never mind the influence of liberals, the Captain himself remained an anti-Dreyfusard. Over and over Clemenceau said that Captain Dreyfus was mistaken. "Dreyfus thinks we are doing this for him. Nonsense. We are doing this for France."

Attorney General Robert F. Kennedy told an American Jewish Congress audience in May, 1963, that the struggle

---

[1] Convention of Student Nonviolent Coordinating Committee, reported in *The Nation*, Jan. 8, 1964, p. 33.

for civil rights in America was an expression of true patriotism, an expression of true love of country.

The late President Kennedy was fully aware that the racial crisis invades America at a time when the country must be united and ready for the most crucial struggle of its history. Even in Jefferson's day, with continents remote from each other and communications primitive, the author of the Declaration of Independence realized that we "must have a decent respect for the opinions of mankind."

Mr. Kennedy knew that in our ideological struggle with the Communist world, our decision to do away with the barrier of a man's color or creed as a measure of his worth will win us friends. Emerson wrote: "Your manners are always under examination and by committees little suspected . . . but are awarding or denying you very high prizes when you least think of it . . ."

In reading Mr. Kennedy's two civil rights messages reproduced in this book, it is clear that the late President saw that our example will help men everywhere who struggle for freedom. It is also abundantly clear that the late John F. Kennedy realized that what the rest of the world sees and hears us do is not as important as what we see and hear ourselves do, and this is not as important as what God sees and hears us do.

The cruel truth and even more cruel coincidence is that our two Emancipator Presidents were assassinated within one century of each other before the fruits of their struggle were realized. Yet neither the assassination of Abraham Lincoln nor the assassination of John F. Kennedy can be traced directly to the race problem. History played us cruelly when Lincoln and Kennedy were taken from us in the midst of a gigantic task. The task of resolving the race problem is central in our history and both men were about the business and politics of racial conciliation. But at least history gave us these men and perhaps we, as a nation, may one day measure collectively to what they measured alone.

Lincoln told his Congress: "The dogmas of the past are inadequate for the stormy present. We must think anew, we must act anew, we must disenthrall ourselves."

One hundred years later, Kennedy told his Congress, "In this year of the Emancipation Centennial, justice requires us to insure the blessings of liberty for all Americans and their posterity—not merely for reasons of economic efficiency, world diplomacy and domestic tranquility—but, above all, because it is right."

MR. KENNEDY'S MESSAGE
TO CONGRESS

February 28, 1963

"Our Constitution is color blind," wrote Mr. Justice Harlan before the turn of the century, "and neither knows nor tolerates classes among citizens." But the practices of the country do not always conform to the principles of the Constitution. And this Message is intended to examine how far we have come in achieving first-class citizenship for all citizens regardless of color, how far we have yet to go, and what further tasks remain to be carried out—by the Executive and Legislative Branches of the federal government, as well as by state and local governments and private citizens and organizations.

One hundred years ago the Emancipation Proclamation was signed by a President who believed in the equal worth and opportunity of every human being. That Proclamation was only a first step—a step which its author unhappily did not live to follow up, a step which some of its critics dismissed as an action which "frees the slave but ignores the Negro." Through these long one hundred years, while slavery has vanished, progress for the Negro has been too often blocked and delayed. Equality before the law has not always meant equal treatment and opportunity. And the harmful, wasteful,

265

and wrongful results of racial discrimination and segregation still appear in virtually every aspect of national life, in virtually every part of the Nation.

The Negro baby born in America today—regardless of the section or state in which he is born—has about one half as much chance of completing high school as a white baby born in the same place on the same day—one third as much chance of completing college—one third as much chance of becoming a professional man—twice as much chance of becoming unemployed—about one seventh as much chance of earning ten thousand dollars per year—a life expectancy which is seven years less—and the prospects of earning only half as much.

No American who believes in the basic truth that "all men are created equal, that they are endowed by their Creator with certain unalienable Rights," can fully excuse, explain, or defend the picture these statistics portray. Race discrimination hampers our economic growth by preventing the maximum development and utilization of our manpower. It hampers our world leadership by contradicting at home the message we preach abroad. It mars the atmosphere of a united and classless society in which this Nation rose to greatness. It increases the costs of public welfare, crime, delinquency, and disorder. Above all, it is wrong.

Therefore, let it be clear, in our own hearts and minds, that it is not merely because of the Cold War, and not merely because of the economic waste of discrimination, that we are committed to achieving true equality of opportunity. The basic reason is because it is right.

The cruel disease of discrimination knows no sectional or state boundaries. The continuing attack on this problem must be equally broad. It must be both private and public—it must be conducted at national, state, and local levels—and it must include both legislative and executive action.

In the last two years, more progress has been made in securing the civil rights of all Americans than in any comparable period in our history. Progress has been made—through executive action, litigation, persuasion, and private initiative—in achieving and protecting equality of opportunity in education, voting, transportation, employment, housing, government, and the enjoyment of public accommodations.

But pride in our progress must not give way to relaxation of our effort. Nor does progress in the Executive Branch enable the Legislative Branch to escape its own obligations. On the contrary, it is in the light of this nation-wide progress, and in the belief that Congress will wish once again to meet its responsibilities in this matter, that I stress in the following agenda of existing and prospective action important legislative as well as administrative measures.

I. THE RIGHT TO VOTE

The right to vote in a free American election is the most powerful and precious right in the world—and it must not be denied on the grounds of race or color. It is a potent key to achieving other rights of citizenship. For American history—both recent and past—clearly reveals that the power of the ballot has enabled those who achieve it to win other achievements as well, to gain a full voice in the affairs of their state and nation, and to see their interests represented in the governmental bodies which affect their future. In a free society, those with the power to govern are necessarily responsive to those with the right to vote.

In enacting the 1957 and 1960 Civil Rights Acts, Congress provided the Department of Justice with basic tools for protecting the right to vote—and this Administration has not hesitated to use those tools. Legal action is brought only after voluntary efforts fail—and in scores of instances, local officials, at the request of the Department of Justice, have voluntarily made voting records available or abandoned discriminatory registration, discriminatory voting practices, or segregated balloting. Where voluntary local compliance has not been forthcoming, the Department of Justice has approximately quadrupled the previous level of its legal effort—investigating coercion, inspecting records, initiating lawsuits, enjoining intimidation, and taking whatever follow-up action is necessary to forbid further interference or discrimination. As a result, thousands of Negro citizens are registering and voting for the first time—many of them in counties where no Negro had ever voted before. The Department of Justice will continue to take whatever action is required to secure the right to vote for all Americans.

Experience has shown, however, that these highly useful Acts of the Eighty-fifth and Eighty-sixth Congresses suffer from two major defects. One is the usual long and difficult delay which occurs between the filing of a lawsuit and its ultimate conclusion. In one recent case, for example, nineteen months elapsed between the filing of the suit and the judgment of the court. In another, an action brought in July, 1961, has not yet come to trial. The legal maxim "Justice delayed is Justice denied" is dramatically applicable in these cases.

Too often those who attempt to assert their constitutional rights are intimidated. Prospective registrants are fired. Registration workers are arrested. In some instances, churches in which registration meetings have been held have been burned. In one case where Negro tenant farmers chose to exercise their right to vote, it was necessary for the Justice Department to seek injunctions to halt their eviction and for the Department of Agriculture to help feed them from surplus stocks. Under these circumstances, continued delay in the granting of the franchise—particularly in counties where there is mass racial disfranchisement—permits the intent of the Congress to be openly flouted.

Federal executive action in such cases—no matter how speedy

and how drastic—can never fully correct such abuses of power. It is necessary instead to free the forces of our democratic system within these areas by promptly insuring the franchise to all citizens, making it possible for their elected officials to be truly responsive to all their constituents.

The second and somewhat overlapping gap in these statutes is their failure to deal specifically with the most common forms of abuse of discretion on the part of local election officials who do not treat all applicants uniformly.

Objections were raised last year to the proposed literacy test bill, which attempted to speed up the enforcement of the right to vote by removing one important area of discretion from registration officials who used that discretion to exclude Negroes. Preventing that bill from coming to a vote did not make any less real the prevalence in many counties of the use of literacy and other voter qualification tests to discriminate against prospective Negro voters, contrary to the requirements of the Fourteenth and Fifteenth Amendments, and adding to the delays and difficulties encountered in securing the franchise for those denied it.

An indication of the magnitude of the over-all problem, as well as the need for speedy action, is a recent five-state survey disclosing over two hundred counties in which fewer than 15 per cent of the Negroes of voting age are registered to vote. This cannot continue. I am, therefore, recommending legislation to deal with this problem of judicial delay and administrative abuse in four ways:

First, to provide for interim relief while voting suits are proceeding through the courts in areas of demonstrated need, temporary federal voting referees should be appointed to determine the qualifications of applicants for registration and voting during the pendency of a lawsuit in any county in which fewer than 15 per cent of the eligible number of persons of any race claimed to be discriminated against are registered to vote. Existing federal law provides for the appointment of voting referees to receive and act upon applications for voting registration upon a court finding that a pattern or practice of discrimination exists. But to prevent a successful case from becoming an empty victory, insofar as the particular election is concerned, the proposed legislation would provide that, within these prescribed limits, temporary voting referees would be appointed to serve from the inception to the conclusion of the federal voting suit, applying, however, only state law and state regulations. As officers of the court, their decisions would be subject to court scrutiny and review.

Second, voting suits brought under the Federal Civil Rights statutes should be accorded expedited treatment in the federal courts, just as in many state courts election suits are given preference on the dockets on the sensible premise that, unless the right to vote can be exercised at a specific election, it is, to the extent of that election, lost forever.

Third, the law should specifically prohibit the application of different tests, standards, practices, or procedures for different applicants seeking to register and vote in federal election. Under present law, the courts can ultimately deal with the various forms of racial discrimination practiced by local registrars. But the task of litigation, and the time consumed in preparation and proof, should be lightened in every possible fashion. No one can rightfully contend that any voting registrar should be permitted to deny the vote to any qualified citizen, anywhere in this country, through discriminatory administration of qualifying tests, or upon the basis of minor errors in filling out a complicated form which seeks only information. Yet the Civil Rights Commission, and the cases brought by the Department of Justice, have compiled one discouraging example after another of obstacles placed in the path of Negroes seeking to register to vote at the same

time that other applicants experience no difficulty whatsoever. Qualified Negroes, including those with college degrees,
have been denied registration for their inability to give a
"reasonable" interpretation of the Constitution. They have
been required to complete their applications with unreason-
able precision—or to secure registered voters to vouch for their
identity—or to defer to white persons who want to register
ahead of them—or they are otherwise subjected to exasperat-
ing delays. Yet uniformity of treatment is required by the
dictates of both the Constitution and fair play—and this proposed statute, therefore, seeks to spell out that principle to
ease the difficulties and delays of litigation. Limiting the
proposal to voting qualifications in elections for federal
offices alone will clearly eliminate any constitutional conflict.

Fourth, completion of the sixth grade should, with respect to federal elections, constitute a presumption that the
applicant is literate. Literacy tests pose especially difficult problems in determining voter qualification. The essentially sub-
jective judgment involved in each individual case, and the
difficulty of challenging that judgment, have made literacy
tests one of the cruelest and most abused of all voter qualification tests. The incidence of such abuse can be eliminated,
or at least drastically curtailed, by the proposed legislation
providing that proof of completion of the sixth grade con-
stitutes a presumption that the applicant is literate.

Finally, the Eighty-seventh Congress—after twenty years of
effort—passed and referred to the states for ratification a Constitutional Amendment to prohibit the levying of poll taxes
as a condition to voting. Already thirteen states have ratified
the proposed Amendment and in three more one body of the
legislature has acted. I urge every state legislature to take
prompt action on this matter and to outlaw the poll tax—
which has too long been an outmoded and arbitrary bar to
voting participation by minority groups and others—as the

Twenty-fourth Amendment to the Constitution. This measure received bipartisan sponsorship and endorsement in the Congress—and I shall continue to work with governors and legislative leaders of both parties in securing adoption of the anti-poll tax amendment.

II. EDUCATION

Nearly nine years have elapsed since the Supreme Court ruled that state laws requiring or permitting segregated schools violate the Constitution. That decision represented both good law and good judgment—it was both legally and morally right. Since that time it has become increasingly clear that neither violence nor legalistic measures will be tolerated as a means of thwarting court-ordered desegregation, that closed schools are not an answer, and that responsible communities are able to handle the desegregation process in a calm and sensible manner. This is as it should be—for, as I stated to the Nation at the time of the Mississippi violence last September:

". . . Our Nation is founded on the principle that observance of the law is the eternal safeguard of liberty, and defiance of the law is the surest road to tyranny. The law which we obey includes the final rulings of the courts, as well as the enactments of our legislative bodies. Even among law-abiding men, few laws are universally loved—but they are universally respected and not resisted.

"Americans are free to disagree with the law but not to disobey it. For in a government of laws and not of men, no man, however prominent or powerful, and no mob, however unruly or boisterous, is entitled to defy a court of law. If this country should ever reach the point where any man or group of men, by force or threat of force, could long defy the commands of our court and our Constitution, then no law would stand free from doubt, no judge would be sure of his writ, and no citizen would be safe from his neighbors."

The shameful violence which accompanied but did not prevent the end of segregation at the University of Mississippi was an exception. State-supported universities in Georgia and South Carolina met this test in recent years with calm and maturity, as did the state-supported universities of Virginia, North Carolina, Florida, Texas, Louisiana, Tennessee, Arkansas, and Kentucky in earlier years. In addition, progress toward the desegregation of education at all levels has made other notable and peaceful strides, including the following forward moves in the last two years alone:

—Desegregation plans have been put into effect peacefully in the public schools of Atlanta, Dallas, New Orleans, Memphis, and elsewhere, with over sixty school districts desegregated last year—frequently with the help of federal persuasion and consultation, and in every case without incident or disorder.

—Teacher-training institutes financed under the National Defense Education Act are no longer held in colleges which refuse to accept students without regard to race, and this has resulted in a number of institutions opening their doors to Negro applicants voluntarily.

—The same is now true of institutes conducted by the National Science Foundation.

—Beginning in September of this year, under the Aid to Impacted Area School Program, the Department of Health, Education, and Welfare will initiate a program of providing on-base facilities so that children living on military installations will no longer be required to attend segregated schools at federal expense. These children should not be victimized by segregation merely because their fathers chose to serve in the armed forces and were assigned to an area where schools are operated on a segregated basis.

—In addition, the Department of Justice and the Department of Health, Education, and Welfare have succeeded in obtaining voluntary desegregation in many other districts receiving "impacted area" school assistance; and, representing the federal interest, have filed lawsuits to end segregation in a number of other districts.

—The Department of Justice has also intervened to seek the opening of public schools in the case of Prince Edward County, Virginia, the only county in the Nation where there are no public schools, and where a bitter effort to thwart court decrees requiring desegregation has caused nearly fifteen hundred out of eighteen hundred school-age Negro children to go without any education for more than three years.

In these and other areas within its jurisdiction, the Executive Branch will continue its efforts to fulfill the constitutional objective of an equal, non-segregated, educational opportunity for all children.

Despite these efforts, however, progress toward primary and secondary school desegregation has still been too slow, often painfully so. Those children who are being denied their constitutional rights are suffering a loss which can never be regained, and which will leave scars which can never be fully healed. I have in the past expressed my belief that the full authority of the federal government should be placed behind the achievement of school desegregation, in accordance with the command of the Constitution. One obvious area of federal action is to help facilitate the transition to desegregation in those areas which are conforming or wish to conform their practices to the law.

Many of these communities lack the resources necessary to eliminate segregation in their public schools while at the same time assuring that educational standards will be maintained and improved. The problem has been compounded by the fact that the climate of mistrust in many communities has left many school officials with no qualified source to turn to for information and advice.

There is a need for technical assistance by the Office of Education to assist local communities in preparing and carrying out desegregation plans, including the supplying of information on means which have been employed to desegregate other schools successfully. There is also need for financial assistance to employ specialized personnel to cope with problems occasioned by desegregation and to train school personnel to facilitate the transition to desegregation. While some facilities for providing this kind of assistance are presently available in the Office of Education, they are not adequate to the task.

I recommend, therefore, a program of federal technical and financial assistance to aid school districts in the process of desegregation in accordance with the Constitution.

Finally, it is obvious that the unconstitutional and outmoded concept of "separate but equal" does not belong in the federal statute books. This is particularly true with respect to higher education, where peaceful desegregation has been underway in practically every state for some time. I repeat, therefore, this Administration's recommendation of last year that this phrase be eliminated from the Morrill Land Grant College Act.

III. EXTENSION AND EXPANSION OF THE COMMISSION ON CIVIL RIGHTS

The Commission on Civil Rights, established by the Civil Rights Act of 1957, has been in operation for more than five years and is scheduled to expire on November 30, 1963. During this time it has fulfilled its statutory mandate by investigating deprivations of the right to vote and denials of equal protection of the laws in education, employment, housing and

administration of justice. The Commission's reports and recommendations have provided the basis for remedial action
both by Congress and the Executive Branch.

There are, of course, many areas of denials of rights yet
to be fully investigated. But the Commission is now in a
position to provide even more useful service to the Nation.
As more communities evidence a willingness to face frankly
their problems of racial discrimination, there is an increasing
need for expert guidance and assistance in devising workable
programs for civil rights progress. Agencies of state and local
government, industry, labor and community organizations,
when faced with problems of segregation and racial tensions,
all can benefit from information about how these problems
have been solved in the past. The opportunity to seek an
experienced and sympathetic forum on a voluntary basis can
often open channels of communication between contending
parties and help bring about the conditions necessary for
orderly progress. And the use of public hearings—to contribute
to public knowledge of the requirements of the Constitution
and national policy—can create in these communities the
atmosphere of understanding which is indispensable to peaceful and permanent solutions to racial problems.

The Federal Civil Rights Commission has the experience
and capability to make a significant contribution toward
achieving these objectives. It has advised the Executive Branch
not only about desirable policy changes but about the administrative techniques needed to make these changes effective.
If, however, the Commission is to perform these additional
services effectively, changes in its authorizing statute are
necessary and it should be placed on a more stable and more
permanent basis. A proposal that the Commission be made a
permanent body would be a pessimistic prediction that our
problems will never be solved. On the other hand, to let the
experience and knowledge gathered by the Commission go to

waste, by allowing it to expire, or by extending its life only
for another two years with no change in responsibility, would
ignore the very real contribution this agency can make toward meeting our racial problems. I recommend, therefore,
that the Congress authorize the Civil Rights Commission to
serve as a national civil rights clearinghouse providing information, advice, and technical assistance to any requesting
agency, private or public; that in order to fulfill these new
responsibilities, the Commission be authorized to concentrate
its activities upon those problems within the scope of its
statute which most need attention; and that the life of the
Commission be extended for a term of at least four more
years.

IV. EMPLOYMENT

Racial discrimination in employment is especially injurious
both to its victims and to the national economy. It results in
a great waste of human resources and creates serious community problems. It is, moreover, inconsistent with the
democratic principle that no man should be denied employment commensurate with his abilities because of his race
or creed or ancestry.

The President's Committee on Equal Employment Opportunity, reconstituted by Executive Order in early 1961,
has, under the leadership of the Vice-President, taken significant steps to eliminate racial discrimination by those who do
business with the government. Hundreds of companies—cov-
ering seventeen million jobs—have agreed to stringent non-
discriminatory provisions now standard in all government
contracts. One hundred four industrial concerns—including
most of the Nation's major employers—have in addition signed
agreements calling for an affirmative attack on discrimination
in employment; and 117 labor unions, representing about
85 per cent of the membership of the AFL-CIO, have signed

similar agreements with the Committee. Comprehensive compliance machinery has been instituted to enforce these agreements. The Committee has received over 1,300 complaints in two years—more than in the entire seven and a half years of the Committee's prior existence—and has achieved corrective action on 72 per cent of the cases handled—a heartening and unprecedented record. Significant results have been achieved in placing Negroes with contractors who previously employed whites only—and in the elevation of Negroes to a far higher proportion of professional, technical, and supervisory jobs. Let me repeat my assurances that these provisions in government contracts and the voluntary nondiscrimination agreements will be carefully monitored and strictly enforced.

In addition, the federal government, as an employer, has continued to pursue a policy of nondiscrimination in its employment and promotion programs. Negro high-school and college graduates are now being intensively sought out and recruited. A policy of not distinguishing on the grounds of race is not limited to the appointment of distinguished Negroes—although they have in fact been appointed to a record number of high policy-making, judicial and administrative posts. There has also been a significant increase in the number of Negroes employed in the middle and upper grades of the career federal service. In jobs paying $4,500 to $10,000 annually, for example, there was an increase of 20 per cent in the number of Negroes during the year ending June 30, 1962—over three times the rate of increase for all employees in those grades during the year. Career civil servants will continue to be employed and promoted on the basis of merit, and not color, in every agency of the federal government, including all regional and local offices.

This government has also adopted a new Executive policy with respect to the organization of its employees. As part of this policy, only those federal employee labor organizations that do not discriminate on grounds of race or color will be recognized.

Outside of government employment, the National Labor Relations Board is now considering cases involving charges of racial discrimination against a number of union locals. I have directed the Department of Justice to participate in these cases and to urge the National Labor Relations Board to take appropriate action against racial discrimination in unions. It is my hope that administrative action and litigation will make unnecessary the enactment of legislation with respect to union discrimination.

V. PUBLIC ACCOMMODATIONS

No act is more contrary to the spirit of our democracy and Constitution—or more rightfully resented by a Negro citizen who seeks only equal treatment—than the barring of that citizen from restaurants, hotels, theaters, recreational areas, and other public accommodations and facilities.

Wherever possible, this Administration has dealt sternly with such acts. In 1961, the Justice Department and the Interstate Commerce Commission successfully took action to bring an end to discrimination in rail and bus facilities. In 1962, the fifteen airports still maintaining segregated facilities were persuaded to change their practices, thirteen of them voluntarily and two others after the Department of Justice brought legal action. As a result of these steps, systematic segregation in interstate transportation has virtually ceased to exist. No doubt isolated instances of discrimination in transportation terminals, restaurants, rest-rooms, and other facilities will continue to crop up, but any such discrimination will be dealt with promptly.

In addition, restaurants and public facilities in buildings leased by the federal government have been opened up to all federal employees in areas where previously they had been segregated. The General Services Administration no longer contracts for the lease of space in office buildings unless such facilities are available to all federal employees wihout re- gard to race. This move has taken place without fanfare and practically without incident; and full equality of facilities will continue to be made available to all federal employees in every state.

National parks, forests, and other recreation areas—and the District of Columbia stadium—are open to all without regard to race. Meetings sponsored by the federal government or addressed by federal appointees are held in hotels and halls which do not practice discrimination or segregation. The De- partment of Justice has asked the Supreme Court to reverse the convictions of Negroes arrested for seeking to use public accommodations; and took action both through the courts and the use of federal marshals to protect those who were testing the desegregation of transportation facilities.

In these and other ways the federal government will con- tinue to encourage and support action by state and local com- munities, and by private entrepreneurs, to assure all members of the equal access to all public accommodations. A country with a "color blind" Constitution, and with no castes or classes among its citizens, cannot afford to do less.

VI. OTHER USES OF FEDERAL FUNDS

The basic standard of nondiscrimination—which I earlier stated has now been applied by the Executive Branch to every area of its activity—affects other programs not listed above:

—Although President Truman ordered the armed services of this country desegregated in 1948, it was necessary in 1962 to bar segregation formally and specifically in the Army and Air Force Reserves and in the training of all civil defense workers.

—A new Executive Order on housing, as unanimously recommended by the Civil Rights Commission in 1959, prohibits discrimination in the sale, lease, or use of housing owned or constructed in the future by the federal government or guaranteed under the FHA, VA, and Farmers Home Administration program. With regard to existing property owned or financed through the federal government, the departments and agencies are directed to take every appropriate action to promote the termination of discriminatory practices that may exist. A President's Committee on Equal Housing Opportunity was created by the Order to implement its provisions.

—A Committee on Equal Opportunity in the Armed Forces has been established to investigate and make recommendations regarding the treatment of minority groups, with special emphasis on off-base problems.

—The United States Coast Guard Academy has Negro students for the first time in its eighty-seven years of existence.

—The Department of Justice has increased its prosecution of police brutality cases, many of them in Northern states—and is assisting state and local police departments in meeting this problem.

—State employee merit systems operating programs financed with federal funds are now prohibited from discriminating on the basis of race or color.

—The Justice Department is challenging the constitutionality of the "separate but equal" provisions which permit hospitals constructed with federal funds to discriminate racially in the location of patients and the acceptance of doctors.

In short, the Exeuctive Branch of the federal government, under this Administration and in all of its activities, now stands squarely behind the principle of equal opportunity, without segregation or discrimination, in the employment of federal funds, facilities, and personnel. All officials at every level are charged with the responsibility of implementing this principle—and a formal inter-departmental action group, under White House chairmanship, oversees this effort and follows through on each directive. For the first time, the full force of federal executive authority is being exerted in the battle against race discrimination.

CONCLUSION

The various steps which have been undertaken or which are proposed in this Message do not constitute a final answer to the problems of race discrimination in this country. They do constitute a list of priorities—steps which can be taken by the Executive Branch and measures which can be enacted by the Eighty-eighth Congress. Other measures directed toward these same goals will be favorably commented on and supported, as they have been in the past—and they will be signed, if enacted into law.

In addition, it is my hope that this Message will lend encouragement to those state and local governments—and to private organizations, corporations, and individuals—who share my concern over the gap between our precepts and our practices. This is an effort in which every individual who asks what he can do for his country should be able and willing to take part. It is important, for example, for private citizens and local governments to support the State Department's effort to end discriminatory treatment suffered by too many foreign diplomats, students, and visitors to this country. But it is not enough to treat those from other lands with equality and dignity—the same treatment must be afforded to every American citizen.

The program outlined in this Message should not provide the occasion for sectional bitterness. No state or section of this Nation can pretend a self-righteous role, for every area has its own civil rights problems.

Nor should the basic elements of this program be imperiled by partisanship. The proposals put forth are consistent with the platforms of both parties and with the positions of their leaders. Inevitably there will be disagreement about means and strategy. But I would hope that on issues of constitutional rights and freedom, as in matters affecting our national security, there is a fundamental unity among us that will survive partisan debate over particular issues.

The centennial of the issuance of the Emancipation Proclamation is an occasion for celebration, for a sober assessment of our failures, and for rededication to the goals of freedom. Surely there can be no more meaningful observance of the centennial than the enactment of effective civil rights legislation and the continuance of effective executive action.

PRESIDENT KENNEDY'S RADIO AND TELEVISION ADDRESS TO THE NATION

June 11, 1963

Good evening, my fellow citizens.

This afternoon, following a series of threats and defiant statements, the presence of Alabama National Guardsmen was required at the University of Alabama to carry out the final and unequivocal order of the United States District Court of the Northern District of Alabama. That order called for the admission of two clearly qualified young Alabama residents who happened to have been born Negro.

That they were admitted peacefully on the campus is due in good measure to the conduct of the students of the University of Alabama, who met their responsibility in a constructive way.

I hope that every American, regardless of where he lives, will stop and examine his conscience about this and other related incidents. This Nation was founded by men of many nations and backgrounds. It was founded on the principle that all men are created equal, and that the rights of every man are diminished when the rights of one man are threatened.

Today we are committed to a world-wide struggle to promote and protect the rights of all who wish to be free, and when Americans are sent to Viet-Nam or West Berlin, we do not ask for whites only. It ought to be possible, therefore, for American students of any color to attend any public institution they select without having to be backed up by troops.

It ought to be possible for American consumers of any color to receive equal service in places of public accommodation, such as hotels and restaurants and theaters and retail stores, without being forced to resort to demonstrations in the street, and it ought to be possible for American citizens of any color to register and to vote in a free election without interference or fear of reprisal.

It ought to be possible, in short, for every American to enjoy the privileges of being American without regard to his race or his color. In short, every American ought to have the right to be treated as he would wish to be treated, as one would wish his children to be treated. But this is not the case.

The Negro baby born in America today, regardless of the section of the Nation in which he is born, has about one half as much chance of completing high school as a white baby born in the same place on the same day, one third as much chance of completing college, one third as much chance of becoming a professional man, twice as much chance of becoming unemployed, about one seventh as much chance of earning $10,000 a year, a life expectancy which is seven years shorter, and the prospects of earning only half as much.

This is not a sectional issue. Difficulties over segregation and discrimination exist in every city, in every state of the Union, producing in many cities a rising tide of discontent that threatens the public safety. Nor is this a partisan issue in a time of domestic crisis. Men of good will and generosity should be able to unite regardless of party or politics. This is not even a legal or a legislative issue alone. It is better to settle these matters in the courts than on the streets, and new laws are needed at every level, but law alone cannot make men see right.

We are confronted primarily with a moral issue. It is as old as the scriptures and is as clear as the American Constitution.

The heart of the question is whether all Americans are to be afforded equal rights and equal opportunities, whether we are going to treat our fellow Americans as we want to be treated. If an American, because his skin is dark, cannot eat lunch in a restaurant open to the public, if he cannot send his children to the best public school available, if he cannot vote for the public officials who represent him, if, in short, he cannot enjoy the full and free life which all of us want, then who among us would be content to have the color of his skin changed and stand in his place? Who among us would then be content with the counsels of patience and delay?

One hundred years of delay have passed since President Lincoln freed the slaves, yet their heirs, their grandsons, are not fully free. They are not yet freed from the bonds of injustice. They are not yet freed from social and economic oppression, and this Nation, for all its hopes and all its boasts, will not be fully free until all its citizens are free.

We preach freedom around the world, and we mean it, and we cherish our freedom here at home, but are we to say to the world, and much more importantly, to each other that this is a land of the free except for the Negroes; that we have no second-class citizens except Negroes; that we have no class or caste system, no ghettoes, no master race except with respect to the Negroes?

Now the time has come for this Nation to fulfill its promise. The events in Birmingham and elsewhere have so increased the cries for equality that no city or state or legislative body can prudently choose to ignore them.

The fires of frustration and discord are burning in every city, North and South, where legal remedies are not at hand. Redress is sought in the streets, in demonstrations, parades, and protests which create tensions and threaten violence and threaten lives.

We face, therefore, a moral crisis as a country and as a people. It cannot be met by repressive police action. It cannot be left to increased demonstrations in the streets. It cannot be quieted by token moves or talk. It is a time to act in the Congress, in your state and local legislative body, and above all, in all of our daily lives.

It is not enough to pin the blame on others, to say this is a problem of one section of the country or another, or deplore the fact that we face. A great change is at hand, and our task, our obligation, is to make that revolution, that change, peaceful and constructive for all.

Those who do nothing are inviting shame as well as violence. Those who act boldly are recognizing right as well as reality.

Next week I shall ask the Congress of the United States to

act, to make a commitment it has not fully made in this century to the proposition that race has no place in American life or law. The federal judiciary has upheld that proposition in a series of forthright cases. The Executive Branch has adopted that proposition in the conduct of its affairs, including the employment of federal personnel, the use of federal facilities, and the sale of federally financed housing.

But there are other necessary measures which only the Congress can provide, and they must be provided at this session. The old code of equity law under which we live commands for every wrong a remedy, but in too many communities, in too many parts of the country, wrongs are inflicted on Negro citizens as there are no remedies at law. Unless the Congress acts, their only remedy is in the street.

I am, therefore, asking the Congress to enact legislation giving all Americans the right to be served in facilities which are open to the public—hotels, restaurants, theaters, retail stores, and similar establishments.

This seems to me to be an elementary right. Its denial is an arbitrary indignity that no American in 1963 should have to endure, but many do.

I have recently met with scores of business leaders urging them to take voluntary action to end this discrimination and I have been encouraged by their response, and in the last two weeks over seventy-five cities have seen progress made in desegregating these kinds of facilities. But many are unwilling to act alone, and for this reason, nation-wide legislation is needed if we are to move this problem from the streets to the courts.

I am also asking Congress to authorize the federal government to participate more fully in lawsuits designed to end segregation in public education. We have succeeded in persuading many districts to desegregate voluntarily. Dozens have admitted Negroes without violence. Today a Negro is attending a state-supported institution in every one of our fifty states, but the pace is very slow.

Too many Negro children entering segregated grade schools at the time of the Supreme Court's decision nine years ago will enter segregated high schools this fall, having suffered a loss which can never be restored. The lack of an adequate education denies the Negro a chance to get a decent job.

The orderly implementation of the Supreme Court decision, therefore, cannot be left solely to those who may not have the economic resources to carry the legal action or who may be subject to harassment.

Other features will also be requested, including greater protection for the right to vote. But legislation, I repeat, cannot solve this problem alone. It must be solved in the homes of every American in every community across our country.

In this respect, I want to pay tribute to those Americans, North and South, who have been working in their communities to make life better for all. They are acting not out of a sense of legal duty, but out of a sense of human decency.

Like our soldiers and sailors in all parts of the world, they are meeting freedom's challenge on the firing line, and I salute them for their honor and their courage.

My fellow Americans, this is a problem which faces us all— in every city of the North as well as the South. Today there are Negroes unemployed two or three times as many compared to whites, inadequate in education, moving into the large cities, unable to find work, young people particularly out of work without hope, denied equal rights, denied the opportunity to eat at a restaurant or lunch counter or go to a movie theater, denied the right to a decent education, denied almost today the right to attend a state university even though qualified. It seems to me these are matters which concern us all, not merely Presidents or Congressmen or governors, but every citizen of the United States.

This is one country. It has become one country because all of us and all the people who came here had an equal chance to develop their talents.

We cannot say to 10 per cent of the population that you can't have the right; that your children can't have the chance to develop whatever talents they have; that the only way that they are going to get their rights is to go into the streets and demonstrate. I think we owe them and we owe ourselves a better country than that.

Therefore, I am asking for your help in making it easier for us to move ahead and to provide the kind of equality of treatment which we want for ourselves; to give a chance for every child to be educated to the limit of his talents.

As I have said before, not every child has an equal talent or an equal ability or an equal motivation, but they should have an equal right to develop their talent and their ability and their motivation to make something of themselves.

We have a right to expect that the Negro community will be responsible, will uphold the law, but they have a right to expect that the law will be fair; that the Constitution will be color-blind, as Justice Harlan said at the turn of the century.

This is what we are talking about and this is a matter which concerns this country and what it stands for, and in meeting it I ask the support of all of our citizens.

Thank you very much.

ADDRESS BY ATTORNEY GENERAL ROBERT F. KENNEDY

at the Law Day Exercises of the University of Georgia Law School, Athens, Georgia

May 6, 1961

For the first time since becoming Attorney General, over three months ago, I am making something approaching a formal speech, and I am proud that it is in Georgia. Two months ago I had the very great honor to present to the President, Donald Eugene McGregor of Brunswick, Georgia, the Young American Medal for Bravery. In twelve bad hours, he led a family of four to safety from a yacht which broke up in high seas off the Georgia coast. He impressed all of us who met him with his quiet courage. And, as the President said, Donald McGregor is a fine young American—one of a long line of Georgians who have, by their courage, set an outstanding example for their fellow Americans.

They have told me that when you speak in Georgia you should try to tie yourself to Georgia and the South, and even better, claim some Georgia kinfolk. There are a lot of Kennedys in Georgia. But as far as I can tell, I have no relatives here and no direct ties to Georgia, except one. This state gave my brother the biggest percentage majority of any state in the union and in this last election that was even better than kinfolk.

We meet at this great University, in this old state, the fourth of the original thirteen, to observe Law Day.

In his Proclamation urging us to observe this day, the President emphasized two thoughts. He pointed out that to remain free the people must "cherish their freedoms, understand the responsibilities they entail, and nurture the will to preserve them." He then went on to point out that "law is the strongest link between man and freedom."

I wonder in how many countries of the world people think of law as the "link between man and freedom." We know that in many, law is the instrument of tyranny, and people think of law as little more than the will of the state, or the Party—not of the people.

And we know too that throughout the long history of mankind, man has had to struggle to create a system of law and of government in which fundamental freedoms would be linked with the enforcement of justice. We know that we cannot live together without rules which tell us what is right and what is wrong, what is permitted and what is prohibited. We know that it is law which enables men to live together, that creates order out of chaos. We know that law is the glue that holds civilization together.

And, we know that if one man's rights are denied, the rights of all are endangered. In our country the courts have a most important role in safeguarding these rights. The decisions of the court, however much we might disagree with them, in the final analysis must be followed and respected. If we disagree with a court decision and, thereafter, irresponsibly assail the court and defy its rulings, we challenge the foundations of our society.

The Supreme Court of Georgia set forth this proposition quite clearly in the case of *Crumb v. the State* (205 Ga. 547-552). The court, referring to the United States Supreme Court decisions, said there and I quote:

"And whatever may be the individual opinion of the members of this court as to the correctness, soundness, and wisdom of these decisions, it becomes our duty to yield thereto just as the other courts of the State must accept and be controlled by the decisions and mandates of this court. This being a government of law and not by men, the jury commissioners in their official conduct are bound by the foregoing ruling of the Supreme Court of the United States, notwithstanding any personal opinion, hereditary instinct, natural impulse or geographical tradition to the contrary."

Respect for the law—in essence that is the meaning of Law Day—and every day must be Law Day or else our society will collapse.

The challenge which international communism hurls against the rule of law is very great. For the past two weeks I have been engaged, for a good part of my time, in working with General Taylor, Admiral Burke, and Mr. Dulles, to assess the recent events in Cuba and determine what lessons we can learn for the future.

It already has become crystal clear in our study that as the President has stated so graphically, we must re-examine and reorient our forces of every kind. Not just our military forces, but all our techniques and outlook here in the United States. We must come forward with the answer of how a nation, devoted to freedom and individual rights and respect for the law, can stand effectively against an implacable enemy who plays by different rules and knows only the law of the jungle. With the answer to this rests our future—our destiny—as a nation and as a people.

The events of the last few weeks have demonstrated that the time has long since passed when the people of the United States can be apathetic about their belief and respect for the law and about the necessity of placing our own house in order. As we turn to meet our enemy, to look him full in the face, we cannot afford feet of clay or an arm of glass.

Let me speak to you about three major areas of difficulty within the purview of my responsibilities that sap our national strength, that weaken our people, that require our immediate attention.

In too many major communities of our country, organized crime has become big business. It knows no state lines. It drains off millions of dollars of our national wealth, infecting legitimate business, labor unions, and even sports. Tolerating organized crime promotes the cheap philosophy that everything is a racket. It promotes cynicism among adults. It contributes to the confusion of the young and to the increase of juvenile delinquency.

It is not the gangster himself who is of concern. It is what he is doing to our cities, our communities, our moral fiber. Ninety per cent of the major racketeers would be out of business by the end of this year if the ordinary citizen, the businessman, the union official, and the public authority stood up to be counted and refused to be corrupted.

This is a problem for all America, not just the FBI or the Department of Justice. Unless the basic attitude changes here in this country, the rackets will prosper and grow. Of this I am convinced.

The racketeers, after all, are professional criminals. But, there are the amateurs—men who have law-abiding backgrounds and respectable positions, who, nevertheless, break the law of the land. We have been particularly concerned lately in the Department of Justice about the spread of illegal price-fixing. I would say to you, however, it is merely symptomatic of many other practices commonly accepted in business life.

Our investigations show that in an alarming number of

areas of the country businessmen have conspired in secret to fix prices, made collusive deals with union officials, defrauded their customers, and even in some instances cheated their own government.

Our enemies assert that capitalism enslaves the worker and will destroy itself. It is our national faith that the system of competitive enterprise offers the best hope for individual freedom, social development, and economic growth.

Thus, every businessman who cheats on his taxes, fixes prices, or underpays his labor, every union official who makes a collusive deal, misuses union funds, damages the free enterprise system in the eyes of the world and does a disservice to the millions of honest Americans in all walks of life.

Where we have evidence of violation of laws by the "respectables," we will take action against the individuals involved, as well as against their companies. But in the end, this also is not a situation which can be cured by the Department of Justice. It can only be cured by the business and unions themselves.

The third area is the one that affects us all the most directly—civil rights.

The hardest problems of all in law enforcement are those involving a conflict of law and local customs. History has recorded many occasions when the moral sense of a nation produced judicial decisions, such as the 1954 decision in *Brown v. Board of Education,* which required difficult local adjustments.

I have many friends in the United States Senate who are Southerners. Many of these friendships stem from my work as counsel for the Senate Rackets Committee, headed by Senator John McClellan of Arkansas for whom I have the greatest admiration and affection.

If these Southern friends of mine are representative Southerners—and I believe they are—I do not pretend that they believe with me on everything or that I agree with them on everything. But, knowing them as I do, I am convinced of this:

Southerners have a special respect for candor and plain talk. They certainly don't like hypocrisy. So, in discussing this third major problem, I must tell you candidly what our policies are going to be in the field of civil rights and why.

First let me say this: the time has long since arrived when loyal Americans must measure the impact of their actions beyond the limits of their own towns or states. For instance, we must be quite aware of the fact that 50 per cent of the countries in the United Nations are not white; that around the world, in Africa, South America, and Asia, people whose skins are a different color than ours are on the move to gain their measure of freedom and liberty.

From the Congo to Cuba, from South Viet-Nam to Algiers, in India, Brazil, and Iran, men and women and children are straightening their backs and listening—to the evil promises of communist tyranny and the honorable promises of Anglo-American liberty. And those people will decide not only their future but how the cause of freedom fares in the world.

In the United Nations we are striving to establish a rule of law instead of a rule of force. In that forum and elsewhere around the world our deeds will speak for us.

In the world-wide struggle, the graduation at this university of Charlayne Hunter and Hamilton Holmes will without question aid and assist the fight against communist political infiltration and guerrilla warfare.

When parents send their children to school this Fall in Atlanta, peaceably and in accordance with the rule of law, barefoot Burmese and Congolese will see before their eyes Americans living by the rule of law.

The conflict of views over the original decision in 1954 and our recent move in Prince Edward County is understandable. The decision in 1954 required action of the most difficult, deli-

cate, and complex nature, going to the heart of Southern institutions. I know a little of this. I live in Virginia. I studied law
at the University of Virginia. I have been privileged to know
many able Southern soldiers, scholars, lawyers, jurists, journalists, and political leaders who have enriched our national life.
From them I have drawn some understanding of the South,
but my knowledge is nothing to yours.

It is now being said that the Department of Justice is at-
tempting to close all public schools in Virginia because of the
Prince Edward situation. This is not true, nor is the Prince
Edward suit a threat against local control.

We are maintaining the orders of the courts. We are doing
nothing more nor less. And if any one of you were in my position you would do likewise for it would be required by your
oath of office. You might not want to do it, you might not like
to do it, but you would do it.

For I cannot believe that anyone can support a principle
which prevents more than a thousand of our children in one
county from attending public school—especially when this
step was taken to circumvent the orders of the court.

Our position is quite clear. We are upholding the law. Our
action does not threaten local control. The federal government would not be running the schools in Prince Edward
County any more than it is running the University of Georgia
or the schools in my state of Massachusetts.

In this case—in all cases—I say to you today that if the orders
of the court are circumvented, the Department of Justice will
act.

We will not stand by or be aloof. We will move.

Here on this campus, not half a year ago, you endured a
difficult ordeal. And when your moment of truth came, the
voices crying "force" were overridden by the voices pleading
for reason.

And for this, I pay my respects to your governor, your legislature, and most particularly to you, the students and faculty of the University of Georgia. And I say, you are the wave of the future—not those who cry panic. For the country's future you will and must prevail.

I happen to believe that the 1954 decision was right. But, my belief does not matter—it is the law. Some of you may believe the decision was wrong. That does not matter. It is the law. And we both respect the law. By facing this problem honorably, you have shown to all the world that we Americans are moving forward together—solving this problem—under the rule of law.

An integral part of all this is that we make a total effort to guarantee the ballot to every American of voting age—in the North—as well as in the South. The right to vote is the easiest of all rights to grant. The spirit of our democracy, the letter of our Constitution and our laws require that there be no further delay in the achievement of full freedom to vote for all. Our system depends upon the fullest participation of all its citizens.

The problem between the white and colored people is a problem for all sections of the United States. And as I have said, I believe there has been a great deal of hypocrisy in dealing with it. In fact, I found when I came to the Department of Justice that I need look no further to find evidence of this.

I found that very few Negroes were employed above a custodial level. There were nine hundred and fifty lawyers working in the Department of Justice in Washington and only ten of them were Negroes. At the same moment the lawyers of the Department of Justice were bringing legal action to end discrimination, that same discrimination was being practiced within the Department itself.

At a recent review for the visiting leader of a new African state, there was only one Negro in the guard of honor. At the Bureau of the Budget, Negroes were used only for custodial work.

The federal government is taking steps to correct this.

Financial leaders from the East who deplore discrimination in the South belong to institutions where no Negroes or Jews are allowed, and their children attend private schools where no Negro students are enrolled. Union officials criticize Southern leaders and yet practice discrimination with their unions. Government officials belong to private clubs in Washington where Negroes including Ambassadors are not welcomed even at mealtime.

My firm belief is that if we are to make progress in this area —if we are to be truly great as a nation, then we must make sure that nobody is denied an opportunity because of race, creed, or color. We pledge, by example, to take action in our own backyard—the Department of Justice—we pledge to move to protect the integrity of the courts in the administration of justice. In all this, we ask your help—we need your assistance.

I come to you today and I shall come to you in the years ahead to advocate reason and the rule of law.

It is in this spirit that since taking office I have conferred many times with responsible public officials and civic leaders in the South on specific situations. I shall continue to do so. I don't expect them always to agree with my view of what the law requires, but I believe they share my respect for the law. We are trying to achieve amicable, voluntary solutions without going to court. These discussions have ranged from voting and school cases to incidents of arrest which might lead to violence.

We have sought to be helpful to avert violence and to get voluntary compliance. When our investigations indicate there has been a violation of law, we have asked responsible officials to take steps themselves to correct the situation. In some instances this has happened. When it has not, we have had to take legal action.

These conversations have been devoid of bitterness or hate.

They have been carried on with mutual respect, understanding, and good will. National unity is essential and before taking any legal action, we will where appropriate, invite the Southern leaders to make their views known in these cases.

We, the American people, must avoid another Little Rock or another New Orleans. We cannot afford them. It is not only that such incidents do incalculable harm to the children involved and to the relations among people, it is not only that such convulsions seriously undermine respect for law and order, and cause serious economic and moral damage. Such incidents hurt our country in the eyes of the world. We just can't afford another Little Rock or New Orleans.

For on this generation of Americans falls the full burden of proving to the world that we really mean it when we say all men are created free and are equal before the law. All of us might wish at times that we lived in a more tranquil world, but we don't. And if our times are difficult and perplexing, so are they challenging and filled with opportunity.

To the South, perhaps more than any other section of the country, has been given the opportunity and the challenge and the responsibility of demonstrating America at its greatest —at its full potential of liberty under law.

You may ask, will we enforce the civil rights statutes.

The answer is: "Yes, we will."

We also will enforce the antitrust laws, the anti-racketering laws, the laws against kidnaping and robbing federal banks, and transporting stolen automobiles across state lines, the illicit traffic in narcotics and all the rest.

We can and will do no less.

I hold a constitutional office of the United States Government, and I shall perform the duty I have sworn to undertake —to enforce the law, in every field of law and every region.

We will not threaten, we will try to help. We will not persecute, we will prosecute.

We will not make or interpret the laws. We shall enforce them—vigorously, without regional bias or political slant.

All this we intend to do. But all the high rhetoric on Law Day about the noble mansions of the law; all the high-sounding speeches about liberty and justice, are meaningless unless people—you and I—breathe meaning and force into it. For our liberties depend upon our respect for the law.

On December 13, 1889, Henry W. Grady of Georgia said these words to an audience in my home state of Massachusetts:

"This hour little needs the loyalty that is loyal to one section and yet holds the other in enduring suspicion and estrangement. Give us the broad and perfect liberty that loves Georgia alike with Massachusetts—that knows no South, no North, no East, no West, but endears with equal and patriotic love every foot of our soil, every state of our Union.

"A mighty duty, sir, and a mighty inspiration impels everyone of us tonight to lose in patriotic consecration whatever estranges, whatever divides. We, sir, are Americans—and we stand for human liberty!"

Ten days later Mr. Grady was dead but his words live today. We stand for human liberty.

The road ahead is full of difficulties and discomforts. But as for me, I welcome the challenge, I welcome the opportunity, and I pledge my best effort—all I have in material things and physical strength and spirit to see that freedom shall advance and that our children will grow old under the rule of law.

ADDRESS BY ATTORNEY GENERAL
ROBERT F. KENNEDY

at the annual meeting of the Missouri Bar Association,
Kansas City, Missouri

September 27, 1963

I am grateful for the opportunity to talk with this distinguished group.

Yours is one of the strongest and most vital bar organizations in the country. That you have won the American Bar Association's top Award of Merit twice within the last four years is an honor that speaks for itself—and I am impressed too by several other examples of your leadership in matters of civic concern.

Your scheduling of a discussion on the representation of the indigent accused is only one such example.

Everything I have read and heard about your activities suggests courage, high principle, and true engagement with the social realities of our time. You are to be congratulated.

But it is regrettable that the same spirit is not shared by all lawyers and public officials throughout the country. If it were, our nation-wide problems in civil rights would be much less severe than they are.

To a far greater extent than most Americans realize, the crisis in civil rights reflects a crisis in the legal profession—in the whole judicial system on which our concept of justice depends.

I'd like to discuss three legal propositions with you. Each of them is part of a time-honored and noble tradition—and each of them, today, is being used to threaten the very foundations of law and order in this country.

The first is the proposition that it is proper and just to avail oneself of every legal defense to test either the validity or the applicability of a rule of law.

The second is that a court decision binds only those persons who are a party to it.

The third is that a court-made rule of law should always be open to re-examination, and is susceptible to being overruled on a subsequent occasion.

All three ideas are basic to our system of justice; none of them needs any explanation or defense to an audience of skilled advocates such as yourselves.

But today we have only to pick up a newspaper to see how these honorable principles—used in isolation, invoked in improper contexts, espoused as absolutes and carried to extremes —have placed the sanctity of the law in jeopardy.

Separately and in combination, they are being proclaimed by lawyers and public officials as the justification for tactics to obstruct the enforcement of law and court orders—as the rationale, that is, for withholding justice and equality from the grasp of millions of our fellow Americans.

We are all familiar with the catch-phrases of that rationale, and with the air of righteous indignation in their utterance.

The argument goes something like this:

Brown versus the Board of Education is not the law of the land; it governs only one particular set of facts and is binding only upon the litigants of that case.

Only when each separate school district, each state, and each new set of administrative procedures has been tested and judged on its own merits can it be said that a binding decision has been reached.

And furthermore—so the argument goes—a decision like *Brown,* repugnant to certain segments of the population and clearly difficult to enforce, may conceivably be overruled as bad law.

To resist it, therefore, is merely to exercise one's constitutional right to seek reversal of a judicial ruling.

When stated that way and surrounded by rhetoric, the argument can be made to have a gloss of respectability. It can even take on the disguise of patriotic, high-minded dissent. Indeed, it is a position publicly espoused today by the governors of two states, by a past president of the American Bar Association, and by a federal district judge who recently overruled the *Brown* decision on grounds that its findings were erroneous.

We cannot blame a layman—even a reasonably fair-minded layman—for being confused and misled by this kind of reasoning.

But to lawyers, it smacks of duplicity. When it comes from the mouths of other lawyers, we must recognize it as professionally irresponsible. And when it comes from the mouths of public officials, we must recognize it as nothing more or less than demagoguery.

Let's go over those three legal principles one at a time. Let's examine each of them and look for the danger that lies within it.

What do we really mean, as lawyers, when we say that it is proper and constitutional to avail oneself of every legal defense?

Surely the Canons of Ethics make clear the impropriety of using dilatory tactics to frustrate the cause of justice.

We have only to imagine that principle being constantly applied across the board, in day-to-day litigation, to see that for all its validity it must be met by a counter-principle—a concept that might be called the principle of good faith.

Every lawyer knows—though his clients may not—that nothing but national chaos would result if all lawyers were to object to every interrogatory, resist every subpoena *duces tecum* and every disposition, seek every possible continuance and postponement, frame unresponsive pleadings, and resist court orders to a point just short of contempt.

We know that tolerances are built into the system. We know what the margins for evasion and dilatory practices are—and we also know that the system would be hard put to stand up under a concerted effort to exploit them all.

There must obviously be a strong element of good faith, of reciprocity and cooperation, if our court system is to work at all. Take away that good faith, elevate the right to avail oneself of a technicality into an absolute—and you bring the very machinery of law to a standstill.

What about the second proposition—that a court decision binds only those who are a party to it? Clearly, this, too is a principle that conceals as much as it says.

Every lawyer knows—though his clients may not—the distinction between the holding of a case and its rationale. We know that although the holding contains a specific disposition of a particular fact situation between the litigants, its reasoning enunciates a rule of law that applies not merely to one case but to all similar cases.

Often there is room for much discretion and honest disagreement as to when cases are alike or unalike. But clearly, in the matter of desegregation, there can be little or no room for argument in good faith as to when one situation is different—in the legal sense—from another in which the law has been laid down.

The county is different, the names of officials are different, but the situation—in all legally significant respects—is identical.

There is something less than truth in a lawyer who insists, nine years after the *Brown* decision and a hundred years after the Emancipation Proclamation, that a law of the land, a guarantee of human dignity and equality, is merely the law of a case.

We come now to the third principle—that a court-made rule of law is always open to re-examination and must be viewed as susceptible to being overruled.

No one can prove in strict logic that any given case will never be overruled. But with regard to the *Brown* decision, I think we can all agree that the probability of its permanence is so overwhelming as to counsel the abandonment of anyone's hope for the contrary.

The decision was, after all, a unanimous one. Since 1954 there have been six vacancies in the Supreme Court, which means that by now a total of fifteen justices have endorsed it.

True enough, it was in itself an overruling of *Plessy v. Ferguson*, fifty-six years before. But that reversal had been widely expected through several generations of legal thought. The whole pattern of American and world history pointed to the abolishment of the "separate but equal" concept; and the reform established by the *Brown* decision was all but inevitable.

Moreover, and more importantly, it is clearly a decision that the vast majority of the American public holds to be morally correct.

To suggest, at this point in history, that there is any real likelihood of the *Brown* decision's being reversed is irresponsible to the point of absurdity.

No lawyer would advise a private client to contest the validity of a decision as solidly established and as often reiterated as this one; he would not want to victimize his client by raising frivolous questions.

Yet a client is being victimized every time this frivolous question is raised today—and the client is the American public itself.

Right now, all over the nation, the struggle for Negro equality is expressing itself in marches, demonstrations, and sit-ins. It seems very clear to me that these people are protesting against something more than the privations and humiliations they have endured for so long.

They are protesting the failure of our legal system to be responsive to the legitimate grievances of our citizens. They are protesting because the very procedures supposed to make the law work justly have been perverted into obstructions that keep it from working at all.

Something must be done—and it's a job that can only be done by members of the legal profession.

First, we have got to make our legal system work. We have got to *make* it responsive to legitimate grievances, and to do this we must work to prevent the unscrupulous exploitation of all the obstructive devices available within the system.

Only when our judicial system offers fair and efficient adjudication does it deserve the public confidence; and it seems to me that American lawyers everywhere have a clear obligation to make that confidence justified.

Second, we have a job of education to do. The public must be better informed about the nature of our legal system—and this includes a better understanding of each of the principles and counter-principles I have discussed with you today.

Only if we are able to instill that understanding will people with grievances begin to realize that there is a practical and realistic alternative to street demonstratons and sit-ins.

But we have to make sure both that there *is* an alternative, and that the nature of that alternative is clearly understood.

If we can accomplish this, I believe we will begin to see a new phase in the movement for civil rights—an increased awareness that sit-ins and demonstrations do not in themselves cure social evils.

They serve to awaken the public conscience, and they can form a means of protest when no other means are available, but they will not dictate solutions; they can only alert us to the problems.

And in the long quest for solutions, we lawyers have a great deal to offer.

We are part of an intricate system that has developed over the centuries as man's best hope for resolving disputes and appraising policies—for working out solutions to problems.

If this system of law—of equal justice for all—can be kept viable, and if people of all backgrounds and of all races and creeds can begin to fully understand and fully take advantage of it, then—and only then—will we stand to realize the promise of democracy, both for ourselves and for the world.

SELECTED BIBLIOGRAPHY

THE LITERATURE on the social revolution of the American Negro is vast. I list here only those materials I specifically used in *Mr. Kennedy and the Negroes.*

Ahmann, Mathew H. (ed.), *The New Negro.* University of Notre Dame, Fides Publishers, 1961.

Allen, Robert S. (ed.), *Our Fair City.* New York, The Vanguard Press, 1947.

Arendt, Hannah, *The Origins of Totalitarianism.* New York, Harcourt Brace & Company, 1951.

Ashmore, Harry S., *An Epitaph for Dixie.* New York, W. W. Norton & Company, 1948.

Barnett, Richard, and Garai, Joseph, *Where the States Stand on Civil Rights.* New York, Bold Face Books, 1962.

Berman, William Carl, *The Politics of Civil Rights in the Truman Administration.* Unpublished Ph.D. dissertation, Villanova University, 1963.

Black, Charles L., Jr., *The Occasions of Justice.* New York, The Macmillan Company, 1963.

Bloch, Charles, *States Rights: the Law of the Land.* Atlanta, Harrison Company, 1955.

Burns, James M., *John Kennedy: a Political Profile*. New York, Harcourt Brace & Company, 1960.

Carter, Hodding, *The Angry Scar*. Garden City, Doubleday & Company, 1959.

————, *First Person Rural*. Garden City, Doubleday & Company, 1963.

Cash, W. J., *Mind of the South*. New York, Alfred A. Knopf, Inc., 1941.

Chesnut, Mary Boykin, *A Diary from Dixie*. Boston, Houghton Mifflin Company, 1961.

Cleghorn, Reese, "The Segs." *Esquire* Magazine (January, 1963), p. 72.

Cook, James Graham, *The Segregationists*. New York, Appleton-Century-Crofts, 1962.

Degler, Carl N., *Out of Our Past: the Forces that Shaped Modern America*. New York, Harper & Brothers, 1959.

Dilliard, Irving (ed.), *One Man's Stand for Freedom: Mr. Justice Black and the Bill of Rights*. New York, Alfred A. Knopf, Inc., 1963.

Douglas, William O., *Mr. Lincoln and the Negroes*. New York, Atheneum Publishers, 1963.

Dykeman, Wilma, and Stokely, James, *Neither Black Nor White*. New York, Rinehart & Company, 1957.

————, *Seeds of Southern Change: the Life of Will Alexander*. Chicago, University of Chicago Press, 1962.

Eisenhower, Dwight D., *Mandate for Change*. New York, Doubleday & Company, 1963.

Elkins, Stanley M., *Slavery*. New York, Grosset & Dunlap, 1963.

Faulkner, William, *The Reivers*. New York, Random House, Inc., 1962.

Fuller, Helen, *Year of Trial*. New York, Harcourt Brace and World, 1962.

Ginzberg, Eli, *The Negro Potential*. New York, Columbia University Press, 1956.

Glazer, Nathan, and Moynihan, D. Patrick, *Beyond the Melting Pot*. Cambridge, M.I.T. & Harvard University Press, 1963.

Golden, Harry, "A Rabbi in Montgomery." *Congress Weekly*, Vol. 24, No. 17 (May 13, 1957), p. 109.

————, "The South Stalls its Future." *The Nation*, Vol. 187 (August 30, 1958), pp. 84-87.

Gregory, Anne King, *History of Sumter County*. Sumter (S.C.), Library Board of Sumter County, 1954.

Griffin, John Howard, *Black Like Me*. New York, Houghton Mifflin Company, 1961.

Guild, June Purcell, *The Myth of States Rights*. Richmond, Anti-Defamation League, 1958.

Gunther, John, *Inside U.S.A.* New York, Harper & Brothers, 1947.

Guste, Robert, *For Men of Good Will*. New Orleans, Catholic Council on Human Relations, 1961.

Handlin, Oscar, "The Eisenhower Administration." *Atlantic Monthly*, Vol. 212, No. 5 (November, 1963), pp. 67-72.

Harrington, Michael, *The Other America*. New York, The Macmillan Company, 1963.

Higham, John, *Strangers in the Land*. New Brunswick (N.J.), Rutgers University Press, 1955.

Hoffer, Eric, *The True Believer*. New York, Harper & Brothers, 1951.

Hughes, Emmet John, *The Ordeal of Power*. New York, Atheneum Publishers, 1963.

Huntley, Martha Williamson, *Koinonia*. Unpublished M.A. thesis, Barnard College, 1962.

Kennedy, John F., *A Nation of Immigrants*. New York, Anti-Defamation League, 1963.

King, Martin Luther, Jr., *Strength to Love*. New York, Harper & Row, 1963.

———, *Stride Toward Freedom*. New York, Harper & Row, 1961.

Kraft, Joseph, "Riot Squad for the New Frontier." *Harpers Magazine*, Vol. 227, No. 1359 (August, 1963), p. 69.

Maston, T. B., *Segregation and Desegregation: a Christian Approach*. New York, The Macmillan Company, 1959.

McCauley, Patrick, and Ball, Edward. *Southern Schools: Progress and Problems*. Nashville (Tenn.), Southern Education Reporting Service, 1959.

McGill, Ralph, *The South and the Southerner*. Boston, Little, Brown & Company, 1963.

Miller, Dorothy, *The Story of Danville, Virginia*. Report for the Student Nonviolent Coordinating Committee, 1962.

Morrow, E. Frederic, *Black Man in the White House*. New York, Coward-McCann, Inc., 1963.

Muse, Benjamin, *Virginia's Massive Resistance*. Bloomington (Ind.), Indiana University Press, 1961.

Myrdal, Gunnar, *An American Dilemma*. New York, Harper & Brothers, 1944.

North Carolina Advisory Committee to the U.S. Commission on Civil Rights, *Equal Protection of the Laws in N.C.* Washington, 1959, 1960.

North Carolina Law Review, "Civil Rights and the South." Vol. 42, No. 1 (Fall, 1963), pp. 3-16.

Ottley, Roi, *Black Odyssey*. New York, Charles Scribner's Sons, 1948.

———, *New World A-Coming*. Boston, Houghton Mifflin Company, 1943.

Pettigrew, Thomas F., and Campbell, Ernest Q., *Christians in Racial Crisis*. Washington, Public Affairs Press, 1959.

Pope, Liston, *Millhands and Preachers*. New Haven, Yale University Press, 1942.

Quarles, Benjamin, *Lincoln and the Negro*. New York, Oxford University Press, 1962.

Quint, Howard, *Profile in Black and White*. Washington, Public Affairs Press, 1958.

Raskin, A. H., "Walter Reuther's Great Big Union." *Atlantic Monthly*, Vol. 212, No. 4 (October, 1963), pp. 85-90.

Redding, J. Saunders, *On Being Negro in America*. Indianapolis, Bobbs-Merrill, 1951.

Roche, John P., *The Quest for the Dream*. New York, The Macmillan Company, 1963.

Sandburg, Carl, *The Chicago Race Riots*. New York, Harcourt, Brace & Howe, 1920.

Schlesinger, Arthur Jr., *Politics of Upheaval*. Boston, Houghton Mifflin Company, 1960.

Sellers, James Earl, *The South and Christian Ethics*. New York, Association Press, 1962.

Sibley, Mulford Q., *The Quiet Battle*. Garden City, Doubleday Anchor Books, 1963.

Sidey, Hugh, *John F. Kennedy, President*. New York, Atheneum Publishers, 1963.

Simpson, George Eaton, and Yinger, J. Milton. *Racial and Cultural Minorities*. New York, Harper & Brothers, 1953.

Smith, Lillian, *Killers of the Dream*. Garden City, Doubleday Anchor Books, 1963.

Sorensen, Theodore C., *Decision-Making in the White House*. New York, Columbia University Press, 1963.

Stone, I. F., *The Haunted Fifties*. New York, Random House, 1963.

Tanzer, Lester (ed.), *The Kennedy Circle*. Washington, Robert Luce, Inc., 1961.

Thompson, W. Hale, *Report on Voting Restrictions in Virginia*. Washington, Civil Rights Commission, April 27, 1958.

Tumin, Melvin M., *Desegregation*. Princeton, Princeton University Press, 1958.

United States Commission on Civil Rights, *Civil Rights.* Washington, 1963.

U. S. Commission on Race and Housing, *Where Shall We Live?* Berkeley, University of California Press, 1958.

U. S. Committee on Commerce, final report, *The Joint Appearances of Senator John F. Kennedy and Vice-President Richard M. Nixon.* Washington, 1961.

United States Court of Appeals for the Fifth Circuit. *U.S. v. State of Louisiana.*

United States Court of Appeals for the Fourth Circuit. *Gloria Brooks v. County School Board of Arlington County.*

U. S. Senate Commerce Committee, *The Speeches of Senator John F. Kennedy: Presidential Campaign of 1960.* Washington, 1961.

Von Borch, Herbert, *The Unfinished Society.* New York, Hawthorn Books, Inc., 1962.

Vorspan, Albert, "The Negro Victory and the Jewish Failure." *American Judaism* (Fall, 1963), p. 7.

Wagenknecht, Edward, *The Seven Worlds of Theodore Roosevelt.* New York, Longmans, Green & Company, 1958.

Wesberry, James, "Court Decision Rocks Georgia." *Christian Century,* Vol. LXXI, No. 33 (August 18, 1954), pp. 986-988.

White, Theodore H., *The Making of the President, 1960.* New York, Atheneum Publishers, 1961.

Wogman, Philip, "Focus on the Central Jurisdiction." *Christian Century,* Vol. 80 (October 23, 1963), pp. 1296-1298.

Woodward, C. Vann, *Reunion and Reaction.* Garden City, Doubleday Anchor Books, 1956.

————, *The Strange Career of Jim Crow.* New York, Oxford University Press, 1955.

ABOUT THE AUTHOR

HARRY GOLDEN is not only a social historian, as the eminent critic Joseph Wood Krutch called him, but one of the best reporters of our day. If his humor has been anthologized, so too have his special assignments, notably his coverage of the Eichmann trial for *Life* magazine.

Mr. Kennedy and the Negroes is Harry Golden's big story, the story of the social revolution of the American Negro. In fact, he may have been the first American journalist to recognize the proportions of the current Civil Rights movement. In May, 1956, when several Southern states were seriously considering the legislation which would curb the activities of the National Association for the Advancement of Colored People, in an address before the North Carolina Press Association at Chapel Hill, Mr. Golden said, "If the NAACP disappeared tomorrow, this movement would hardly miss a beat. This is a social revolution of monumental proportions and it will not come to an end until the Negro finally leaves the periphery of our society and enters caste."

Harry Golden is 61 years old and lives in Charlotte, North Carolina, where he writes and publishes his personal journal, *The Carolina Israelite*. His books include *Only in America, For 2¢ Plain, Enjoy, Enjoy, You're Entitle', Forgotten Pioneer,* and *Carl Sandburg*.

Mr. Kennedy and the Negroes is a serious analysis of the entire Negro movement in the United States and an in-depth study of the late President Kennedy's total commitment to that social revolution. Imperfectly understood till now, because it was inadequately and scantily reported, this is one of the great stories of American history. Harry Golden has been writing the background of this story for twenty-two years and from his vantage point of critic, historian, and reporter, he has written a book that is significant and important social history.

Not only does Mr. Golden describe how John Fitzgerald Kennedy became the second Emancipator President, but he also pinpoints why the civil rights movement demanded nothing less in the White House in 1960. More importantly, his book outlines the remarkable victory the Kennedy Administration was able to achieve within a period of only two years and ten months. "While the struggle is by no means over, the end is now inevitable," says Harry Golden, "made inevitable by Mr. Kennedy and the Negroes themselves."

The civil rights story is traced from its
(*continued on back flap*)